RIVERS

By the same author

To the Baltic with Bob
Semi-detached
Mountain

Griff Rhys Jones

RIVERS

A Voyage into the Heart of Britain

HODDER &
STOUGHTON

The right of Griff Rhys Jones to be identified as the Author of the Work has been asserted by him in accordance with the Copyright, Designs and Patents Act 1988.

Edited by Gill Paul
Designed by Antigone Konstantinidou
Map on page 8 by Neil Gower

By arrangement with the BBC

The BBC logo is a registered trademark of the British Broadcasting Corporation and is used under licence

BBC logo © BBC 1996

A CIP catalogue record for this title is available from the British Library

ISBN 978 0 340 91863 0

Typeset in Adobe Caslon Pro by Antigone Konstantinidou

Printed and bound by Graphicom, Italy

Hodder & Stoughton policy is to use papers that are natural, renewable and recyclable products and made from wood grown in sustainable forests. The logging and manufacturing processes are expected to conform to the environmental regulations of the country of origin.

Hodder & Stoughton Ltd
338 Euston Road
London NW1 3BH

To Paul and to Cadbury

CONTENTS

9   Starting Out

14   Across the Centre of Scotland

68   From the Mersey to the Humber

126   The Severn and Wye

178   The River Lea

230   East Anglia

283   A Word of Thanks …

284   Picture Acknowledgements

285   Index

STARTING OUT

It was late. I got to Suffolk from London well after dark. I was tired. I was only there to pick up my canoes and load my stuff and we had a long trip ahead. I also needed to pick up my driver, a quasi-recalcitrant eighteenth-century manservant called Paul, plus a semi-amphibious chocolate Labrador called Cadbury, and a minor department store of clothing smothered in plastic toggles and logos. But I found someone had parked a grotesque and silly 4x4 SUV in front of my gate.

I conscientiously worked myself up into a state of proprietorial outrage before I realised that this was in fact my own, new, rivers-expedition vehicle, selflessly loaned to me by a major car firm.

It was a blockish, purple, four-wheel-driven tin shed on wheels. Admittedly it seemed to have less room inside than it promised outside, like an exo-Tardis. In the front there were two over-large armchairs for fat men to watch football matches, and, in the back, well, pretty much nothing at all except brick-thick walls and a sofa, but I rather liked it. Usually I would have despised the thing but with the key in my hand I changed my mind.

Mind you, there was hardly room for my stuff, and none at all for Paul. Paul is a "medical giant". This is the official designation for a person over six foot six inches tall. Paul is two inches into the category. He gets a grant from the government for his shoes. And no doubt he intended to bring his shoes. There was going to be no room for me at all if we took the dog.

We were taking the dog. This was more impulsive TV behaviour. I thought he would prick his ears and look winsome for important cut-aways. But as I walked on towards the house I began to recall, too late, what sharing a small hotel with a big dog can be like. He gets over-excited, wakes up in the middle of the night and licks any naked hands or feet that hang out from under the duvet. Damn.

We meant to sleep in a tent some of the time. Would he want to come inside? Is it legal to leave a dog overnight in a car? If you leave the windows open and let robbers steal it, will he protect it? He won't bark at robbers. Can I fit the car with a letterbox? I went to bed.

I was starting my voyage from my house overlooking the estuary of the Stour not far from Ipswich. The mud that eventually reaches the water begins a few short yards from my back door. If I planned the tide accurately I would be able to end my journey here too. I would work my way back to the house by paddle, canoe and tidal stream, because in a very real sense, the river runs through me – or, at least, it could do if global warming continues.

I was starting in the Western Highlands seeking wilderness. I would cross from the Mersey to the Humber. I would head out to the far west to the Severn, the longest and most British of rivers. I would descend to London to explore how rivers made our towns, and eventually I planned to take to the slow waterways of East Anglia back home. That, I thought, should be quite enough for everybody.

The voyage was going to take six months or more, not travelling all the time but roaming back and forth, not always on the river, but dropping in and out. I wanted these rivers to carry me into the overgrown bit of the back garden of Britain, but we were making a film for the BBC and I knew everything would be circumscribed. This is a fragmented account of an illusory experience made over a disjointed period of time, not really a guidebook. In case you were wondering.

The next morning an off-putting, grey, sluggish sky hung over the house. It had only intermittently stopped raining. I gazed up. For television purposes rain has to look like broom handles or it doesn't show up. Perhaps that had changed with High Definition. The camera would prefer highly defined water drops rolling down my nose and glossy matted hair slapped to my skull. They'll get that if I fall in, of course. That's what they wanted.

And so did I.

Paul helped me strap the canoes on to a black metal cradle joined to the car. It was about twenty feet long. To make it turn backwards one had to revolve the steering wheel in the opposite direction to the way one wanted to go. As long as you started with a straight rig, and as long as you had more than twenty feet to turn into, and as long as you moved the wheel with the very slightest of adjustments, it was fine.

I explained this to Paul as we readied ourselves. The dog had taken up the entirety of the back sofa. The rest of the vehicle was stuffed to the plastic panels. We could not see backwards at all.

"Don't be cool. You have nothing to prove. We can always disengage the cradle and lug it round and hook it on when we have turned," I said.

Paul started by trying to reverse down the farm track and into the hawthorn bush.

I let him play the game for at least ten minutes before we disengaged the trailer and lugged it round by hand.

It was a portent.

But I wanted to get on. Sometimes, whatever Robert Louis Stevenson might have said, it is better to arrive than to travel hopelessly.

ARGYLE-SHIRE.

FORREST of MAMLORN.

GLEN-LOCHAY

BREADALBAN

LOCH-TAY

CONRISH

GLEN-LOCHART

GLEN-DOCHART

GLEN-FALLACH

LOCH-ERN.

LOCH-VEOIL

LOCH-DOIH

LOCH-KETTERIN.

Glen Finlas

LOCH-VENACHAR.

LOCH

Ben-Lomund

Chapter One

ACROSS THE CENTRE OF SCOTLAND

HORSEPLAY

I could hear the waterfall, but I couldn't see it. We were parked in a broken asphalt car park in front of a faceless, empty white house. It was raining steadily. We had climbed up from Loch Leven and were now about 250 feet up the side of a mountain.

Ben Starkie and Mike Clifford were standing by their Land Rover boot, furtively clanking shackles and coiling hideously coloured ropes.

I stood on an empty rucksack and dragged off my clothes. Teetering in my thermal underwear I inserted my chubby legs into a red and blue drysuit, trying not to put my stockinged feet into the puddles. The rain was still falling. I was getting wet before I'd got my wet protection on.

I was not going over the top of the Grey Mare's Tail. It was too powerful after a flood. Instead it had been decided that I would abseil down alongside it.

After the usual uncomfortable moment when I had to stick my neck through the tight black rubber Durex top, I was finally sealed in an unbecoming, breathable, human-shaped waterproof bag: a drysuit.

I was in sombre mood. This means I was becoming passive-aggressive with a little bit of aggressive-aggressive thrown in.

"I thought we might film the opening sequence just before you go over the edge."

"In this?"

"Er, no. Perhaps in the original gear you came in ... you could ..."

Ross, the director, looked into my eyes and faltered. "Well, maybe not. Let's pick that up later."

We trudged off down a woodland path following Ben and Mike. I wasn't brooding on the fall, or the abseil, or the height; I was brooding on the discomfort. Already I was chafing and stumbling and I was simply trying to walk the tourist path. Ross told me he had already moved all the camera positions and the abseil points because overnight the drenching rain had boosted this natural power shower from "punishing tingle" to "overwhelming crunch".

Cadbury ran ecstatically through the rain. "You'd better get hold of him," someone said. "We don't want him to slip over the edge."

We tied on. Ben strapped me in to a harness. It was a black plastic nappy that went around and under my arse. Two loops went over my thighs and a belt tied the whole thing together at my waist. At the front was a webbing loop with a strong metal ring. The rope was clapped on to it.

Ben, wearing a bright yellow diver's suit, was going first. "It's a bit complicated through the heather to begin with, but then you'll get to the face of the rock and you just have to lower yourself down," he bellowed. "Mike here will have the safety rope but he won't be able to see you so he'll be slackening off by feel."

I nodded. It was difficult to speak above the racket. If I looked over his shoulder, I could see a massive gout of white foam, like a broken water main from hell. I was mostly looking at that.

The ropes were anchored to a pine tree. We had to slither down a steep incline to get to the vertical face. Ben leaned back, fiddled at his waist and jerked downwards into the haze of mist and spray. He left me to ponder my abseil gizmo under the dripping pines.

This is a simple "figure of eight" ring made of shiny steel. A rope threads through it. One end is attached at the top, the other reaches all the way to the bottom. By applying force on the lower end of the rope the friction is reduced and the rope begins to slide through the ring. Since you are attached to the ring, you go down. Naturally you are anxious to control the slide. This is perfectly possible. You have to lean back into empty space and drop the arm controlling the rope. This will bring the braking mechanism into play. Easy.

But you have to lift it first to release the brake. You have to experience that first sliding, shuddering fall.

I felt less secure than I had when abseiling before. Maybe it was the weight of rope beneath me. Perhaps the rain had soaked into the lines and made them slippery, swollen as they were by the water. When I first lifted them upwards to release myself, the rope felt massively heavy and unyielding and the first jerks down were fast and uncontrollable.

The trees overhanging the lip twisted me off balance as I lolloped backwards down an almost vertical crest towards the edge. I had to push out to one side and through the undergrowth. My feet were scrabbling on the thick wet pine needle blanket. I could see the water squeezing out of the rope as it slithered through the ring.

"Pull down," I kept muttering to myself, "it will brake." And it did, but now the edge of the precipice was directly beneath my feet, or at least one of my feet. The other was flailing in space.

Cliff abseils are rarely straightforward. These are not buildings or climbing walls. The face was broken and bowed. I had to negotiate an overhang, with one foot a little above waist height trapped under a bit of old root, and I desperately wanted to get both my feet onto something solid. The noise had grown. The air was thick with spray. The great white gout of the falls themselves was spewing past a few feet to my left.

This was the moment I had to put my trust in the mechanism. It was also the moment when an unacceptable fear rose up and gripped me by

WATERFALL FACTS

The Grey Mare's Tail waterfall on the River Leven just outside the village of Kinlochleven was given its name by King Edward VII, who said it reminded him of his own horse's tail.

It is not, however, the only Grey Mare's Tail waterfall in Scotland or even the highest. At 80 feet Kinlochleven's Grey Mare's Tail is less than half the height of its namesake near Moffat. Even this is dwarfed by Eas a' Chual Aluinn in Sutherland, which at 658 feet is the highest waterfall in the United Kingdom. And the UK's champion is no match for the highest waterfall in the world, the 3,212 feet drop of Venezuela's Angel Falls!

Nevertheless even a small river falling over an 80-feet drop can involve a considerable weight of water. You only need 44 cubic feet of water to make one ton in weight. So even if you stand beneath an apparently insignificant waterfall, several tons of water could be crashing down around you.

Theoretically it is safer to jump down a waterfall into the river below than to do the same jump into standing water. The theory involves factors such as the movement of the water and the softening of the water because of the amount of air that the waterfall is forcing into it.

Don't try this at home, though. A lot may depend on the depth of the water at the bottom.

The Grey Mare's Tail is only 80 feet tall, but fierce after heavy rain.

the throat. I knew the theory. I had to take the pressure off and let myself over the edge into the overhang. Further down I could make contact again, but I was not sure how much I had to release. It was like untying a heavy sack. Too loose, and the weight might slip out of control. But how much was too loose? I was sliding very gently downwards, gripping so hard I could see water oozing out of the knuckles of my glove.

I tried to summon logic. I summoned funk. I loosened the rope. I swung down. I bumped against the edge and dropped a few feet. My feet came up against rock that was green with mould and fluid and they flailed, failing to adhere at all. I crashed into the cliff and then bounced backwards and wobbled out swinging and twisting into space. Now I was directly hanging over the void, and that should have been easier. I could use one foot at a time to push me in the direction I wanted to go. The mass of the waterfall was crashing down behind me. The slimy wall of rock was sloping away in front of me and the river was thrashing itself into a tantrum eighty feet below.

For a while I dangled in the sopping air. Trying to control my breathing I yanked myself around to make my observations to the camera, noting, ruefully, how Richard had quietly come down the same route, ten yards to my right, with a camera balanced on his shoulder, making a record of every cowardly impulse flitting across my features. As I did so I felt a searing pain in my groin.

I blame the safety rope lifting me slightly sideways, or perhaps the dry suit bunched under my belt. My total weight seemed to jolt onto one of the straps in the leg harness. It lodged itself up under my thigh. A sharp unyielding edge of thick nylon webbing sawed up into my scrotal region.

"So the Western edge of Scot- arrrgh!" I began. "Are… arrgh!" Something had me with a hook through the flesh of my inner thigh and was bouncing me about on it.

"Arrrrrrgh! Arrrrrrrr! Arrrrrgh!"

I realised something significant. It was me that was doing the bouncing. Every time I lowered myself a little more on the abseil, the rope twisted round and dug into me.

"Arrrrrgh."

But if I stayed still, it steadily pinched harder.

"Arrrgh."

At least it banished all imagined horrors of vertigo. I dropped swiftly down the whole cliff, alternately grimacing and roaring at the uncaring waterfall. Each slithery jerk pinched my poor, tender flesh and I landed in a foul temper at the bottom. Most of my imprecations were drowned by the sound of the fall crashing all around us. Tons of water threatened to sweep us off our feet.

Grumbling and harrumphing I slithered into the freezing torrent and followed the yellow-suited Ben along the river and back to an earthy bank under dripping oaks.

Had I managed to find a shred of self-composure, I had intended to point out that the rivers of Scotland are generally shorter and faster in the west than they are in the east. This is because, geologically speaking (and I apologise to all geologists before I say this because I have no right to be speaking geologically at all), the north of Scotland is like a sloping table.

The table was created over a period of 3 billion years. It was tipped up on edge, however, a mere 60 million years ago, when Scotland separated from the eastern edges of the United States and they began to drift apart. (The islands of the Inner Hebrides are little volcanic dribbles that show where this fracture took place.) The very old rocks to the west were lifted up by molten rock. This created a slope that had a steep edge on the western side and a longer, more gradual slope to the east.

This table of rock was made by a hugely complex and erratic process. It involved volcanic eruptions, drifting continents, great ocean beds, mountain ranges as big as the Himalayas, huge lakes, rivers, and tropical forests. The final touch to Scotland's landscape, however – the picture we see behind the cow with the long horns on the tea tray – was made much more recently by global climate change and the Atlantic climate, or, more specifically, the huge amounts of water that all that stuff creates. The icy periods within the ice age of the last two and a half million years gouged out the glens and dug the lochs. (A major glacier can scrape away its bottom at the rate of a few millimetres a year.) The meltwater and the rain smoothed and rearranged the rest. The force of this single compound, water, sliding, flowing or grinding, had rearranged everything beautifully and haphazardly, thanks to the many different ingredients that had been baked into the table over the preceding three billion years.

As the ice melted, massive rivers did most of the rest of the work. They wore away rock and smoothed out valleys with deposits of stones and gravel. The fall at the Grey Mare's Tail was a dribble compared to the great torrents that charged through the landscape at the end of the last glacial period, 12,000 years ago.

The rivers I intended to follow across Scotland were mere trickles: the last gasps of past gigantic movements of water. But, like fine sanding after a chisel, water was still smoothing out the scenery. Ice was still doing its winter masonry work, chipping out blocks, levering out faults in the rock and grinding away exposed granite.

I had intended to say all of this as I came down the waterfall. I only got as far as "Arrrgh".

I dragged myself out of my drysuit, rubbed my sore groin and hobbled over to look at my maps on the bonnet of the car.

Thanks to the upheavals 60 million years ago the first part of my journey would be up steep inclines to a nearby watershed. Then I would follow a much gentler declination, but one that would meet great lochs and strong swooping rivers. At the mouth of the Tay, ninety miles further east, more water than in the Severn and Thames put together flowed out to the sea. It came, however, from a catchment area a quarter of the size of the Severn. A steep and wet basin, it would seem. Up, down, up again and round: this was going to be a rollercoaster ride across Scotland.

DOG ON AN ARGOCAT

Along the banks of Loch Rannoch cascades of golden showering birch and explosions of bright red beech provided a massive and unending firework display. We made our way up to Rannoch Station. "Arguably the most remote station in the world," the guidebook says. I was inclined to argue. There were stations on the Trans-Siberian Railway further from real civilisation than Rannoch, and the sign said that Glasgow was only eighty-seven miles away.

I took the dog and drove up the mountain in an Argocat. And they let me drive. Well done. An Argocat like this has eight wheels, two handlebars and six seats. It sits very low and has no fear of heights. Twist the throttle and the wheels grind forward, pull it back and they grind more on the left. It's like steering but it's not. It's more like grinding. It's like a boat in a storm. You don't point it, you generally direct it. And it will churn up the landscape as if it were water, leaving a permanent wake in the mud.

Cadbury sat alongside me and quivered. When I set off downhill he buried his head under my arm like a cartoon dog.

This was "down" as understood by a bungee jumper. I wondered, fleetingly, whether the machine could get out of control and become a Runaway Argocat, so I throttled back, but the machine's grip was Velcro tight. It was my trousers that were failing. It was all very well the vehicle gluing itself to an incline. I wasn't glued to the vehicle.

I hardly had time to examine the valley I was lurching into. Like all Scottish hillsides it looked deceptively smooth. This was what made it so beautiful – the gently rounded hills in the foreground and the snowy peaks in the background – but when you are in the foreground you realise that the surface is not a surface at all: it was a pitted, hummocky booby-trap of sods and puddles. The Argocat whined, roared, groaned and heaved and I just hung on, pitying poor Cadbury with every jolt, as it juddered towards a blissful blue loch.

Yes, blue. The mist had burned off. A few white clouds hung in a perfect sky. The loch sat like a desert oasis in a valley of yellow grass. We could have been in Africa. We lacked only an elephant grazing by the water.

This was the Loch of the Sword. The Camerons and the Atholl clansmen had once agreed to meet here to settle a dispute about who could graze all these hopeless sopping tussocks. The Atholl clansmen broke the agreement and turned up in a mob. The Camerons had guessed they might misbehave and had hidden some extra clansmen behind the rocks, who then leapt out in such large numbers that the Earl of Atholl threw his sword in the lake. (Shouting "Aw heck, we never wanted the grazing in the first place!" I imagine.)

A dinky train suddenly rattled past. It was a Sprinter. The West Highland Line went straight through the moor. It looked utterly alien. And, as suddenly as it rattled up, it rattled away again. Silence returned.

Someone had planted a flag on a little island. There were deer hoof marks in the sand of a little beach on the shore. But it wasn't this pristine blue loch I had come to see. I was actually looking for another patch of water some 200 yards further west. I nearly fell in it. In contrast to the loch it was a black and putrid boggy mess of water oozing from the ground and littered with whitened roots.

Cadbury plunged about in the black mud and started chewing rotten logs. You might have expected this bog to drain down and fill the loch, but it didn't. There was a hump of land between. The water flowed in the opposite direction. A few feet to the east of the bog there was a definable burn, trickling into the mist of Rannoch. I was beyond the watershed. From here the water would seep down to the sea, seventy-five miles to the east, through Loch Rannoch and then into the River Tummel. It was downhill all the way.

CANOE INSTRUCTION
AT THE BRIDGE OF GAUR

First of all, it was downhill the wrong way and I had to turn the canoe in the narrow lane that ran along the side of Loch Rannoch. I was getting good at this now; a perfect move forward, a little kick to straighten the wheels (most important when doing a mirror reverse trailer turn), slip backwards, easing the wheel in a clockwise direction. Push the Nissan arse against the tow-bar and turn the thing. Almost instantly straighten the wheel and then back we slip into the driveway. Except that the canoe trailer hit a nicely painted black gate with an audible clang and we were stuck straight across the road. There wasn't enough room to go all the way round. We couldn't swing it any further. We had to go on and look for somewhere else to start all over again.

My canoes are only sixteen feet long. Mere twigs. Dave Latham had several times been across the whole of Canada on thousand-kilometre races in a six-man, twenty-six-foot canoe. It involved pulling the canoe out and carrying it round rapids.

He explained this as he helped me get my canoe down to a frothy curve of water just down by the Bridge of Gaur.

"So when you portaged it, did you carry all your stuff in it?" I pronounced the word port*age* with a long faux French 'a'.

"Yes, we port*aged* it."

Dave was imitating me now. He'd come over all pretentious and French too.

"Sorry, I just pronounce it that way because I read about it first in John Keegan's book about the Anglo-French Wars," I explained as pretentiously as possible. "I thought it was a French word, and now I pronounce it as if I was trying to rhyme it with *ménage*. It's probably as bad as calling it a gar*age*."

Dave was gallant. "You may be right. I went on my trip with English Canadians not French ones."

Now, clearly, neither of us was ever going to use the word again. Portage means carrying your canoe and everything in it for a distance. We established that the canoe is a symbol of the Canadian backwoods.

This is because native Canadians travelled thousands of miles by canoe through their uncharted forests. They would paddle the river and then take long paths through the thick forest that linked one waterway to another.

Trappers and then French and Scottish fur traders adopted the birch bark canoe for their explorations, eventually crossing from one side of the continent to the other. This was only possible because the Canadian landscape had been formed by glaciers, which had carved out long shallow rivers that travelled great distances. The canoe had been the ideal boat for navigating them, being shallow and long-nosed and able to point its way between the rocks.

Dave told me that this was the reason why the canoe is called "the Canadian canoe" in Britain but just "the canoe" everywhere else in the world.

I had told everyone my canoes were made of polythene but in fact they are made of some type of modern plastic sandwich. This has a cellular structure that can remember its own shape, hence the value of this new system over real old-fashioned polythene canoes which wobbled, the fibreglass ones which cracked and the aluminium ones which were rattly; though not, of course, over the original birch bark canoes which were traditional, very beautiful and highly valued by everyone associated with canoes, even though I assume they were as fragile as a teapot.

I was a wholly untutored canoeist. I had improvised all my "techniques". I bought my canoes in a job lot including the trailer, and (I was beginning to understand) naff and unsuitable plastic spade paddles. I had just set out and started paddling. How difficult could it be? You had a paddle and you stuck it in the water. I had idly read that there were other skills, but I was all puffed up and canoe savvy. I thought

I had most of the necessary knowledge, with the possible exception of single-handed portaging.

"Can you do that with a big canoe like this, Dave?" I asked, fully expecting the answer "no".

"Yes," he replied.

"Oh, right."

Dave swung into action. He twisted his canoe upside down at the nose end, lifted it up on both arms, and gracefully propelled himself forward with the body of the canoe above his head.

"You go on until the weight is evenly balanced and you'll find a strut that crosses the width of the canoe at exactly this point," Dave boomed in a hollow echo from somewhere in the bowels of his own canoe. "Some have a special yoke."

I looked at my own canoe. It had a special yoke. "So that's what that is!"

"And then you lift the other end…"

Dave put two hands on the outer edges and lifted. The canoe was now balanced upside down on his back. It was a canoe with legs. It was a double-beaked green toucan roaming around the lawn.

My turn.

I got it turned alright. It rolled right over. It did this a couple of times. There's a lot of weight involved. But finally I got both hands under the edges and, with a succession of ungainly heaves, I humphed my way down to the centre point. Dave was smaller than me. He was clearly a wiry little man of the backwoods. The thing weighed a ton and the yoke dug into my neck. None the less, with a final "hup!" I became a canoe-backed little-legged beaky thing myself.

I roamed around the lawn under the trees and executed a cautious two-step dance of triumph.

It was back-breaking to put the thing down, though. I had to roll it off my head and onto my thighs and then onto the ground, but I felt a little better for having done it. Now in an emergency portage, somewhere in the primeval Canadian forest, I might be able to hump my own canoe for at least five or six yards before collapsing. This was good stuff.

We launched the canoes and drifted off towards the Bridge of Gaur. Dave had more handy hints. He showed me how he semi-knelt in the canoe rather than sitting upright on the little wicker seat. He disparaged my spade paddles. His was round-ended, with a "beaver tail" blade.

"Much easier going and less tiring for long journeys," he said.

I tried it out.

"You've got big whitewater paddles there," he observed.

So that was alright – I had macho paddles.

"And this is an otter tail." He showed me another paddle shaped like a lawn-turfing tool. "And *this* is a racing paddle." He propelled his canoe sideways across the water, which was pretty neat, and handed me an otter-tailed paddle with a bent handle.

I tried it. It felt good.

"You have it upside down."

"Oh." I turned it round.

"It's counter-intuitive because you're reaching forward with a paddle." Unlike a scooped oar, the racing paddle was designed to reach into the water ahead, so the handle emerged from the blade at an acute angle. "I used this particular one for those thousand-kilometre treks," he said modestly. I nodded approval.

However Dave suddenly got devastatingly personal. "But I'm afraid you are paddling all wrong, Griff," he told me.

I drifted and turned towards him, a half smile playing on my rugged features.

Me! Paddling all wrong! I had been paddling my canoe round the rivers of East Anglia for years. I had been in small boats all my life. I paddled with grace and elegance. "But, Dave, I can manoeuvre my canoe on a Canadian dollar…"

"You don't have to reach across to the other side as you do. You should take one stroke cleanly and just twist the handle downwards like so." He demonstrated. "And use the flattened blade of the paddle to correct your direction." He executed his smooth, one-sided paddle and serenely canoed ahead.

I gazed after him. "Yes, I see. But I actually rather like my way. Because I can get more purchase and steady myself."

"No, not when you're practised. It saves huge amounts of energy… see." He paddled and twisted. "It's the correct way to paddle."

"Is it? Right."

I tried it and banged my knuckles. "I've banged my knuckles."

"You will to begin with, but with practise it becomes second nature. In a while you won't be able to do it any other way."

But the way I did it already had become second nature. This was like being told I slept on the wrong side of the body.

I bashed my hands and twisted too little, too much and not at all for a while, as we paddled along together.

There was no point in arguing. Dave had trekked across the whole of Canada with real Canadians in proper travelling racing canoes of high technical merit. He was a canoe mensch.

I was a self-taught amateur. I would have to relearn my most basic skills. I would have to admit sheepishly that I should have taken instruction years ago.

I bid farewell to Dave and paddled away. Applying myself ponderously to my stroke I juddered into a freshening easterly headwind, scrupulously banging my knuckles on the foam sandwich of my canoe and ponderously adjusting my direction by flattening the blade.

Slowly, clumsily, painfully, I crept along and after several hours of effort finally turned out of sight of the Bridge of Gaur.

Then I went straight back to my old ways.

There's always a bend in the river.

I assume I can re-educate myself when I go to the Rockies.

RIDING THE TUMMEL

We arrived at Dunalastair at the far end of Loch Rannoch. A passionate canoeist called Mary Conacher was taking me to canoe down the River Tummel. A little dam at the end of the loch supplied electricity to the grid, and according to Mary the hydro people were responsible for releasing spates into the Tummel. These powerful floods had worn away the banks, and the result was an obstacle course of half-submerged trees and tangled branches that was becoming a trap for the unwary paddler.

Mary wanted me to experience the difficulties of the barrage for myself so that I could broadcast its terrors to the world, and was anxious to hurry me along to my canoe down the side of a concrete wall and into the black and wreathing stream of the Tummel.

Before I hopped aboard, I couldn't help noticing that this five-foot elderly lady was wearing a drysuit. I had one myself, with rubber collars and boots and massive hard-to-pull zips. It was waterproof in situations of total immersion and much-used by oil rig workers and underwater people.

"Do you think I should wear one?"

"Oh yes. And buoyancy, of course."

As I pondered this, I fingered her impressive Mae West-type life-jacket and its zippers and pockets, until it occurred to me that this might be presumed a little intimate.

Clearly we were off on an adventure.

We debated whether to take Cadbury. He had a life-jacket, but there is no sub-aqua drysuit for dogs. Cadbury is the size of a small donkey, especially when prone. I could almost guarantee that as we entered the danger zone, facing submersion in the roaring torrent, Cadbury would sit up to have a look, or shift from one side of the canoe to the other, mainly because the motion somehow reminded him that he could.

"He won't stand up," I explained. "He's most unlikely to leap from the boat in terror, but he does squirm."

Given this ballast nightmare I'm not sure why we eventually pushed off into the Tummel with Mary up front and the dog lying in the waist of the canoe. We were heavily laden and a little bow-down. And we went at a terrifying rate, alone except for the camera boat, on a river that was surging downstream.

"I started by kayaking," Mary explained. "I taught canoeing for many years. Er … We must break for the other side now."

"Break? Yes." I suddenly realised that Mary thought I knew what I was doing.

She dipped her rounded paddle in the inky stream and we veered out to the left. We were going at an unacceptable speed without paddling at all. There was something ahead and we skidded within inches of it. I had time to register that it was the whitened beak of a submerged log.

In England and Wales what we were doing would be considered trespass. We would have been invading the privacy of the landowners. But in Scotland the right to paddle had been won alongside the right to roam. Some landowners still did what they could to stop people getting to the river, and prevented unloading and parking, but we were legally allowed to do what we were doing. The privacy issue was such poppycock anyway. Had we all fallen in and drowned horribly nobody would have been there to see us. We were as insignificant as the leaves dancing in the eddies and about as disturbing to fish as the log tumbling alongside us.

"We have to show due consideration," Mary said. She had clearly been made aware of her obligations as well as her rights, so she was talking Committee Talk now.

"Can you make long treks around here?"

"Oh, you can canoe across the whole of Scotland. But I don't do it any more. I like to do short hops and stay in warm hotels."

Mary was sixty-eight.

"There we are. Ahead!"

Mary had talked airily of twenty minutes, but we had covered the miles far more quickly than that. The bank had been lined with a golden parade of larches, alders and beeches. It was achingly beautiful. Ahead of us was a bend in the river and a web of channels round an island of white stones which was crowned with more lovely trees: the very trees that created the log jam directly ahead.

Mary directed us to the island. We slewed out of the growing torrent and thumped up on a shore of big flat pebbles. It was not easy to get out without losing the canoe to the current, but I wanted to get a handle on the obstacle ahead. What was our line? How were we going to negotiate this? I had expected something nicely ordered: like those log jams from dimly remembered films where men in tartan shirts hopped about over floating islands of pines. This was an utter mess. Nobody had stripped these trees or cut them away from their roots. They were a tangle of semi-submerged, clawing branches and herbage.

She pointed at a substantial larch lying half out of the water. "We should try to go on the other side of that," she said. The water was boiling in mid-stream. How did she know there was a way round on the other side? What if there were branches underneath?

Mary indicated another slew in front of another island straight ahead. "We'll want to break to the right and get down there and the current will do the rest."

I was already blustering – not directly to Mary but to the camera crew and myself. "Quite honestly I'd be happy to do it on my own, but there are two of us in the boat and we barely know each other. Mary and I simply haven't done enough practise paddling in tandem."

Obviously I was scared. I was flinging some persiflage about to try and scare everybody else. But we had come this far.

"No one will take responsibility for clearing the trees away. And this is an issue to do with safe navigation," Mary said. There had been a nasty incident involving a father and son earlier in the year.

"I've been to the hydro people. They are sympathetic. The landowner is helpful, but it will cost thousands to get them all removed and the whole thing is only going to get worse if nothing is done."

I was on the point of offering the money but Mary already had her helmet on. She handed me another one. I strapped it on and we pushed out into the current.

I was right to be scared. The canoe was impossible to control. It rushed out into the maelstrom and skewed past the first log at an acute angle. It was surely inevitable that we were going to end up in the branches. If we did, I knew what would happen. The branches grab at you but the boat carries on.

With inches to spare, we swung on our axis and flung ourselves downstream, rocking wildly. I was using my paddle to try to stop our progress, paddling backwards to slow us down and then just as wildly digging to get the bottom end of the boat to turn to the right. It wouldn't come and we were simply careering sideways. Now there was a savage spike of branch at the apex of the current. With a frantic effort we managed to avoid hitting it beam-on, but then we plunged forward.

We were in the current now. Wallowing from side to side, we shot down the last sluice and pranged straight on top of a submerged branch. It quivered beneath us. We hung for a moment, twisting round and tipping sideways, until, with a last lurch, we fell off it and plunged on into the lower river and the pool beyond. The energy dissipated as it always does. The river spread wide and the rush subsided. Now we were cushioned by the waters instead of buffeted and we swung lazily across the dark water towards a grassy yellow bank on the far side. The dog stood up.

The river was deep black. The name Tummel means "the dark one". The water was clear to a great depth, penetrated by sharp autumn sunshine which picked out bright yellow birch or red beech trees twirling upwards from far below on disturbed eddies like kaleidoscope fragments flying out of space in slow motion.

CRANNOGS ON LOCH TAY

Paddling up … (I nearly wrote "rowing up". That's a sin in canoeing circles. The tao of paddle must be obeyed.) … paddling up Loch Tay brought me to the eastern end and a village on the shore. There were two islands there. One that had to be looked for carefully and could be spotted as a barely visible dome of trees against a wooded background on the north shore. The other was some forty feet into the loch with a couple of big pines. It is believed they were both largely man-made.

Clansmen had used the tree-dome as a fortress in relatively recent historical times – that is, about 300 years ago. The other was more distinct and rocky and uninhabited. Both dated from before history was recorded. They were built originally as settlements out on the river probably in about 600 BC, and they are two of eighteen that have so far been discovered along the fourteen-mile length of Loch Tay.

These crannogs were constructed at significant points or perhaps clustered in the wells of bays so they could be easily seen, or so that the next settlement up the loch, as it were, was easily visible to the last settlement. It might have been an early warning system. Or perhaps the sites were chosen because of the shallowness of the water, which would have made building them easier. Nobody can be certain.

I was visiting a reconstruction of a crannog on the south shore, towering over my canoe and the black water in the gloom of the late afternoon. A nest of alder stilts held up a platform of logs some ten feet

IRON AGE HOLIDAY HOMES?

Hundreds of crannogs have been found in Scotland, thousands of similar constructions have been found in Ireland and one has been discovered in Llangorse Lake in Wales. Older crannogs were timber roundhouse structures built on stilts to stand above the water. Later crannogs involved thousands of tons of rock being piled onto a loch bed to create an artificial island on which buildings could then be constructed.

The oldest crannog found in Scotland dates back to around 3,000 BC. Crannogs were still being built and used in the country up until the seventeenth century and even more recently the Scottish Crannog Centre at Aberfeldy has reconstructed its very own crannog complete with a thatched roundhouse on stilts on Loch Tay.

There are various explanations for the use of crannogs. They may have been created as homesteads for farmers, as hunting and fishing stations, to afford protection in times of trouble or because of a shortage of open land on which to build. These Iron Age lake dwellings may even have been used as holiday homes or because they were a form of status symbol.

Perhaps the crannogs simply testify to the enduring nature of a couple of popular selling points for property: lake views and no near neighbours.

Reconstructed crannog on Loch Tay. Crannogs were ahead of their time in their use of decking.

above my head, and on top of this was a sturdy house with a great conical roof, thatched with reeds. The reeds were not authentic. The roof would probably have been made from bracken, rushes, and probably also straw, continuously renewed. The walls were made of hazel woven together and bracken had been properly used there, stuffed in like a sandwich; an early, organic cavity insulation.

Wild, romantic and clumpy, this place could have taken a starring role in *The Lord of the Rings*.

Barrie Andrian, an American archaeologist, ran the centre. Archaeologists have to spend half their lives speculating, and the other half refusing to speculate at all. They are martyrs to the either/or, and Barrie's greatest desire was to find a body.

The Iron Age Celts on the edge of the Caledonian forest just didn't seem to leave enough of themselves around – except, of course, in these crannogs. That was why they were so exciting. Their inhabitants had thrown what little rubbish they had over the side and into the loch for 900 years. The dark icy fresh water had helped to preserve a lot of this detritus, even smears of butter in a wooden pot. With 30,000 other lochs, and crannogs in most of them, there were thousands of other heaps of ancient trash to be investigated – eighteen in this loch alone.

Barrie had previously worked on the *Mary Rose*. There, underwater, she had helped discover an archer pinned to the deck by a cannon, still wearing his quiver, so she was well used to mind-boggling discoveries. She had fervent hopes for these un-explored mounds beneath the freezing waters. Archaeologists had already found out that the dwellings were supported on alder poles. They had discovered a jet bead, probably from Whitby. They knew that the people kept animals in the house, that they farmed the land on the shore, that they used a lot of bracken and that they made fire by the laborious method of rubbing sticks together at warp speed using a tool that involves a bow string and a specially created hole. I had a go at it and singularly failed to produce a spark. I will never handle matches and rolled-up bits of newspaper in a cavalier fashion again.

Given the difficulties of dealing with the ordinary business of life, in a countryside just as soggy then as it is now, it is hard not to salute these distant ancestors. Nobody really knows why they built their huts in this way. They may have made their crannogs to protect themselves from predators both human and four-legged. They may have built them far out over water just to get away from the midges. They may have built these splendid things just to show off. But they also built them to be close to the simplest means of transport that they had – the river system.

When Barrie and her husband were exploring the location for their reconstructed crannog they came across another find just off the shore. It was a canoe, buried in the silt. It still sits there. This is a vessel from before the man-made islands were constructed. It dates to about 1500 BC and it is at least thirty feet long.

That was longer than any of the few boats moored in front of the village at the end of the Tay.

ELECTRICITY GENERATION

Even in the wet this was an incomparably beautiful place. We took the road to Kenmore, at the bottom of Loch Tay, where we hunted along the lochside for the road up to Fortingall. I thought we would be climbing up the side of the valley, but in fact we passed into another glen – Glen Lyon – which immediately took its own course northeast, with its own river, flowing out towards the Tummel.

Instead of being up on a slope, we were down in a valley and turned into an estate with a spectacular avenue of trees, a handsome crow-stepped house and a knot garden courtyard, to look at the hydroelectric plant.

Alastair Riddell had been brought up on the estate and he remembered how, as a boy, he had been called out of bed by the estate manager in the middle of the night to go up into the hills to clear ice and leaves from the intake so that there would be electricity in the morning.

Stepping out in the rain, he enthused about how he had followed his uncle up the canyon in a troop that they called "The Glen Lyon Commandos", how they opened the sluice gates and let the water charge into the leat to turn the old decrepit mill wheel one last time, and how the place had been a constant adventure for him and his brothers.

Before there was a National Grid his family had used their London money to provide electrical power for themselves, and the local village, by damming the burn some way up in the hills and running a turbine.

It was first installed in the 1930s and had continued running, with ten-year maintenance overhauls, until early 2000. Now it had been replaced and the system was working again.

Alastair had another scheme, a much bigger one, already in progress, which would make use of seven separate streams and link up to the National Grid. He was confident that these miniature local hydro plants could make significant contributions to national power requirements and could do so at a profit. He was a hydro enthusiast.

And so was I. As it happens, I have a mill pond on my farm in Wales, and a barn that used to be a mill. With the high price of oil, with Canadians trying suck the stuff out of sand and a vociferous public confusing atomic power with atomic bombs, I was interested in the possibilities of saving money on my energy supplies. And, of course, I also want to have renewable energy that will save the Earth from exploding in a puff of hairdryer heat. I'm not selfish. I want to be a hydro person myself. I listened to his fervent spiel with more than usual intensity.

But there were disadvantages. Alastair thought being woken in the middle of the night to go and clear ice out of the intake header pond was terrific fun. Myself, I have not been in the army. When Alastair talked of the intake supply being up on the hill, he actually meant about a thousand feet up on the hill. It must have been a long climb in a howling gale. It was long when we went in a Land Rover past herds of deer through field gates and more plantations to a bare damp upland.

Mind you, the inlet seemed a modest enough proposal; not as slight as a beaver dam, but a good deal less imposing than a wind turbine. There was a small concrete wall, "which could be less" and a low enclosed "housing", not even a hut. The grille that we had come to clean was clean anyway. We went through the motions of brushing it down for the camera, and I waffled on about the necessity of inventing a self-cleaning system.

The system was reassuringly simple but hugely expensive. The water passed into a pipe which snaked down the mountainside. For reasons of environmental concern the pipe had to be buried. Burying pipes up a mountain tends to cost a mountain of cash.

Then again, it was not considered politic to take all of the water. For environmental reasons, the stream below the dam had to remain a stream. Some of the water went down a pipe and did a bit of work but a thousand yards of stream had to be left flowing, which rather diminished the efficiency of the system – though it in no way diminished the enthusiasm of Alastair.

On the way back he became more candid about other costs too. The most expensive part was linking up to the National Grid. Pre-planning had required intensive measurement of a year's water flows. The government had shown very little sympathy at all until the Scottish Nationalists arrived, and now, more optimistically, there was "cross party support" for this particular bandwagon.

Alastair was now talking quietly about millions of pounds of investment. "You have to work at it. If you don't look after it when it's up and going then you will start to extend the time it takes to get back your investment."

I was more thoughtful by the time we got to the hut next to the farm which held the turbine. Millions of pounds seemed quite a lot to spend on free electricity.

Alastair cocked his head. "Listen. You see? Wonderful. You can't hear a thing by the hut."

He was right. And the impact on the environment that everybody is seeking to protect was so slight, so localised and so unobtrusive compared to the industrial propellers marching across the ridge lines of Britain.

It was pretty noisy inside the hut, but it was also more dynamic than I had expected. On one side was a blue machine. The pipe came out of the wall and then split into two and entered a humped casing. To the side of that a large spinning cog and axle disappeared into the green casing. This was machinery running for ever and ever (or at least ten years or so before they have to change the bearings). The water (by the time it got here) had developed huge pressure. If they had to press the emergency button and disconnect the machine the water would fly out of an emergency hole with enough force to cross the canyon outside. "You can break a crowbar on it," Alastair enthused.

Big black power wires emerged from the green casing and ran into a more conventional cream metal box. On the side there was a dial. Alastair went over and beamed approval at it. "See there. Not full power, but good stuff," he said.

The read-out was flickering at about 500. I peered at it. "What does that represent?"

Each one or two of those kilowatts was roughly enough to run one house. We were looking at enough electricity to power up to 500 houses, generated by one mountain stream. How could you not be overjoyed?

I was overjoyed. I was only trying to power one house. Hey, I could look at a mini system. Maybe at a 500th of the price. I took Alastair's details, thanked him warmly and set off into the rain again.

TAKING THE WATERS OF BRUAR

We were in a major romantic chasm, visited by every early tourist with rapture in their hearts – except that they invariably seem to have found it a little disappointing. That tireless eighteenth-century gazeteer of the notable view William Gilpin admired the waters but felt the surroundings lacked proper cladding. In those days the falls were simply a fault in a bare mountainside. Then Rabbie Burns wrote a poem to the landowner purportedly from the waters themselves, urging him to plant some trees on the banks to make them more conventionally beautiful, and he complied. Who wouldn't with such urging?

But we weren't there to discuss poetry. We were there to explore the geology of the place with Duncan Hay, who was waiting patiently to one side in a brown knitted beanie and a wetsuit. He was going to take me where Rabbie had never been – straight down the falls, a handy way of getting close to the powers of erosion.

On the way down to the icy torrent, Duncan had to put up with my thin grasp of the last 600 million years of geology. (I thought we had better get that out of the way first.) "It's like a cake, isn't it, Duncan?" I opined.

He smiled bemusedly up at me from where he was hanging on to a slimey pine root. "I guess…"

"No, I mean some of the rocks here are very old but all this stuff has been pressed and crushed and filled with little explosions of lava for hundreds of millions of years so that there were loads of different ingredients in the mix like a Ben & Jerry's ice-cream."

I had not so much mixed metaphors as coagulated them. I slid down a bank of pine needles and tried to get a grip on a slab of wet green rock.

"But then along comes the wet climate and pours all this hot chocolate sauce over the cake and that works its way along the crust washing away some ingredients and leaving the crunchier bits exposed as mountains."

Duncan knew exactly what I was talking about even if you don't. He was now slithering along a long spur of wet schist. And this effectively got 600 million years of extremely complicated geology, involving collapsing oceans and colliding continents, out of the way. I sat on my arse and bumped down to the edge of the cataract. We were both happy.

As we plunged into the ice-cold foaming torrent, Duncan explained that the waters of Bruar had basically torn their way through the surface soil to the bedrock.

We followed the route, wading down the waters and clambering over a series of semi-upright flags, grappling with humps and miniature gullies all the way down. Given that it kept threatening to lift us up and hurl us down the canyon, it was quite easy to see the work that a flood of water like this could do.

We pushed across surging waters and looked into a nicely hollowed-out cauldron by the edge of the cliff. This was a bowl carved out of the rock by an eddy to the side of the river. The smooth large pebbles that were revolving in it and shaping it, which might eventually bring more slabs crashing down, were sitting there placidly waiting for the level to rise so they could get to work.

This is simple rock erosion. It takes time. We could see plenty of other dramatic examples of this around us – arches, buttresses, hollows and great overhangs leading to falls. In fact, the director was keen that we plunged over the examples and swam right into them. So we did. It was wrenchingly cold.

The river was flooding hard but it was as nothing to the gouts of water that ran through the landscape during the great melt after the last glaciation. Everything we saw now was magnified. Even now in the warm interglacial period in which we are living, ice still does the real damage. It seeps into cracks. It expands to break off lumps of rocks. It crumbles granite faces.

"I want you to plunge into the water down the bottom there," Ross, the director, said.

Duncan and I made one final sally, swimming out across a yellow pool and commenting on the black arch that soared above our heads. In fact, both of us were thinking that Rabbie Burns had hardly got close to the real spirit of the waters. Quite honestly that water would have been totally unconcerned about the trees and bushes on its banks. It would have been far too cold to think about anything. It probably just wanted to get on and reach the nice warm sea.

SEX WITH SALMON

We must not talk of a cold fish. A cold fish is, so it would seem, a hot fish. We are wrong to associate fish eyes and wet slabs with lack of ardour. Salmon are driven by sex. They leap cataracts for sex. They travel thousands of miles for sex. And they don't even think of sex until the water temperature gets down to about eight degrees centigrade.

I was going to investigate fishy raptures. I had to get to the River Garry and we were leaving before breakfast. This is film-making. We leave hotels before they are ready for breakfast and arrive back after they have finished serving dinner.

Within half an hour the sun had burned up the early-morning fog. A few patchy drifts hung around like smokers in a back alley. The sky broke out a clear blue day. The gateway to the Highlands was looking like a National Trust calendar. This was the best weather we had had since early June. I knew this because I had been out all year, filming things in out of the way places in continuous rain.

A group of men were standing conspiratorially around their SUVs. They were wearing khaki fatigues and rubber suits. They were there to gather in salmon in what might seem a wholly unfair manner.

We were a few miles from Pitlochry, on the edge of the Blair Atholl estate. One of the salmon men, Dr David Summers, explained that this was a sizeable chunk of land but no longer controlled by the duke. The old duke had died and left all his land to a close female relative who was closer to him than the proper duke who got the title.

The views were impossibly clean. No blear, just golden trees and shining hillsides and slanty light. It was distracting and enviable, but as I dragged out my own rubber suit, I decided there was no point in owning such a place. We could all walk around it, thanks to proper legislation, and somehow the responsibility for such beauty must be a burden.

Lee Fisher led us down to the water's edge so that we could begin netting salmon. It was a big operation. The team threw a net out further down the river to span it from bank to bank and then began a slow progression towards it with another net and their zapping machine.

"You'd better tie up the dog," Lee said. "The power won't be enough to hurt him but he might feel it if he's in the water."

He had already been yapping at wavelets, so I led him away. "What about me? I'm wearing a rubber suit. Is that going to protect me?"

Lee laughed. He handed me his own stick of beeswax to lubricate and seal my zips. I had a nice long zip that ran across my shoulderblades and a smaller one hidden by a flap at crotch level. It was the toughest trouser zipper I had ever encountered and clearly required watchfulness. It had amputation capacities.

"You're perfectly safe, and you're mostly rubber-insulated anyway."

I was. The drysuit ended in two absurd flappy rubber socks, which were now stuffed into my rugged cross-country trainers. Technically I was totally waterproofed. But the water was so cold that when I stepped into the Garry I became convinced that the boots were leaking.

It felt like walking into the river in your shoes and socks. The toes froze just the same.

Lee showed me the net. It had long electric strands dangling from the top of it.

"So these stun the fish?"

"No." It was some magnetic method. "They just seem to attract them."

Our power source was a generator which was sitting in a rubber dinghy. It was strange to be discussing getting electricity from a river one day and literally pumping it back in the next.

Willie Tritton had hold of the other end of the net, on the other, deeper side of the river, and he was up to his chest in the water. He was going to walk down that bank. I was going to hold a rope across my back and walk down my bank. We would progress down the river in a stately manner, dinghy and all, attempting to lure salmon into our trap with our electric force-field.

Off we went. "Fishing!" Lee shouted loudly, and the generator grumbled. "They can be pretty good at getting round the edges so we want to be as tight as possible," he explained.

"Are we after both sexes?"

"We want cocks and hens," Lee said. "We want to breed them."

I should have worked that out. The life cycle of the salmon is one of arduous toil. Anglers particularly seem to admire the muscular wild salmon that has made the extra effort to get as far as possible upstream to his spawning grounds. Was this because they were more sportive as they were yanked out of the water or more delicious when they were plonked on the salver? Quite possibly both.

There are still salmon being taken from the Tay, though anglers are supposed to "carefully release" the first one and not to take females full

A sexual thrill for the salmon: the River Garry in winter.

In the Argocat on Rannoch Moor. Thunderbirds are go.

Free power at a million pounds a shot from the dam at Glen Lyon.

The Grey Mare's Tail, Lochleven, in a frisky state.

The Loch of the Sword. All it lacked was a grazing elephant.

Sightseeing at the Falls of Bruar the cold way.

Queen Victoria's favourite view of Loch Tummel.

The Falls of Tummel by Nasmyth. His favourite view.

Bridges over the River Tay at Perth in warmer weather.

AN OBSTACLE COURSE FOR SALMON

The Pitlochry salmon ladder was built by Wimpey Construction between 1947 and 1950. Wimpey were not, of course, primarily engaged in the business of building climbing tools for fish. Their main objective was the construction of the Pitlochry Dam, which was created as part of the snappily named North of Scotland Hydro-Electric Board's River Tummel Hydro-Electric Power Scheme.

The salmon ladder enables the fish to bypass the dam, which at 54 feet they might have found a bit challenging as a high jump. The 34 steps or chambers of the ladder are vital in enabling the salmon to complete their 3,750-mile journey from the Atlantic to their spawning grounds.

Atlantic salmon are able to find their way back to their spawning grounds with incredible accuracy. Over 90 per cent of salmon then die after their first spawning. The young salmon stay in the river for up to five years before returning to the ocean for perhaps three or four years then it's time for another climb up the Pitlochry ladder.

Over 7,000 salmon have been counted ascending the ladder each year, as have around 500,000 tourists. The latter, however, seem to be a lot easier to spot than the former. Even though it takes each salmon about twelve hours to ascend the ladder very few visitors ever manage to catch sight of them through the observation window.

The Pitlochry salmon ladder: easier to swim down than up.

of roe. They cannot fish in the spawning season. So, by now, in early November, the anglers had left the river, leaving it free for Lee and his men to do their work.

It is over ten years since the Tay was a commercial salmon fishery. Anglers have been forbidden to sell their fish since 2002, even though they still catch around 10,000 a year in this river (which must mean a lot of frozen salmon in stockbrokers' mansions in the Home Counties). But stocks have declined.

The salmon, as every schoolboy used to know, swims hundreds of miles out of the river to live near Greenland. It goes to the icy waters of the North Atlantic at the age of two or three. So energetic and muscular are these salmon that they are considered genetically different and certainly not to be confused (or bred) with flabby, farmed salmon.

The salmon that we were hoping to catch were not going to be farmed. Milked yes, farmed no. They were simply bred privately. Lee was their madam. He was going to take them to stay in his Tayside fertility clinic, milk the hens of their eggs and introduce those eggs to the milt of the cocks so that he could nurture the fry away from the ravages of nature. Later he would reintroduce the infant salmon back to the river at an age when they might have more of a chance of survival. As far as I could see this huge enterprise was undertaken mainly to provide better sport for the fishermen.

The salmon we were seeking now had already come back from Greenland. They had jumped their way up the Tay to the place where they were born, and the hens were now looking for the perfect place to make a little bed in the gravel with their tails and lay their eggs. They would do this a couple of times then the males would do their stuff, in a state of high excitement, not over the female herself but over the roe.

This would happen once, or possibly twice, before the cocks quietly expired, apparently of exhaustion. Sex is a remarkable trigger.

"Fish in the net" shouted Ronnie Whytock, who was the manager of a Country and Western band when he wasn't up to his waist in a rubber suit in the Tay. He waded forward and grabbed the edge of the net and there was a plump salmon.

"He's a cock," said Lee. "He's gone pink."

"That's a good sign?"

"Yes, salmon that are ready for sex go pink."

How similar to bankers and stockbrokers. He was cut out of the float net, transferred to a big shrimping net and carried with great care to the holding tank.

There were no more salmon in that pool so we moved on to the next where our trawling procession began again. This time we caught two fine hens of at least fifteen pounds each, and another cock.

Lee was pleased. "It's two matching sets," he beamed. "A good morning's work."

Salmon Central Headquarters was just outside Perth. It was a Saturday morning when I got there. Everybody had brought dogs. Lee seemed to have about six. They were running around the car park in amongst the trees, so I left Cadbury with them. I went inside and peered into a big black round plastic tank. The fish I had helped to catch were going to be attended to some other time. Lee had two others here, lurking on the bottom. "Nice big fish," he crooned as they fished them out. Both the cock and hen had been caught in the same stretch of river. They wanted to avoid genetic mismatching. Who knows what lurks in the DNA of those eggs? Nobody wanted neurotic, displaced salmon, uncertain which river to return to.

Mum was ready, or "pregnant", I suppose. She was lightly drugged, but otherwise this was going to be a New Age natural birth. They even had a birthing pool. Davie held her over a colander. Lee reached down and gently squeezed her lower portions and a stream of pink roe poppled out of a little hole about two-thirds of the way down her stomach.

"We have to keep them dry." Lee was mopping the bowl with paper towels. "The eggs open up in the water to accept the sperm, and we need to keep them closed for a while longer."

By now he had pretty well drained the hen and she had stretch marks to prove it. Her lower abdomen was flat and flabby. "Like an empty purse," Lee said, transferring the eggs into a bowl. It looked like an ordinary kitchen bowl, because it was an ordinary kitchen bowl.

And now we had to milk the cock salmon. He had a big up-thrusting lower beak and sharp teeth. "Mind, cos he'll bite," said Lee and he showed me where he wanted me to press while he held the fish over the eggs. So I pressed and Lee directed the result, a milky white spurt, rather too familiar in some respects, which mingled with the roe. One, two, three spurts later Lee was satisfied, and so, we assume, was the salmon.

"In the wild there may be a lot of visitors to the redd [the nest where the eggs would have been laid] so each egg would have got a fair chance, but here I want to mix up this lot properly." He did so with his free hand and then added the water. "Watch it fizz."

Our primeval soup started bubbling.

"That's the eggs opening up in the water."

It seemed a deeply unscientific scrambling of the eggs, but Lee only ended up with a very small number – less than one per cent, he reckoned – that didn't get fertilised.

The result was ready to be transferred to a hatchery. In the hut next door, quietly germinating, in rows of trays fed with fresh running water, lay a million eggs. Each would become as hard as a little marble and develop eyes before being transported back to the river to face the herons and the kingfishers and the anglers.

A BEAVER ON THE LOOSE

The valley we were in – the house and the pampered fields, the neat stone walls, the plantations, the gardens, the trim sports grounds and the expensive shops – seemed to imply that Perthshire was almost suburban in nature. But in reality this northwest corner of the county is a thinly populated place, and the lochs run up through valleys into bare outlands which have been losing population since the nineteenth century; not just because of the Highland clearances but also because of the simple difficulties of life in a post-industrial nation. Now it is a place of second homes and retired people and outward-bound hotels.

These changes had brought difficult decisions to the countryside. The great sloping sides of the valleys were sequestered for a variety of single interests.

"There is too much overgrazing." John put it simply. In his opinion the subsidy system that used to exist had encouraged overstocking. Farmers had been encouraged to bring flocks into areas that remained difficult to farm and produced animals of little value. "There was a big fuss about the sea eagles over to the west. They do take the occasional lamb but it is hardly their main food."

Where there are no sheep there are deer. Sporting estates dominate great swathes of land. Their parks are fenced off to allow for another commercial concern: forestry. Bare, black geometric slabs of alien spruce still disfigure the hillsides of the Highlands. Once, this area was covered by the great, natural Caledonian forest but almost nothing remains. What was not grubbed up for pasture before the tenth century was chopped down in the seventeenth and eighteenth, before the process began a gradual reversal.

The "Planting Dukes" of Atholl put in over 27 million trees in the eighteenth and nineteenth centuries. These included larch, first imported from Austria. Larches blazed great yellow seams across the woods. They complemented the burning red of the beech trees. But these were alien too.

What we look on in the glens is hardly "natural" even when it is beautiful. Most of it has experienced continuous change. The climate itself has altered. Before the last ice age, trees grew to a height of 3,000 feet. Today they go little higher than 1,500 feet. Yet game-fishing interests, shooting interests, forestry interests, nature conservancy groups, farmers and bureaucrats still argue the toss about what is natural and right, or traditional, or best for the area.

John Mattingley and his wife Wendy took me for a walk round the gardens of Cluny, which are unashamedly alien themselves. There are several huge sequoias from California, with red, fire-proof bark, and mountain trees from all over the world – cherries from the Himalayas, pines from California, beeches from Chile.

We were there to catch the last red autumnal fire storms from exotic acers and birches. There was snow in the air. It was promised for midday. The clear skies that had brought the fall in temperature had also let the sunshine in, and set the garden ablaze with colour.

This little pocket of six acres was a defiant arboretum of alien species and yet it thronged with wildlife. Waxwings, fieldfares, redwings and tits flitted through the lower branches gathering up the berries. There were red squirrels everywhere. I put Cadbury on a lead. He hates grey squirrels. He has never caught any but he likes to threaten them and drive them up trees. But he hardly noticed the red.

The morning before I went to Cluny the newspapers had carried the story of plans to try to reintroduce the European beaver into Angus. Wendy was keen on the idea.

"We saw them up in the Alps and they were surprisingly near the city," she said. "There's always opposition. There was opposition to the sea eagles."

There had been an outcry about the reintroduction of the beaver. Forestry interests pointed out that a couple of beaver can clear ten acres a year. Fishing interests were worried about the effects on "their" salmon.

"Which is a typical misunderstanding because the beaver is a herbivore," Wendy said.

"They're worried about dams disrupting the breeding grounds," John pointed out.

"They're ones to talk about balance. It's a term they like to use. But in fact these commercial interests are considerably imbalanced." Wendy was unrepentant.

Personally, I would love to see more of the hillsides taken out of the monoculture. I think it would be good for the Highlands to be less of a deer park or a sheep run or a spruce plantation, and become a proper forest. If the birds and squirrels hopped around there, as they did in the garden at Cluny, and we had to keep a look out for wolves, then that would seem an excellent adventure. But I don't live there. I don't farm there. I live in London. I am just a romantic.

What is disheartening is that the debate is forced down to pure economics. The beaver plan was accompanied by a po-faced estimate of their economic benefit to the region. If beavers were released in the wild it could apparently add two million pounds to the tourist economy each year.

But people who live by the sword may die by the sword. Never play economics with the political classes; they use statistics as weapons. Once you are in there, you descend to those terms, their terms, and their terms alone. Economics cannot rule Nature, or our natures. That way leads to wind farms on every ridge. (But I thought you wanted the Highlands to pay for themselves!)

There were very few trees at all in the Highlands at the beginning of the eighteenth century. They were planted partly to make the place more romantic for would-be Highland lairds from Lancashire. As Wendy said, just before I left Cluny, "One of the most important values is what you feel is good and right."

THE TAY IN FLOOD

We were twelve miles upstream of Perth. Across a muddy field I could see the bank of the Tay, built up like a dyke, curving round in front of the hills. There was a washed blue sky, a little sharp light with dank, sun-shot clouds and a high north-westerly wind. We turned off into the drive of a row of estate cottages.

Fourteen years before, Roy Hutton, an engine driver from Perth had bought this terrace. He and his wife Val had converted it into a single house. Then three years ago the river came over the bank.

"We got a call from Charlie. He's the flood co-ordinator. And he said the river was threatening to burst its banks, so I went down to have a look. Mind you, he'd called before. There had been false alarms, but this time I could see that it was just under the top. Usually the river is fifteen feet below us, and now there was no more than a couple of feet in it, so I reckoned this was probably the real thing."

Roy ushered me in the side door. There were two black biro marks on the frame. The top one was at waist height. This was where the water had come in 2006. The one below it was a little lower. This was the first visitation, in 2005.

"We hung on as long as possible, and took all the stuff we could."

The house was essentially a bungalow. There was no upstairs except an attic. There were mouldy marks up the side walls and the floors were bare of carpet.

"But what can you get in a couple of cars? We had to leave all the furniture, the sofas and the like."

There was no furniture in the bare damp rooms now.

"In the end the police told us we had to leave. The water was just across there on the other side of the road. I remember my son and I stopped on the rise above the back field and we could see the water roaring across the top of the bank."

Roy's house was built about a hundred years ago. When he bought it in the late 1990s, his survey had told him that he was in a flood-risk area and there had been bad recent floods in Perth, in 1993 in particular.

But then Perth has often been flooded in the past.

A few years after the Smeaton Bridge was built in 1771, heavy ice build-up blocked the arches completely and the back-up took the water to one of the highest levels recorded. All through the nineteenth century there had been intermittent inundations. The great valleys of the mountain area are like a wash basin, filling suddenly and violently, swirling water down a narrow plughole. All this has long been true. Significantly, however, examining the marks on the side of the bridge, it seemed that four of the highest floods ever recorded have happened in the last twenty years.

"There had been two days of continuous rain," Roy told me.

These were the conditions that John had talked about in Cluny House Gardens in Aberfeldy. Snow fell heavily but didn't stay.

"There's no frost to hold it." Roy obviously knew about this too. "These days the snow can fall one day and completely melt the next."

We had walked to the far end of the house, through blue and straw-coloured rooms, now discoloured by spotted streaks of mould and damp.

All the ordinary possessions of a family, the toys, cushions, wastepaper baskets, curtains and clothes, were piled in the far bedroom, but John was anxious not to draw too much attention to them, because they had been burgled after the last flood. And yet the reason they were here was because they loved the open countryside and had hated living in the town.

The house had been strongly built. Their neighbours had been less fortunate. The bungalow next door had been lifted and turned on its foundations. Nothing now remained of it except a dirty depression in front of an overgrown garden. The occupiers had abandoned it and moved away completely to start again, but Roy and Val were utterly determined to stay. They were living in a caravan with their daughter Naomi, their son Garry and the dog Missy. Over coffee, beneath a shelf holding Val's collection of model cars, she told me their plans. They had applied for planning permission and were going to build up, almost abandoning the lower floors, so that they could live above it all.

"You're Queen Canute," I said.

Val was giggly. "This is my home. We've been here fourteen years. We built this place. It's not just bricks and mortar. They're not going to help us. The government have abandoned us, really. They're concerned about the town but they don't care what happens to us, but we're going to stay here. This is our home."

They weren't going to get any more insurance, however. The company had abandoned them too. The landowner had spent some money repairing the bank, but I sensed that it was only a matter of time before the water came back, dirty and full of sewage; the water that had layered their garden with straw and mud and destroyed all the precious things they had forgotten to take (the children's pictures from school and the train ticket they had kept from their first date); the water that had simply lifted up the table where they had put things for safety and thrown it down in the filth; that had left them with a mortgage and no house on a bit of soggy threatened land.

Sometimes at night in their caravan the family could hardly sleep for the noise of the geese. Formations were flying up above the house as I left. A flock of about a hundred Canada geese were preening on the far side of a shingle bank in the river bend. They were there as a little primeval warning. They come every year from Siberia to what had been marshland long before the local famers tried to reclaim it for agriculture. About 3,000 years ago the Bronze Age civilisation that lived and farmed along these valleys was driven away by the climate. A volcano erupted in Iceland and brought freezing winters and crop failure. A few thousand years before that, the last glacial period had made this area completely uninhabitable. Some sort of climate change will come again, perhaps induced by us, perhaps as another part of a cycle that started two and half million years ago. Officially, despite global warming, we are still in an inter-glacial pause. The geese are ready to adapt. We might find it less easy. Not all of us will be as resilient as Roy and Val.

A FROZEN LEG OF HUMAN

I didn't want to swim in the Tay. The idea seemed horrible to me. I'm not really an action man. I hate the cold. I don't want to be cold. I want to be warm.

In fact, I had spent a lot of the previous evening walking up and down my hotel complaining about the radiators. It wasn't as devastatingly cold as it would have been in a tent at the North Pole. There was no threat of blackened toes. I knew I was in Scotland, home of the goose-pimpled. (Men arrive for work on the mountains with three top buttons undone and sleeves rolled up. Sexual excitement is generated by chapped legs in a short skirt and a brisk nor'easter.) But I was cold. Was it August? No, it was November. I could expect some rudimentary internal heat in November, even in Scotland.

I went to reception. They fought back. They totally ignored my first visit. After supper I went again. The owner glowered at me from a distance and hitched up his chef's trousers. A man was sent to find the hotel's portable

SWIMMING WITH THE PHIBBIES

The members of Ye Amphibious Ancients Bathing Association (or Phibbies, as it is known) have been swimming in the icy waters of the River Tay since the club was founded in Broughty Ferry, near Dundee, in 1884.

Phibbies is now the only open-water swimming club in Britain. Nevertheless its members are still as keen as ever to encourage others to join them in the Tay, if not the even less warm waters of the open sea and the Scottish lochs.

Members say that wild swimming provides the body with a rush of endorphins. Swimming in open water results in extra blood going to the brain, heart and lungs to protect them from the cold and this in turn produces an exhilarating "tingly" feeling.

In the late nineteenth century it was not unusual for 60 swimmers to gather for a morning dip in the Tay. Nor did it seem to do them much harm. In 1889 the Phibbies appointed John Barrowman as their first Chief Ancient or President. He held the post for 25 years until his death at the ripe old age of 79.

Joyce McIntosh, the club's first female president, has seen interest rise in recent years. When she joined in 1982 she says there were just eight members. Today more than 200 people take part while several thousand others come to watch. It's always fun watching someone else plunge into freezing water, isn't it?

Phibbies enjoying a traditional New Year's Day "dook" in 1889.

electric heater. He took an hour. This was a vain attempt to batter me down, to make me get used to the nip in the bathroom, but I waited, rubbing my hands, until they allowed me to plug it in and huddle over it.

The following day, with a high blue sky and a bite in the air, I met up with a crowd of people in tracksuits from Ye Amphibious Ancients Bathing Association, in front of the Perth harbourmaster's office. They were the oldest open-water swimming club in Scotland. The "ye" gave them away. It was a "ye" from the Victorian era when men jumped into the Tay on New Year's Day and swam to the other side. I suppose they were drunk, but I had no such excuse.

The sun was already going down. After all, it was half past two. The water was looking progressively more frozen. This was snow melt.

The harbourmaster gave me somewhere to change and regarded me with an expression that I recognised as pity.

Frank Chalmers from Kentish Town, though originally from Dundee, had been a member since he was a boy. He had big shoulders and was quite short. He was a good friend of my ex-girlfriend from university.

"She says she'll never forgive me if I kill you," Frank said. This sounded like an improvement in relations with my ex-girlfriend, but it was a disconcerting proposition.

"Is there a chance of death? Nobody spoke of death."

Frank laughed heartily. "No, no. Well … I mean there could be a chance of a heart attack. But you're fit. It will be good for you. It's a wonderful stimulus to the nerve endings."

"What is?"

"The pain."

Already there were several assumptions that I wanted to tangle with, but I started with the most obvious one. "Pain? Is it painful?"

"It's very cold." Frank paused significantly as if flippancy were not enough. "Very cold," he repeated, so that I understood. "And it is a bit of a hammer blow to the system."

"Is it best that I jump in and charge away?"

"No." Frank was oddly emphatic. "No, don't jump in."

I didn't like this new tone. Seriousness was laying a clammy hand on our badinage.

"Far better to slide in carefully," Frank continued thoughtfully. He was chewing his lip with the concentration of a hippo. "Sometimes the shock can close up the windpipe and I wouldn't want you getting into difficulties at the beginning."

"No." And I meant no. Up until this point, I had been buffoonishly exaggerating my distaste for the whole experience. I didn't fancy it. I was recalcitrant. I was a prima donna. This was mere childish hysteria. I value childish hysteria when it serves my own interests. But I had used up my supplies of temper. I was exhausting even myself. I had graciously agreed to be cold and wet and uncomfortable if the director really, really wanted me to be cold and wet and uncomfortable for no good purpose at all.

But this was different. Frank was now ringing an ambulance bell and sounding his siren at the same time. There was that word again. "Shock." I was shocked by my bedroom the night before. That was the sort of shock I liked to moan about. This was more akin to "shock" as understood by medical practitioners. I had been fed up. Now I was looking at him seriously.

But Frank was taken off in a car to somewhere up river, because he was planning to start our relay by sliding in from the bank. I was going to join him by boat.

Another man in a red and white tracksuit came along to mark my bare wrists and shoulders with a magic marker. I had to take off my fleece. The air was savage. The number was "3". That was my place in the relay. They promised I would be in for about five minutes and doing the fastest bit.

"Why do you need to mark me?" I asked.

"So that we can spot which one you are in the race."

"You won't recognise me?"

"I'm sure we will, but the judges might not."

I saw what he meant. We all look pretty much the same in the water, and this would identify me fairly quickly. I was still trying to work out why it was necessary, in an eight-person relay. My number felt disconcertingly handy for a lifeboatman dragging a bloated icy corpse off a sandbank somewhere in the mouth of the Tay estuary.

But now I was hurried away myself. I got in a RIB with a man in a complete drysuit and helmet and Beth McDonough, who peered out at me from under a yellow bathing hat with a black logo on the side I think it was advertising some children's swimming club.

"I've got one of those," I ventured.

"You'd better have one like this," she said. "It's thicker."

Like Frank, Beth was not a lithe young slip of an athlete. She was wearing a tracksuit and a look of inner resolution on her face.

"Do you do this in November a lot?" I asked.

"No, never," she said firmly. "The season usually ends around September."

There was a pause. I felt that I was in some way to blame. Or my producer was to blame. We said very little as the RIB sped up and alongside Tay Street, except to compare more kit. Nose plugs, no. Goggles, yes.

"Put on some Vaseline to protect against chafe."

Was I going to be in long enough to chafe? We were travelling fast. My big green fleece began to feel wholly small and unfleecy.

I wanted the speeding to stop because I felt too cold. And this was on the boat, and dressed.

The inflatable reached Smeaton Bridge and revved up to shoot through what appeared to be fierce rapids between the pink granite arches.

"He's gone in," someone said suddenly. I looked across where Beth was pointing and there was Frank.

He had got in to the water from the side of the river above the bridge and was now striking out for the middle arch. It was all happening very quickly. I had expected more preamble, more time to brood. The current was racing Frank along. He was producing a strong steady crawl. His little yellow head in the bathing hat was bobbing along and his limbs were thrashing steadily through the black water. As we approached more closely I could see that the arms were already a flayed pink in colour.

I could also see that the hugely experienced Frank was pausing from time to time, steadying himself, to retain control, not only of the current that rushed him through the eddies but also, I suspected, of his own resolve. Then he swam remorselessly on.

Beth started to take off her tracksuit. She had a blue swimsuit. Her voice had the hard tone of a person about to undertake a disagreeable task in the name of duty. "You'll have to help me here, because I've never been over the side of a boat before," she said. Murmured voices of concern guided her to the side. Beth was number two. I watched her prepare. And helped her over. She slid in.

"Oh," she said simply, and began to breaststroke with a slight look of bewilderment on her face.

I started to dwell on the significance of the number three on my wrist. Frank was one. Beth was two... But now with Beth gone, I had to help Frank aboard and we hauled him up, a shower of silver water cascading off his red raw frame.

"Ahharrr," he gasped. "It's like fire."

He sat for a moment on the black cushion of the boat hull and blinked water out of his face. He didn't reach for a towel or robe. He just sat. I would come to understand why. He was, by sitting there naked in the bitter air, much warmer than he had been a few seconds ago.

"It is cold enough for three things," he rasped. "One, it's like being set on by a blowtorch. Two, it's so cold that even the enamel on my teeth hurt. And three, I lost my penis on the bottom of the river there." We covered him in the dressing gown I had brought to hide my man boobs.

Beth was plugging on. After five time-bomb minutes, I noticed that the other support boat was alongside Beth and realised that it was now my duty to join the relay. I had to slip into this freezing water. I seriously considered backing out, even at this stage. Both Frank and Beth appeared wounded by their encounter. But the routine was un-resistable so I slipped over the side.

It was fiery. And it did reach up and hold me in shock. I didn't feel particularly panicky but the symptoms were exactly the same. My breath came in short rasping gasps. I felt light-headed. I felt that my arms had no power in them. The cold began as a blistering pain and then got worse. I had fully intended to do the crawl but I simply couldn't. I couldn't bring myself to force my head under the water, so I swam down the river using breaststroke. I very rarely swim breaststroke. It usually seems such a slow and clumsy way of propulsion, but now, like an old woman with a new hairdo, I kept my turtle head stretched out of the freezing water.

After three or so minutes I nearly called it off. I nearly said "You've got your shots, I've had it!" – but I knew that would be cowardly. I knew what it took to get men over the top. I had to stick it, and I paddled on. The water seemed supernaturally clean. Even the bits in it were clean. Leaves were not disintegrated pulp but spiralling frozen crystals. The freshness of the water made it seem less buoyant. At one point I turned and swam a bit on my back, but I was never going to stick my face in that ice bath. Never.

On we went. I have been in cold water before, but this water never warmed me. My thrashing didn't generate heat. I never got used to the cold. It simply got colder and colder and colder. It was sucking the body heat out of me.

The last few minutes were the worst. I thought of sailors on the North Atlantic convoys. I thought of the passengers on the *Titanic*. I thought of giving up. If you fall in the North Sea, even in summer, the hypothermia will kill you in an hour. The current was not at its fastest on my bit of the relay. My bit turned out to be the longest leg. Frank had made a little miscalculation. I was in the Tay for more like ten minutes and when I came to drag myself out over the edge of the RIB my poor red thighs pulled across the rubber like a windscreen scraper.

It would have been nice if a brisk rub-down with a rough towel had brought on a sudden rush of exhilaration to rival the high from class A drugs. But after I got out, I got colder. I noticed that Frank was now bluer than when I had got in.

I was put ashore. I went back to the harbourmaster's office, I sat by his blow heater. I put on six layers of clothing and a puffa jacket and I shivered ceaselessly for forty-five minutes.

I had reached the end of my Scottish journey. The river had claimed my inner warmth and carried it down to the sea.

Detail from "Trent Waterways from Nottingham to Newark", 1531.

Chapter Two

FROM THE MERSEY
TO THE HUMBER

AMLWCH. PILOT BOAT. 3 A.M.

It was dark. It usually is at three in the morning, but this felt darker, partly because there wasn't a moon and partly because I would rather have been in bed. I was off in a thick, countryside blackness, along deep lanes bordered by high-hedged fields. We were crossing Anglesey in a convoy of Mercedes vans and Nissan SUVs, bound on what was apparently routine business. We were going to ambush a ship.

I suddenly recognised where we going. Five years before, Amlwch Harbour had been one of the candidates on the first series of *Restoration*. It had tall, inverted slate walls and a deep basin, like a castle sink. It was built for ships exporting copper from a strange spoil heap called the Parys Mountain. "That must be around here somewhere too," I said. Too dark to see, of course, but no doubt it loomed against the sky somewhere. The harbour and the mountain had been a joint candidate. They didn't win the competition, but I remembered the eerie fascination of the place: a copper mine that had been worked for nearly 3,000 years and had shut up shop in my own lifetime. Even people with a bone for a pickaxe had bothered to work that mine, but we had lost interest. It had quickly become a huge and austere monument – unloved, unused and, in the end, un-voted for.

Except that it wasn't unused. We arrived, breaking out of the dark onto a dazzlingly bright wharf in a harsh floodlit island. A familiar orange Nelson launch sat in the black plughole of the harbour. This remote corner of Anglesey was being temporarily used to pick up pilots to guide ships through the difficulties of the River Mersey.

The safety lecture was quick and efficient. We buckled into lifejackets and loaded kit. The pilots were on important business. We were just tagging along. They revved the engine and we dropped down a twenty-foot ladder onto the deck. Ladders were a significant part of this trip. There was another, longer one ahead.

We swung out in a welter of eddies and white water. We were crammed into the darkened cabin, lit only by the green light of the radar: something tiny going out to meet something enormous. As soon as we had passed the shadowy point, the skipper gunned the engine and we charged out into an ethereal smoking darkness at twenty knots. The sky already had the shiny petroleum-blue edges of approaching dawn. But the flat sea was a little disappointing. We had been hoping for some action. We knew we had to catch our boat as she swept in. We had to daringly come alongside, and the pilot would have to daringly leap for the ladder and I was daringly going to go with him.

I had imagined stormy conditions when the boats would clash and the jump would be terrifying. But today would surely be easy.

"Have you ever fallen in?"

"Not yet."

Geoff Rafferty the pilot looked unsuited to great feats. There were no drysuits and waders and no safety helmets. A dignified chap, he had come down from his farm to do a week's shift, dressed for work, as he always was, in a suit and tie with sensible leather shoes. His one concession to the sea was an overcoat.

Once aboard Geoff would take over from the ship's captain and have full responsibility for getting one of the biggest ships on the Atlantic safely into the River Mersey and then into dock. Neither were simple tasks.

And there she was. I missed her until she was almost upon us. We were both going at speed and we had smoothly crossed paths as planned. The *Atlantic Conveyor* had been built as a replacement for a vessel that went down in the Falklands. Over to our port, she was swinging round on a converging course, a huge slab of metal with the profile of a floating box. She was blacker than the black of the sky. She had powerful lights in her castle that threw an off-circle of light, making her commanding and irreproachable.

As we got closer, so she got bigger. The hull loomed over us and diminished us further. Somehow, on this calm night, it was as if we were approaching a massive object floating in space not the sea. But we could see that the water was surging past her hull now. We were converging to match our speed to hers. She was hardly going to pause. She was on a tight schedule and we had to hop aboard.

The flat plane of the ship's side was broken by a perfect square – a door cut in the hull. Two figures in orange boiler suits and helmets were standing high above us, with a rope ladder lying flat against the side beneath them.

Geoff stepped out of the warmth of the cabin and edged around the narrow lip of the pilot boat with practised speed. We wanted to stop and take stock, but Geoff was ahead of us, stepping onto the ladder and clambering up in one fluid movement. I followed. Two members of crew hauled us into a metal cubbyhole. Another vertical ladder led up from the boarding platform and through a hatch. Geoff went up that too. I followed, but by the time I got to the top he had hurried on. Like the white rabbit, he was gone. Andy the cameraman called me back. He wanted to catch more shots.

The pilot boat was already disengaging. The rest of the team were aboard. I climbed the ladder again and tried to get some semblance

Lost Atlantic Empires. The Liver Building and Mersey Ferry.

A long way to breast-stroke. Across the Mersey to the Anglican Cathedral.

One way to attract the ladies.

Containers in Seaforth bring more goods to Liverpool than ever before.

The Albert Dock. Built out into the river to take bigger ships.

The Manchester Ship Canal slides past Old Trafford.

The River Irwell still looking vaguely poisonous in Manchester.

The Canal Bridge, Salford by Lowry.

Kitted out for underground river exploration. Batteries not included.

Stagnant water navigation at Standedge Tunnel on the Huddersfield Narrow Canal.

of continuity but the *Atlantic Conveyor* was picking up speed. Geoff wanted to catch the tide.

I helped haul the kit up on deck and we were led off deeper into the great metal world of the ship. "It's a good setting for a horror film, isn't it?" I said to Andy. "You know – like a space station." This was an enclosed community, who rarely even got ashore, on a great labyrinthine darkened moving platform, sweeping across enormous distances.

A hundred yards of dimly lit walkway stretched between a metal bulwark and the scuffed rusty edges of the containers above us. We dipped through a safety door into a suddenly over-bright corridor and took a lift to emerge into what felt like an early 1980s office, following our guides as they snaked down passages and climbed more steps, crossed a plastic wood-veneered mezzanine, and stepped out into the enclosed bridge, where the daylight was now breaking through. Five or six officers and crew were standing silently in a long lateral gallery from which plate glass gave a view out on all sides. The starboard passage behind the navigation room was lined with exotic cacti and succulents sitting in pots on a ledge: the spare captain's hobby. (The ship had two captains who took turn about. The indoor-plants man was currently on leave at home in Sweden, where this vessel was registered, and the other, Stefan Johansson, was standing just beside Geoff.)

Once aboard, Geoff effectively took complete control of the ship. Somewhere about fifteen feet away one of the crew was holding a small lever. It was the steering mechanism. Geoff would occasionally talk into a hand-held radio device. But mostly he just looked ahead and then down at his watch.

"We're a little early," he explained, "So I'm slowing down."

He pointed to the screen nearest to me. It was a GPS reading of our position. The *Atlantic Conveyor* appeared as a black, arrow-shaped oblong on a map of the coast, overlaid with radar. "We have to be careful because we actually only clear four feet over the sand bar at this stage of the tide."

It was a tiny margin. But this was a world of tiny margins, realised by long practice and super-efficiency: the margin of tide, the margin of time, the margin of size, the margin of dockage and the margin of profit. The *Conveyor* had come from Antwerp and timed her journey exactly so that she would enter the complicated arrangement of sandbanks at a precise moment, give or take three or four minutes. Ahead was a big red and white buoy.

"That's the centre ground," said Geoff. He pointed to the radar where it stood out as a giant black shadow. But Geoff was still looking out at the sea and visually judging the lie of the waters. The Mersey Estuary is not a funnel, like most entrances, but an hourglass. Two bastions of headland pinch the opening. It widens into a great expanse once it has gone beyond Liverpool. We were going to dock just before it closed up and became a harbour.

"The entrance to the port of Liverpool is very dangerous without a skilful pilot, and many ships and lives have, of late years, been lost owing to the negligence and ignorance of persons taking upon them to conduct ships and vessels into and out of the said Port." This was how the Act of Parliament relating to Pilotage at Liverpool addressed the matter in January 1765. In the previous year eighteen ships had been stranded on the sands and fifty lives had been lost and in 1766 an official pilotage service was set up.

As it happened, Geoff was not part of the Mersey pilot system. As a "Liverpool Pilot" he has a private arrangement with several companies, including the one that owns the *Atlantic Conveyer* and that was because, having successfully negotiated the narrow channel and pushed the speed back up, we were now hurrying towards the most complicated part of her journey: squeezing into the Royal Seaforth Docks.

I clambered up onto the top of the bridge and stood amongst the radar scanners to watch the *Conveyer* meet her tugs and turn in the river. The lock at the entrance was a tight fit. The ship went in with her tugs, one at either end, squeezed right up. They almost touched, but they didn't. That was the skill. There were no more than a few feet on either side. Using the bow thrusters and the forward engine, Geoff edged the ship to a stop by lining himself up with a mark on the dockside.

That was it. There was no waiting around. There was very little fuss. Everything was achieved in low voices and with redoubtable efficiency. The ship tied up in the main dock and, even as she did so, her stern doors opened, lorry-loads of goods were driven aboard, men started marching in and out, forklift trucks buzzed everywhere and mobile cranes began selecting and lifting the red and yellow boxes off her deck. Geoff was back in his coat and disembarking, his job done, almost before we had managed to pick up our stuff. There were good reasons for this rush. The ship would pay a prohibitive parking fine for each day spent at the wharf. It needed to leave at the next tide. The captain and crew would barely walk ashore. Everything that was needed would be lifted off and stored on the quays for further dispatching.

The Royal Seaforth Docks were built in the 1960s, opened in 1972 and have been growing ever since. They are barely in Liverpool at all. A ship arriving in the Mersey when the pilotage service was first set up would have gone right up into ten miles of docks built on both sides of the Mersey and might have taken three or four weeks to unload, but these docks had effectively been rendered redundant by the invention of containerisation. The river had moved on. A working river is constantly reinventing itself.

A DIP IN THE MERSEY

That evening, I went for my daily run in the rain, padding alongside the remains of one half-drained basin, over smartly laid granite setts, out past groups of disconsolate tourists scuttling around the Cunard, Liver and Port Authority Buildings.

These great grey monoliths face the Mersey like part of a vanished Egyptian dynasty – a Lost Empire of the Atlantic. They were separated from the city itself by what every provincial council in Britain seems to desire most in life – a six-lane highway right through the middle of town. Local motorists were careering through Liverpool at seventy miles an hour. The pedestrian traffic lights weren't working, so I stayed on the dock side of the road, jogging past the nearly finished entry to the Mersey ferry and on around a boardwalk in to the Albert Dock, originally built next to the site of the first commercial wet dock in Britain, and on this damp summer evening thronged with people.

The Mersey had provided a safe harbour for eight centuries. The Romans preferred Chester a few miles to the south, but that harbour silted up in the 1700s. As ships got bigger and the productive possibilities of the north of England increased so trade gradually moved to Liverpool.

The newspapers of the nineteenth century were in no doubt as to why. The waterway itself was treacherous and difficult, but it was the courage of Liverpool businessmen that made the Mersey successful.

The sides of the river were shallow. Boats became larger and the docks were built further out into deeper water to accommodate them. This had been an enterprise of courage and resourcefulness. It had certainly resulted in some magnificent, robust warehouses, the most instantly accessible of Victorian architecture: simple, strong and adaptable.

I panted through pastel-coloured crowds staring at clothing shops and trinket supermarkets festooned with Chinese-made imports. The old docks were obviously still a trading post. It was just retail rather than wholesale now. There were restaurants on the wharves and tugboats and heritage sailing vessels tied up in the basin.

The decline of these docks has been played out as a tragedy for the city. It left thousands redundant and changed a way of life. But the goods on show had in all probability still come ashore in Liverpool. That was what the *Atlantic Conveyer* was doing at the Royal Seaforth Docks. Liverpool today handles more cargo than the old docks ever did. Trade is unloaded further out towards the sea by a new improved system that employs fewer people and uses less of the river.

I ran beyond the Albert Dock and stopped. Ahead lay acres of freshly prepared building space. The ground had been cleared and neatly parcelled up. There were roads and canals, and a few new glass façades, but, as yet, no coherent commercial city. The way ahead ended in car parks and hoardings. I turned right and ran alongside the walls that had once rigorously kept the general public out. Now it kept me out. There was no way through along the river. I was forced to turn and run back the way I had come. I had reached the limits of the redevelopment.

To take my journey onwards the following morning I had to cross to the other side of the river. We disembarked in Ultra Mersey. As we travelled on to my next appointment with the river, we glimpsed bits of the elegant squares of one of the earliest planned cities in Britain poking through the ruins of Birkenhead, turned through an official-looking gate and came down to a granite launching jetty by a regenerated red brick dock.

Scraps of garden centre whitebeam, of the variety that redevelopers use to mark out their suburban ambitions, were thrashing in a force five wind. I was in a mood as foul as the weather. It made me crosser to see an ambulance and three safety boats standing by, so I launched into various absurd statements. "What are all these here for if I'm only going for a swim?" and, almost in the same breath, "You can't possibly expect me to swim in that!"

"That" was the murky, storm-tossed expanse of the estuary. From our restored wharf vantage point the Albert Dock was a mere smudge on the other side. As usual, I hadn't been listening when they told me what was planned. Now I began to focus.

"What do you mean it's a mile? Yes, of course I could swim a bit if the weather was better. I agreed to do this because it was going to be sunny. Look at it!"

Breakers were crashing on the launch ramp. Dirty, yellowy-brown water was heaving and swirling with a froth of unsavoury white foam.

"We've been across in far worse than this," said Dave Sandman, my companion from the Liverpool Open Water Swimming Club.

I scowled at him.

"But I don't think this is going to be easy for you," he chuckled. "We begin the cold-water training in April."

"In April! What training?"

"It's a long way and once you get really cold you can't do it. So we work up to it. We train in the Albert Dock.'

I turned to Jim, the director. "I'll go in for a little dip," I whined, "But surely you can get what you want and fake the rest?"

Dave was an engineer who worked for North West Water. He kept all the mechanisms going. He was justifiably proud that the water that now flowed into the Mersey from his machines was sparklingly clear. Five million people lived upstream of where we were now and in the old days most of their bodily waste was simply pumped into the estuary. "My dad used to take me down to the waterside at Otterpool and you could see… well, it was indescribable."

"Shoot me from the neck up only." I irritably instructed the cameraman. We stripped off. It wasn't really very cold. Not cold enough to tone up my bosoms anyway. Get your shoulders back! Posture! We picked our way down the jetty towards the sludge-coloured briney.

It wasn't just the human waste. The river has also been a great disposal drain for the manufacturing heart of Britain. Everything that could be swilled away went straight down this plug: originally, all the liquid by-products of a massive textile industry – foul-smelling dyes, bleaches and washing agents – and more recently the toxic by-products of the great chemical works at Runcorn. DDT had been developed on the banks of the Mersey. There was mercury in the sediment and the tide was certainly capable of dragging that up. I stood looking at the mustard-coloured stream, still boiling away in front of me. The water had been mixed with "persistent organic contaminants". My super-duper favourite was the by-product of the plastic industry: the endocrine inhibitors that changed the sex of fish. Perhaps it would change my recently pregnant woman shape and my tits back into something more manly. I was crouching and hobbling towards the edge.

"We jump in," Dave explained. "But don't dive. You don't know what's down there."

Proud of their super-clean-up of the dirty old river, the water company had rustled up some willing employees to go for a plunge ten years ago, reminding me of the Mexican mayor who drank the water to prove there wasn't any cholera and promptly dropped dead. Dave had been one of the volunteers.

It was supposed to take about twenty-five minutes. "It's sixty-four lengths of a pool, that's all."

"An Olympic pool…"

"No, just an ordinary pool."

I tried to work out what that was. Not a garden pool I suspected. We dragged on rubber hats, pulling hair.

Then he jumped.

I followed.

It was cold. That familiar crushing ice headache hit me, and then the panicked thrashing. I was bobbing around, somehow over-animated and feeble at the same time, flailing at the water. I could see it seeping through my goggles into my eyes. It filled my mouth and blew into my windpipe.

I hate swimming in the sea, except on a soft warm beach with nice blue breakers. And as I cleared my vision and struggled to get my lungs to operate in a less intrusive and demanding way, I noticed out of the corner of my opaque goggles that Dave was already powering away. Christ.

"Don't leave me, Dave!" I shouted and thrashed after him, plunging my head into the water, conscious only that my usually smooth, powerful crawl had become a dachshund's paddle. My casual, effortless breathing technique had become a rasping snatch. My whole chest seemed to have shrunk in the cold. I couldn't get air into it. I plunged on for what seemed like hours. It was minutes. Where was the end of the pool? There was nothing to measure. I trod water.

Dave was a distant white blob. I couldn't seem to breathe, even just floating. For God's sake, why wouldn't my body just relax and breathe? I breast-stroked for a bit.

The people in the safety boat looked worried. (Or more worried than usual. Safety people are paid to worry.) I hadn't got more than a few yards from the shore. But gradually I settled. It was like going for that run. At my age the whole body goes into shock even though it does the same thing every day. ("Not this again!") But then it gives in. I powered on. I hit a rhythm.

Dave turned round. I joined him. We pressed on together. He was still far too strong for me, but we were keeping up a steady pace. At this rate we would be across within a week or two, as long as the tide didn't change and drag us both out to Ireland; except that, slowly, I became aware of a dark shadow falling over the proceedings. The attention drifted away from me. There was a lot more shouting. It was a massive, black-hulled, bob-nosed oil tanker and three attendant tugs. I was surprised to see it for two reasons. First, because I had spent half the day pontificating on how the river had lost most of its commercial traffic (and this was clearly not a pleasure boat); and, secondly, because it seemed remorselessly and improbably to be moving towards us at speed.

Everybody wanted us out. Dave thought we had better get in the safety boat, director Jim was beginning to fuss politely, the safety people were on the point of sending up flares, so we headed for the safety boat, crawled up a toe-numbing ladder and I was handed a scrap of flannel to dry myself with.

That was that. The whole cross-Mersey swim was abandoned – and not because of any negativity on my part. What a pity. Because I have to say, when I took stock, I found I was in a much, much better mood.

THE MANCHESTER SHIP CANAL

I had experienced the Liverpool Mersey. I had swallowed quite a lot of it. I wanted to get on and across England. That night, I lay in bed at my hotel and fell asleep over a dull book. It was an account of the diligent bureaucrats and local government officials who built the Manchester Ship Canal. The next day I went to see it, and rather liked it.

We arrived at the heavily fenced entrance some six miles upstream from Birkenhead, unloading all our equipment in the full expectation of hitching a lift on a ship going to Manchester. Despite the traffic sliding busily in and out at high tide and despite all the pipes and the men in day-glo vests, this was a deserted twentieth-century area, with paths that nobody walked on where the asphalt was disfigured and erupting with moss.

The paintwork was patchy or disintegrating. Massive galvanised pipes wound themselves into forgotten intestinal complexities. The hard surfaces had none of the charm associated with the flagged passageways of the old Merseyside docks. Here was a harsh, inhuman environment built for fuel oil and aggregates.

Great barges called *Cormorant* and *Kestrel*, swilling with chemicals and sporting hatches with "emergency shower" written on them, slipped past on unregarded missions. They were probably on their way to Runcorn, where they would be pumped out to create plastics, or bleaches, or soaps or toothpaste or paints; all somehow made silently

LINKING MANCHESTER TO THE SEA

Industry on the Ship Canal in the mid twentieth century.

The Manchester Ship Canal was one of the last major canals to be constructed in Britain. The scheme to build it was hatched at Manchester manufacturer Daniel Adamson's home The Towers, Wilmslow Road, Didsbury on 27 June 1882.

There was fierce opposition to the project from the city of Liverpool as well as from the railway companies because it was felt that the new canal would inevitably take away their business. Nevertheless an Act of Parliament enabling the work to begin was passed on 6 August 1885.

Sixteen thousand navvies, some aged as young as twelve, were employed in the construction, along with 97 steam excavators, 174 locomotives, 6,300 wagons, 182 steam engines, 59 pile engines, 196 horses, 212 steam pumps and 194 cranes.

Railway bridges had to be raised and miles of track on either side of the canal had to be torn up and re-laid.

It was estimated that it would take four years to complete but in the event the canal was not finished until 1894, four years after the death of Daniel Adamson. Costs for the project had also risen to £15 million. Vastly over-running budgets – why does that sound familiar?

and without fuss, on an unimaginable scale, so that we don't have to pay too much for our basic household concoctions.

"Come from Rotterdam, probably," Alan Feast, the deputy harbour-master, explained in his control room. His colleague, Trevor, was the all-seeing canal controller of the moment. He was watching a bank of computer screens, which monitored thirty-six miles of canal. We sneaked away so as not to disturb him.

Alan had originally run away to sea himself. He got his ticket in the Merchant Navy and then worked in the Far East serving on oil rigs. We stood on the wharf to watch the lock gates open and he went a little soppy as he recalled his golden days in exotic ports and distant lands.

"But that's all gone now, Griff," he said. "Ships don't call at ports along the way these days. They just bash on."

The crews never even saw the container port where they offloaded cargo. Everything was getting longer – not just the voyages but the boats as well. Even the shifts and the tours were a trial, because the managements wanted them to travel more slowly to save on fuel.

The sailors we could see sliding past didn't look much like sailors, in their hard hats and orange boiler suits. They stood on the bows and threw huge cables on to the lockside, and then winched them back in when the gates at the far end of the lock opened. Thus another ship entered this huge man-made river, a river that was far more useful than the unreliable, shallow, uneven, unnavigable upper Mersey.

The Corporation of Manchester had deliberately undertaken their mammoth enterprise, a third of the length of the Suez Canal, in an attempt to best the Corporation of Liverpool. They wanted to steal business from the Mersey docks. But the whole venture had been touch and go. Just because it was a new and improved system, it didn't mean that trade was going to use it. The railway companies fought back. They refused to build lines to serve the canal. The Liverpool docks retaliated by dropping their rates. I had read the night before how the Corporation tried to get frozen meat to come right up to Manchester. They built refrigerated warehouses for it. Alas, frozen meat stayed loyal to its old routes. It was considered a major success to get the Egyptian cotton trade to use the canal.

And now? The Port of Liverpool and the Ship Canal are owned by the same organisation. Alan was very optimistic. Things had slowed a bit, but a rise in fuel prices meant that goods were returning to the canals. Tesco had just started shipping tanker-loads of wine up to thirsty Mancunians.

This seemed an invigorating prospect, but we couldn't get on it ourselves. At the last minute and at the highest level, our request was turned down. We were devastated. I didn't think they'd want me to paddle about on the "greatest engineering feat in the north" in a canoe, so we got back in the car and drove inland instead, another cargo lost to the internal combustion engine.

GOING UNDERGROUND

Posthumously, the painter Laurence Stephen Lowry seems to have Manchester in his grip. The new Arts Centre is named after him and so is a smart white hotel where I was staying. I don't remember. Did Lowry paint any leathery women in chrome-fronted dresses teetering up to glass-fronted bars? I could only think of Beryl Cook. But perhaps "the Beryl Hotel" lacked gravitas. Lowry's vision of a Manchester sunk in smog and dirt was clearly the preferred reference point for its glitzy regeneration.

We were there in preparation for a piece of film we never used. I needed to get inoculated for rabies. Something stirred in my memory. Didn't this involve a long needle stuck straight into my stomach? It was a well-known, ghastly ordeal, wasn't it? While I waited, I paced around my orange leather chaise longue and pulled back my grey hanging slash blinds. I peered out at a gloomy stretch of the River Irwell, six stories beneath me. It ran through a high-sided embankment and curved out of sight with no towpath or bankside walk. It was black and cold. Slabs of offices rose on the banks. The hotel seemed marooned beside it, waiting for some of the vacant areas nearby to be developed.

Over the last ten years people have moved back to live in inner-city Manchester and a new, brave, white basket of a Millennium footbridge crossed to our hotel, but the red pavers, trees and benches laid out by the river seemed wet and threatening. Everything was dominated by towering blank buildings. The Irwell obstinately refused to become an amenity. I was surprised to see a single sculler rowing past, like a gawky insect; an incongruous human touch. For the rest of the time the river sat and glowered between its high banks.

Unlike the poisonous green waters you see in Lowry's paintings, Manchester's rivers were once famous for their liveliness. The town had been founded by a bridge, which crossed a profusion of waterways rushing out of the nearby hills. These had eventually powered the mills that brought industrial pre-eminence to the city. There had been a smooth transition from ancient wool mill to linen mill to cotton gin. Water had been invaluable in this city. But where was all that water now?

Walking in the town I only came upon its rivers by chance. Manchester waterways run through ditches and culverts, behind walls, under shopping centres and down canyons of back alleys.

It was time for my rabies injection. Two kindly nurses arrived and I discovered that the needle in the stomach was only necessary if one had caught the disease. The inoculation was a simple, standard jab. So I only needed three people to hold me down while it was administered.

Later I asked my taxi driver if he knew the rivers of Greater Manchester. He did. He could take me to pretty bits if I wanted, he said, no trouble. There were pleasure boats on them in the summer. I was underestimating them. But as we drove along, heading north and east, we passed the routes of others that we couldn't spot at all. The Irwell he could name. The Mersey. But he got stuck on the Irk, the Tame, the Goyt, the Medlock and the Roch. There are twelve in all, running out of the hills and through the town.

And these are only the main ones. The team I was on my way to meet were responsible for keeping all the mini-tributaries, streams and brooks running underground. Fifteen strong, they went out in storms to clear drains and pipes, to make sure that 7,000 separate culverts ran freely. If they got blocked, the results could be catastrophic.

I changed into a drysuit and we marched off to find the entrance. We lowered ourselves down an overgrown bank and into Morton Brook. It stank. It was a nose-wrinkling stench, full of ammonia tinges – the smell of raw sewage. The bed was littered with plastic waste, gently swaying in the current. I could make out most of a child's bicycle.

"Mattresses, furniture, wheels, fridges, pallets, drums or just trees," Mark Whittaker said, "and there's a lot more fly-tipping recently. I think the biggest thing we ever had to get out of one of these tunnels was an entire Mini. We had to cut it up and take it out piece by piece."

Despite the stench this wasn't a sewer, but there had been a lot of rain and that could cause the effluent to overflow and pour into the river system. The foetid water beneath our feet was essentially on its way into the Mersey that I had swum in a few days ago. Gradually, sewer systems are being improved to stop this happening but in the meantime it added to the discomfort and danger of Mark's job.

I had been squeezed into a complete waterproof suit, zipped up at the chest with a rubber seal at the neck. I had a helmet, rubber gloves and wellington boots.

The brook ran beneath a low wide arch. His team was doing a routine check. They left men on the surface at the exit manhole, where their unit was parked up, and they stayed in constant radio contact. They carried gas monitors to test the quality of the air. These beeped. Red lights flashed continuously as we slithered into the darkness. It was like entering a level of Dante's inferno. We were a military patrol on a smelly tributary of the Styx.

The brook was not as littered in the tunnel but the bed of the river was a mess of bricks and slabs. "Careful how you go." Mark kept looking out for me.

The sewage waters no longer carried the danger of cholera or typhus. The drainage systems were kept scrupulously clear of the drinking water systems, but that didn't mean there wasn't disease down here. We never saw them, but the Norway rat certainly lived in these underground systems. Rats have killed millions by spreading bubonic plague. Today they continue to infect the water with Weil's disease, which is carried in their urine. It is the world's most widespread zoonosis (a disease caught by humans from animals) and 15 per cent of cases are fatal.

"You just have to watch yourself, Griff." A colleague of Mark's in Cornwall had got splashed in his face. "That's all it was, and he got

THE TROUBLE WITH RATS' URINE

Weil's disease is a severe form of leptospirosis. Traditionally infection with this bacterium was associated with miners, fish workers and sewer men. It is caught most frequently on muddy riverbanks, ditches and in livestock-rearing areas, and there is a direct correlation between incidence of the bacteria and the amount of rainfall.

The disease is transmitted to humans by contact with the urine of animals such as rats, mice and voles. Other animals, including rabbits, cattle and dogs, can also carry and transmit it. Dogs, for example, could contract the disease after swallowing water containing the urine of an infected animal.

Leptospirosis causes flu-like symptoms such as fever, headaches, muscle pain and skin rash around two to three weeks after contact with the bacterium. The more severe form, Weil's disease, affects only about 15 per cent of those who catch leptospirosis but its symptoms include jaundice, liver damage and internal bleeding.

While it's not a good idea to drink river water, I wouldn't get too hypochondriacal about it. Over the last decade, an average of 54 cases of leptospirosis per year have been diagnosed in England and Wales. That's about one case per million people.

A ratcatcher in the sewer, 1870, demonstrating how to catch Weil's disease.

the disease. It didn't kill him but he was off work for months and hasn't fully recovered. Careful how you go."

That was difficult to do. The stinking water ran and gurgled over greasy stones and deep hollows. My wellingtons didn't feel entirely secure. The torches and headlamps reflected off the dark green goo. They made the shadows blacker and more difficult to penetrate. Most of the time, however, the lights were focused above our heads.

Mark's job was to check the brickwork for signs of subsidence. He swept his torch over thousands of bricks, packed delicately into a continuous undulating roof.

"You can see the more modern work there, Griff, but essentially this is the same structure that was put up by the Victorian engineers." Mark flashed his torch into an elliptical hole about two feet high. It was made of red bricks, wet, clean and glistening. It narrowed slightly, curving away and out of sight: a squashed tube, but a tube made of bricks, an impossible construct to imagine. Organic in shape, it was made entirely out of oblong segments. What a thing! It could have been an installation in a contemporary art museum. It was a monument to an anonymous bricklayer, one of thousands of such tunnels, painstakingly pieced together, utterly unseen in the darkness and oddly moving.

Mark splashed away. I stepped after him, caught my boot on a rock and fell sideways into the murk.

"Shit!"

I put out my hands and crashed into the water, banging myself on unseen slabs. I had fallen into the putrid stream. I could feel that my rubber glove had burst. I lay struggling on my side. The water was running over my suit and hands. I pushed myself up.

"Alright?" Mark shone his torch on my hands.

"Yes. Yes. Fine."

I felt stupid. After everything they'd told me, I had fallen straight in the sewage. I was anxious to play it down. "I didn't get anything on the face."

"Good. No rips or anything in the suit?"

There weren't. I held my hands in the light. They looked bleached white and frail. I turned them over. "Luckily there aren't any cuts or scratches," I said.

"No, but we'll wipe them in antiseptic just the same."

Quite frankly I was surprised I had stayed on my feet so long. My ankles were sore where they were rubbing against the boots. The trudge was exhausting. The concentration was wearying.

In fact we were nearly at our destination. The ceiling suddenly rose up. There was a massive, rusted, round portal ahead of us, operated by huge iron cogs. It was throwing gothic shadows about in the glare of the torches. To the left and right were balconies surmounted by balustrades hung with the remains of tassels of used lavatory paper. It was part of the flood relief system. Mark pointed downwards. He shone his torch and we knelt and looked into a much smaller, lower tunnel, which ran on as far as the light could reach.

"That's where the brook goes. We'll be going down there soon to check that out."

It was knee-high. The team have to clear spaces as low as three feet tall.

"But not today, eh?" Mark laughed and turned. He took me up a set of steps, smeared with a thick layer of pustular mud, to the balcony and then through a low arch. Another set of steps led down. "Pop down there and have a look to the right," he said.

I teetered down the goo-encrusted treads into the dark and shone my light where he directed. A long tunnelled slope descended at an acute angle.

"That goes down sixty foot to the lower-level sewers," Mark shouted from behind.

I figured that when the water reached a certain height they could shut off the outlet with the big door and it would shoot through this pipe to some unimaginable horrid drain far below. The team had sent one of their camera robots down there. A long way below in the depths of the treacherous sloping tunnel I could see another light and another network of culverts leading away into the darkness.

"I love this." Mark said, and meant it. "It's a fantastic place. It's all that planning and building."

And I was pleased to have seen it. I admired the work he did, day after day, night after night, down there in his Mancunian Hades, but I was already exhausted and a little scared and disgusted by the smell. I was pleased to come back up the stairs and see the well ahead, like a sentry box set into the glutinous walls. It was a tiny space; big enough for two of us. I stepped in and looked up. High above me there was a small circle of light.

"Keep your hands crossed in front of you and don't try to use the built-in ladder holds on the way up." Mark shackled me to a wire. "Unfortunately some of them aren't very secure."

He signalled, the wire tightened and I lifted off. Like an unwanted sack of potatoes I began to grind upwards, a slow ascent up a long manhole, to the light, the cars and the fresh air.

EAST AT FOUR MILES AN HOUR

Forget Me Not had a tapering bow and a hull caked with years of crackled pitch. Her cabin's painted flowers were faded. Her sides were scuffed. She was one of the few remaining working barges. She still cleared litter for a living and had a proper hold, currently loaded with old bikes, broken fridges and tyres. I clambered aboard and Andy let me drive her away.

To do this, I had to pull on a round handle sticking out of the cabin housing. It needed gentle, toggling persuasion to get her into gear. Finally there was a big clunk. A waft of black diesel smoke blew across our faces from the chimney (ah, the seductive stench of diesel engines) and we eased out. Not without difficulty, because we were aground.

"It's silted up a bit here close to the bank," Chris Leah said, jumping off and pushing at the bow.

Like all engineering systems, canals require constant maintenance. The whole network quietly died with the coming of the lorry after the Second World War. By the late 1960s it was in crisis. But here, for once, was a major waterway success story: the leisure industry saved our canals. Thousands of miles have now been restored.

Chris pushed her out into the middle of the channel, where it had been properly dredged. We chugged at four miles an hour under a bridge to join the Huddersfield Narrow Canal. Even here, in this run-down area, Chris was able to point out locks, turning bays and stonework, all painstakingly restored, although some of it, he admitted, to specifications which were a liability to him.

The system had originally been designed for boats that were seventy feet long. The designers allowed a small amount of clearance in locks and at basins. Alas, boat builders and canal companies decided that they could use that clearance if they were clever, so they added the extra three feet to the boat. *Forget Me Not* was seventy-three feet long. She fitted this canal to the inch and sometimes, after canal restorations, not quite to the inch.

We ducked down to get under the first bridge. Footbridges, road bridges, pipes and carriageways permit no more than you need and apparently you don't need to stand up. We swung out through the Portland basin and into an even narrower cut.

We were perched on a narrow platform at the stern of a narrow boat. The tiller handle swept the entire available deck. Andy pointed out that I could only control the barge by standing in the hatchway above the steps that led down to the tiny cabin and reaching behind me to the tiller. Otherwise I would push myself over the side as I tried to turn the boat.

Even though I kept forgetting this fundamental instruction, and had to dance and squeeze around the tiny deck, I liked steering *Forget Me Not*. It was a battle. Everything had to be anticipated. Her great length would come round quite smoothly, but only if allowed time. Getting her straight was a geometric puzzle, and entering a lock without scraping the hull required minute, exact judgment. The first lock had to be negotiated through a long, low tunnel.

"There's a Tesco built on top of us," Chris explained, peering up from under his fedora as I wrestled to turn our length and straighten up fully before we dived underneath.

"Not bad," he said, but then there was an ominous thud and, because that is the way of such matters, the thud was followed by a succession of scrapes, bangs, crunches and judders. I realised that we would take a little time to ram our way into the available slot. In fact, we were going to bounce our way in, like a stick up a pipe.

There wasn't much time to commiserate about the paintwork or note, comfortingly, that it was already pretty battered, cracked and scuffed, before I had to stop. The tunnel came straight into the lock. I reached for the big black round handle and shoved it forward. We slowed.

"That's reverse," Chris said. "We're going out now."

I pulled it back, forwards, then back again. There was a tiny gap in between forward and reverse where the gears fitted into neutral. It was a slight dip, which I could feel if I concentrated very hard indeed. After about half an hour of churning and thudding we finally settled. I climbed the ladder up the side of the lock and, watched in utter silence by a posse of lads with glazed eyes, I wound the lock gates shut behind us and released the water into the pound.

We rose six or seven feet and then, with another pall of choking black smoke, we chugged on.

We were making our way steadily upwards, rising out of Manchester, heading northeast towards the distant hills. The locks came regularly every few hundred yards. On either side we passed a phalanx of abandoned factories and mills: hundreds and hundreds of mainly derelict buildings. Sometimes they had been replaced with new corrugated sheds but for the most part they were bare façades with blank smashed windows, sprouts of buddleia in their upper gutters and overgrown yards on the canal side. Sometimes little mini canals shot off to service their back entrances. There were big pipes that led into the water, presumably to suck it up, and others with rusted trumpet bell ends, to drop something back in.

We kept passing over real rivers running out of the hills. Later, on another canal at Marple Junction, twelve miles to the south, I looked down into a deep valley at what seemed to be the least explored and exploited river in Britain. It was the Goyt – quite difficult to get to, hemmed in by trees and tumbling down over stones to Manchester. It would have been impossible to use this river for transport. The navigators who built the original canals dug alternative rivers around the hills for the benefit of manufacturers. They extended the navigable river systems in order to bring coal from Huddersfield and to carry goods inland or across the neck of England to eastern ports.

Sometimes the aqueducts we passed over in *Forget Me Not* were only a few feet high, but the river below was still a rushing, shallow unuseable stream. It was easy to see why Manchester was the birthplace of stagnant water channels. But it was rushing water I was moving on to find and to do that I had to go up higher than the canal could carry me.

THE FURIOUS DERWENT

The Derwent hurries fifty miles out of the Peak District to meet the Trent. Daniel Defoe called it "a frightful creature when the hills load her current with water" but it has been a working river all its length.

I joined the Derwent above the Ladybower Reservoir, trudging down over blanket bog to join the stream as it gushed through a steep valley, which was difficult to get to without slipping on the yellow grass into the chocolate-brown water. It was hard to imagine that here, in this inaccessible place, they had once mined for lead. And they had used the Derwent to drive their engines.

A drain on the Ladybower Reservoir on the Derwent.

A 'nick' in the Derwent, where a weir could have been made.

Kayaking not drowning and not me, near Matlock.

The Emperor's Fountain, Chatsworth. And a baby. Not to scale.

Chatsworth House and its artificially gorgeous river valley.

Passing through Megawatt Alley but not at record-breaking water-ski speed.

Swarkestone Causeway lying athwart its flood plain.

Work in progress at Joe Irving's boat yard, Barton-upon-Humber.

The Humber Bridge; and worth every penny.

Further downstream, I encountered its driving force, hidden away behind tree-lined banks. The Derwent is crossed by "nicks" – narrow points across the bedrock, which were used to dam and drive mills – and these weirs still exist. I walked along the top of one silted up, bulging and leaking, and sprouting with vegetation. Surrounded by thick wood it had almost become part of the natural landscape.

Derwent Hydroelectric Power is installing mini-hydro schemes on these old mill dams. They reckon that each of the major weirs could provide enough power to light a village. It seems ridiculous that we don't re-employ them, given the hideous alternatives marching across the skylines. But waterpower is the forgotten baby brother of the renewable industry. This certainly wasn't true when the river was the only source of energy.

For thousands of years, there have been flour mills all along the Derwent, but in 1771, just down the river, a former wig-maker, a technician in fiddly things, decided to build a Heath Robinson device even more complicated than a flour mill. He called it a water frame.

Richard Arkwright wanted to spin yarn to make cheap calico, using a machine. He needed a power source and so he sought out an old mill and built Cromford Mills to use water power (having previously tried horses at Nottingham). He mechanised what had previously been a hand process, and in so doing completely changed his own economies of scale. He revolutionised all industry, by making a purpose-built place for his equipment and his ambitions.

I went to revisit Cromford, recognised by many as the first factory, sitting in its grey, tree-covered gorge with its grey stone buildings ranged around a large grey courtyard in a grey dusk. It was closed. The visitors had left. But we sneaked in through the green gates past the cleaner's children playing in the yard. You can see how the idea worked. The factory became a visitor attraction when it opened. Arkwright guarded his secrets jealously, driving on through the night, with lights blazing, to produce more and more cotton, because the machine, unlike the flour mill, seemed to have endless possibilities. It grew itself. The buildings which had been erected steadily, year on year, round the yard attested to this.

By the end of the century there were thirty other mills down the same short stretch of river, but what is most memorable about any visit there is the sound and sight of running water. A canal runs through the centre of the factory, under the first building, and drops into a black and ominous weir. It reminded me that the "dark satanic mills" that Blake decried were not belching chimneys but water mills – then unnatural interferences with nature, now quaint, green and pollution-free, the essence of clean power.

SLEEPING ARRANGEMENTS

The Duke and Duchess of Devonshire invited me to Chatsworth to take part in a water-tasting exercise. I rolled up at the front entrance, properly miked, having been told the Duke himself was going to let me in. I had been advised to call the Duke "Duke". I was told he didn't care for "your grace". (I subsequently discovered that only servants ever used the term.)

I was a TV presenter by appointment, perhaps a superior tradesman, but I balked a little at the proposed address. "Duke, hi!" It sounded like he was John Wayne or something. You wouldn't call Sir Alan Sugar, "Knight". "Listen, Knight!" He wouldn't like it.

I comforted myself by imagining that the whole arrangement must be a bit like school. There was a robust, no-nonsense directness there, with perhaps a touch of role definition. "Could I have a word, headmaster?"

So what would it be? "Good to be here, Duke. Do call me 'Presenter'." I would manage somehow. I have been in the presence of royalty, and I know that addressing HRH as "HRH" or more commonly "Sir" comes very readily to anyone who has been to a sufficiently out-of-date school. You can even sling in a little peremptory familiarity if you're feeling daring.

As I stood in front of the grand entrance with the camera rolling I decided to call him absolutely nothing at all when he swung open the large paned door.

The first thing he said was "Call me Stoker."

"Pleased to meet you, Stoker," I said.

I was shown upstairs, up another flight, then left, left again, along a corridor and in the sixth or seventh door along to my quarters.

This was the Sabine Room. I went through a little ante-passage, opened a large door and gazed twenty feet to the ceiling. When I finally got my eyes there, it was worth looking at. The entire room had been painted by Sir James Thornhill, three hundred years ago, with a lively representation of the Rape of the Sabine Women. Men in grey Roman breastplates were carting off semi-clad women thrashing big white legs. I was to overnight in one of the greatest achievements of English high baroque.

At the window, the grounds lay spread out in a vision of riverside fantasy. The Derwent slipped between fields of grazing sheep, artfully dotted with clumps of great oaks. If I twisted to the right I could make out a fine, stone, three-arched bridge that led a country lane to the front entrance. It was as pretty as a picture, which was exactly as intended.

The landscape was created by Capability Brown, who had dammed and altered the flow of the river and moved the bridge (the new one was designed by James Paine) and utterly done away with a mill and an area of kitchen gardens to the left. He demolished most of the village of Edensor and transferred it out of sight. He planted hundreds of trees to create a perfect vision designed to echo a fantastical eighteenth-century notion of the landscape as the abode of gods and satyrs. The room and the grounds were of a piece and the river was a key part of this scheme.

It all did the job. A survey has shown that much the favourite element of any visit today is the setting in the landscape. Here was a river put to work in a different way, as an adornment and amenity. For once nobody was talking about this becoming redundant, and it was a continuing economic resource. Beauty can pay its way.

The estate was making use of the Pennine water in more prosaic ways too. It bottled its own spring and served it in all the restaurants, competing with nearby Buxton which had been a spa since Roman times. The Duke and I had a tasting in the library (and agreed only that flat de-ionised pure H_2O with every chemical and mineral removed for use in irons and batteries is quite the strongest-flavoured water you can drink), filmed during the rest of the day, dined with the Duke and Duchess and went to bed.

I followed that carefully articulated route again: up two flights, left and left again – along the corridor flanked by portraits of family friends like John Betjeman and Patrick Leigh Fermour, painted by other friends like Lucian Freud. In the bedroom, more friends were perpetrating muscular rape. Would I be able to sleep surrounded by such a mountain of intimidating flesh? Luckily I had my own flesh to intimidate in return.

I had decided, over dinner, not to mention the last time I had visited the house. This was in the time of the Duke's father. It was when I was presenting *Bookworm* and I had come to talk about Georgiana, the flamboyant eighteenth-century Duchess of Devonshire. My meeting must have taken place on a floor below.

While we had waited for the then Duchess, I asked if I might use the lavatory. The guide was clearly perturbed. We were just visitors.

I couldn't believe that anybody would mind. I was told to hurry up. When I emerged the Duchess had arrived in my absence and was startled to see me emerge from her lavatory. Perhaps she did mind. They were not public conveniences. Perhaps she was embarrassed by the roaring noise it made.

I decided to risk the lavatory again and stood for a while fiddling with the ancient plumbing. This was going to be very embarrassing. I was standing here unable to flush the thing once again. I would forever be known as that man who visited Chatsworth and made embarrassing use of the facilities – the lavatory man from the telly.

I depressed the handle slowly. I pushed it down quickly. I lifted it slightly. I did it suddenly, hoping to catch it off guard. I yanked, coaxed and dandled it, but nothing came. Bafflingly, it was simply a handle in a wall. There was no visible cistern. There was nothing to lift in order to depress ball-cocks or elevate levers. I was about to go back to the Sabine room, pack my bag and sneak out into the night through the carpentry shop, when I decided on one last push. I depressed the handle and at last something happened. There was a far-off gurgling, as if in some distant tower. The faint rushing sound began to grow and a few seconds later a great gush of water descended and washed all away. What a relief.

I knew that this water had travelled nearly five miles down from the East Moor to work all manner of ingenious systems in the big house but I hadn't imagined it would take most of the evening to get to me. But at last I could sleep soundly.

THE EMPEROR FOUNTAIN

Perhaps the delay meant someone had been fiddling with the Emperor Fountain. The next morning I went to take a look at Chatsworth's water power source with Sean Doxey, the Comptroller.

This extraordinary geyser was built after the sixth Duke of Devonshire had been on a visit to Russia. He saw the fountains at Czar Nicholas's palace at Peterhof, and in 1843 when he heard that the czar was coming to England (and likely to visit) he decided he would build a bigger and better spout for himself.

Joseph Paxton, his head gardener, was given six months to do it (work had to continue at night by the light of flares). The water, however, could not simply be allowed to drop down the mountain and shoot up the fountain. It had to feed a variety of other ingenious water features on the way, some already in existence.

Above the house, in thick woods, on a plateau, beneath the moors, there is a series of man-made ponds. Sean and I wandered up a leaf-strewn path and stood looking out over the Emperor Lake, misting slightly in the cold morning air. This was the eight-acre lake that had to be constructed 381 feet above the house, which with two miles of piping could deliver 4,000 gallons per minute.

A narrow open channel ran off to one side. We followed it to a confluence, where Brian and Henry were standing by. They were often standing by. One the continuous problems of any water system (should you be thinking of "doing a Paxton" yourself) is leaf rubbish. You have to keep clearing those pesky leaves. Or at least you have to employ a Brian and Henry to do it for you.

I was invited to start up the Emperor. To do this I had to lift a bar sticking out of a metal plate. The camera rolled. I tugged and pulled. I yanked. The veins stood out on my forehead. Brian and Henry looked on with pitying expressions. It wasn't just heavy. The plate was iron and a little rusty and seemed totally jammed into its socket.

This was the second time I had had to struggle with some mechanical object in this place. What sort of a country house visit was this? I had expected social humiliation and I was getting mechanical humiliation. I waggled it from side to side, lugged and hauled and finally, grunting obscenely, I lifted the plate and, at last, what seemed a pathetic stream of water gushed through the gap. But it was enough. We were off.

We ran, following the water down the hill. They call them follies, but this was mucking about in the garden developed to an epic obsession.

"What say we have a flat sort of rocky dish thing, up here right at the top of the cliff? The water hits it and then tumbles over, as if we were in a fairy grotto."

The water made a simple waterfall to begin its journey. We had to scramble down through rhododendron bushes to get to the next invention.

"Your Grace, I thought that we'd build an aqueduct."

"A Roman one."

"In the antique fashion, but just to make it even more Roman we'll make it look like a ruined one. The sort you might stumble upon in some overgrown forest."

"Love it."

"And then the water can shoot off the end and cascade a good fifty feet into a rock-strewn chasm."

And there it was, halfway down the hill: a totally barmy toy that must have cost a fortune to build. We weren't even halfway there yet. The water passed through a temple, one which Thomas Archer had provided in 1703. There was a secret lever to one side.

After another breathless rush across a road and through the trees, coming out at the beginning of the park, Sean scurried off to show me that the lever still worked. He returned and we stood at the base of the temple.

"Wait," said Sean. "Here it comes."

Two mythological creatures started to dribble, gush and then spout projectile vomits of water. Above our head trickles ran out of the gutters and as the water coursed through a siphon, driven only by gravity, every stage of the stepped roof began to run with water, like a fiendish version of a tower of champagne glasses in a thirties film. The water began to go everywhere. Roof, statues, walls, foundations became immersed in it. Down it fell, surging into a pool at our feet.

"But you know the hill directly leading away from the main house, your Grace. What I had in mind was a gigantic set of steps. They will be some hundred feet long and fifty feet wide and the water will cascade over them."

"Can you make it 200 feet?"

"Done."

The massive cascade, which has been voted the greatest water feature in Britain, was originally built for the Fourth Duke in 1696 and was then rebuilt on a larger scale five years later. Then in around 1830, Paxton rebuilt more than half of it to align it better with the house.

It dwarfs human beings. The water, having now engulfed the temple, was sluicing down these steps. And not a drop had so far been lost. The weight of the water was all still available. It could be diverted to run the sawmills, turn the spits and fill the grey water plumbing systems of the estate, but it could also be taken down a pipe beneath a harmless-looking manhole cover under the trees by the great lake.

Sean handed me a metal lever. I poked it into a socket somewhere in the darkness. I heaved it round, and finally felt it give. There was a subterranean roaring and gurgling. The mouth of the fountain started gushing.

"Keep turning."

Under my control the fount grew. It lost its tap water spout and began to feather. The wind caught it and it whitened. It went on climbing. It towered over 200 feet above us, spreading its spume all across the garden.

"I can pretty much guarantee that you will end up with a fountain that will be over 250 feet in height, your Grace."

"That will show the czar."

As it happens, the czar never saw it. His diary took him elsewhere at the time of the scheduled visit. Or perhaps he found out what had been going on and wisely decided he didn't want to see a fountain so much bigger than his own.

SLALOM ON THE DERWENT

The Matlock section of the Derwent is a picture of incident and romantic charm. We stood and waited in a car park, as filming people do, while above us a tiny orange figure clambered up a great grey wall that rose beyond the fringe of green trees. The river passes through a great chasm and we were there to take part in a canoe slalom – an exacting sport, so I was informed.

"No canoeing upstream." The sign was direct. We were allowed to launch and go downstream, but even then only by dispensation of the council because the council owned the land. They had decided, presumably after some deliberation, that canoeists might be allowed to use the waters – as long as they didn't interfere with the dye works or any other factory waste system. But nobody should dare to think that they might go on beyond the second bridge and certainly never explore beyond the bend in the river. That was private water.

The first kayak the Matlock canoe club provided for me was narrow and made of fibreglass. It was a proper slalom kayak with a small hole halfway along the top. I had to get my big arse in the small hole. First I had to get my fat thighs through and into the narrow bit up the front. We were already afloat, or nearly afloat. The bottom of the thing was resting on a few stones. I toppled forward and slid in and then got stuck. There was some debate and I was ignominiously pulled out like a rat out of a drainpipe. Little footrests deep in the hull were adjusted and I tried again.

"OK?" Chris Martin asked.

"Yes."

I didn't really think so. I was just saying it. My giant thighs were pressed up against the fibreglass and incapable of movement. One of my feet was lightly skewed at an acute angle. You have to sit bolt upright with your legs straight out in front of you and your back vertical. Like a duck or seal, the kayaker sacrifices dignity on land for later waterborne mobility.

I was given a bright orange helmet. I strapped it on. My face became a ripe ogen melon wedged in a basin. I was wearing a wetsuit and a skirt. The skirt was pure Vivienne Westwood. It was made of black stretch rubber with a flexible belt that had to be pulled up tight around my proper waist (high up under my ribs). The skirt had a heavy elastic band built into the hem. This gave it what I think Madame Westwood would call "a bias". It hung all curly-wurly. I looked like a self-conscious 1980s pop star dressed as a Liquorice Allsort. Still, soon I would become a dashing swan scudding through the billowing torrent.

It took at least five minutes to squeeze me into my fibreglass cocoon. I huffed and puffed and managed to pull my skirt into place, attaching the hem around the raised rim. With the help of three others I was finally sealed in. We set off, pushing successfully away from the little rocks and into the relatively calm waters above the rapids. These waters were simply coursing along, not boiling, as they were further down, waiting for me to be the carrot in their pot, but still I went shooting into them at an unacceptable speed, wobbling dangerously from side to side.

I needed to turn. I deftly wielded my double-ended carbon-fibre super-slalom paddle and toppled sideways. It was instantaneous. I had been aware that I was merely balanced on a biro case. Now the thing rolled into the stream and I was left hanging upside down, with my twelve stone underneath acting as a sort of keel. I surmised that it was not going to roll back upright unless I pushed it there with a huge muscular upper body. Unfortunately I did not have a huge muscular upper body.

I was still shooting downstream at a tremendous rate, though now underwater. This was where my instruction had to come into play. All I required was a cool head and my head was cool. My head was semi-frozen. I leaned forward, scrabbled at the front hem of my skirt, let go a stream of bubbles and then, rapidly running out of breath, struggled to release myself.

I was supposed to do a forward roll, but my legs needed a shoe-horn to extricate them from the fibreglass shell and none was available. With commendable presence of mind, I panicked. I thrashed about and finally popped out. It was like getting out of a pair of wet, fibreglass, hipster trousers.

I broke the surface, gasped and stood up. Oh. It wasn't that deep then. Still resembling an album cover for the Plastic Allsorts, I waded back to where I started. The instructor looked worried. We were on television after all. Everyone was solicitous. I spat out some water, adjusted my skirt and they squeezed me back into the hole again.

It was only after I toppled over a second time and they had dragged me out and lain me on the bank in a semi-comatose state that it was decided, with a bit of chin stroking, that I should perhaps try a "novice kayak".

I understood their dilemma. We were being filmed. The best slalom could only be achieved in a state-of-the-art biro case with carbon-fibre trimming that weighed less than a leaf. However, given that I was capsizing and I hadn't been on a six-month training course and wasn't at the absolute pinnacle of fitness, some sort of compromise was probably acceptable. We compromised.

I capsized this barque a further three times, but I finally learned that you raise the inner knee as you circle in a rushing stream.

Or was it the outer knee?

Anyway, it became reasonably instinctive. I found that I could get down the slalom course. I couldn't get through any of the gates but I could get down the course. Sometimes I was foolish enough to think about what I was doing, and at that point I toppled over again.

Afterwards we took a much simpler straight route on through Matlock, past the beautiful walkways and under the elegant iron bridges. We slipped half a mile down this charming river and then had to stop. That was as far as I was allowed to travel by the council. I had to get out and walk.

I wasn't entirely sorry.

CANOEING ON THE TRENT

The Trent is a serious river, it might have fewer furious rapids and less white water than the Derwent but it roils along with a steely purpose.

By the time I joined it at Shardlow it had already come a long way from Stoke, the pot place, and Burton, the beer place, both of which originally owed their fortunes to this eddying motorway. The river had already run a lot of mills, washed a lot of gravel and carried huge quantities of trade, and it still had more than a hundred miles to go to the North Sea. It cut a deep wandering channel across the working heart of England.

It felt almost presumptuous to venture onto this massive flow of water in my tiddly canoe. I remembered Maggie Tulliver, who takes to the flood at the end of George Eliot's *Mill on the Floss* (the Floss being a fictional version of the Trent). Her sweeping current was a metaphor for death as it carried the heroine to her watery end. It picked me up now and hurried me down to lunch, but it felt deep and determined.

I must have crossed the Trent many times, but I had only consciously gazed upon this mighty giant once before, thirty-five years ago, when I was a student performing sketches at the Robin Hood Theatre in Averham. The theatre, set down in a country churchyard not far from the river, doubled as a dormitory. Little more than a tin-roofed shed, it was miles from "nearby" Newark, and miles more from tantalising Nottingham. We didn't have a car. We couldn't be bothered with a bus. We had heard that Donald Wolfit started his career in the Robin Hood Theatre. What on earth did the great man do with his spare time?

One afternoon we decided to walk down to the river. What could be more charming? The girls put on white dresses. We carried beer. We tramped across five desolate fields and came to a massive galvanised pylon. A short distance beyond that we nearly fell down a nasty steep cliff studded with stones, from the top of which we gazed on a forbidding prospect. Following the route of the National Grid in a vaguely easterly direction was a grim brown torrent sluicing along a huge winding ditch. This was the Trent.

My reaquaintance was not entirely as uninspiring as this. This is flat countryside. There are lots of pylons. Newark itself is delightful. But the river is relentless. You look forward to its mouth, because that at least will be an incident. Now I canoed down a misty section under white skies with a slab-like black flow sliding under me.

In the thirteenth century England was officially split into two regions: Citra Trent and Ultra Trent. "This side of the river Trent and the other side of the river Trent." They meant "the far side", "the bit beyond", the uncharted world, where naughty Northern barons lived. Just getting across it was a major undertaking, and I was paddling my way towards a thirteenth-century solution to that particular problem. Swarkestone Causeway happens to be one our finest medieval monuments. It is also one of the most neglected. Listed "Grade One", the equivalent of York Minster, it is regularly battered, assaulted, hit, scraped, bashed and nicked by passers-by. That is because it is still in daily use as a road bridge.

The river flows under a fine Georgian replacement section, a mere 200 or so years old, because a massive flood built up a raft of timber that carried most of the original away in 1795.

I approached the bridge gingerly. There was an alarming little race under the third arch, but I wobbled through that and headed sideways, furiously paddling against the current, to squash against the muddy bank, crash through reeds and sting myself on nettles getting to the road. But now I could walk up past the pub and see the medieval causeway, battered and buttressed and spectacular. It is Britain's miniature Great Wall of China. A raised thoroughfare of yellowing stone traversing almost a mile of low-lying flood plain full of gravel pits. It was those pits I was heading to next.

CARP

"You see what it is, Griff…" Gary Banks paused and cackled slightly. "You know when you were a boy and you went for that fish, and you caught it but there was always one that you wanted that was bigger than that one? Well, that's the one we're after."

I didn't know, because I had never caught more than three fish in my life and I can't really remember how big they were, but I nodded encouragingly.

"These fish are the ultimate! They are absolute monsters."

"I'm guessing here but if you've had a bad day, and things are going badly in a relationship, or you lose your job, then you could always think, 'At least I landed that 600-pound fish.'"

"That's exactly it. You've got it in one."

We were waiting for a pot to boil and Gary was mixing bird food, fruit oils, mealy powder, strong-smelling oils and unguents into a bowl so that he could mould them into little balls which he would then cook in a pan. He was making "boilies". This was food for carp.

It was late afternoon and we were sitting by the side of a completely placid lake on a well-mown stretch of grass. I was planning to be there for the night, but these guys were quite content to wait longer than that for a giant carp.

"Three hundred hours."

"For one fish?"

"That's how long it took. But it was worth it. What a beauty!"

Jonny Bannister was less fevered about the whole obsession. Jonny wrote poetry about the experience: not just about the carp, you understand, but the bushes and trees and the lake and the outdoor life by the deep fish pond. He was keen that I try to appreciate the heartache involved.

"This is a mental battle, Griff. I'm trying to calculate how to lure the carp onto my hook. I know they are out there. I even know their names. The carp I am going to try to catch has probably been caught before."

QUEEN OF THE RIVERS

Izaac Walton wrote in *The Compleat Angler* that "the Carp is the Queen of Rivers: a stately, good and very subtle fish. The Carp, if he have water-room and good feed, will grow to a very great bigness and length; I have heard, to be much above a yard long."

Carp were believed to have been brought to Europe in 1227 and to have been bred for food by monks, although it has also been argued that an indigenous carp population had existed in the Danube since the last ice age.

Despite being large and muscular carp are, like goldfish, members of the minnow family. European carp can readily grow to 10 pounds in weight. They are among the longest-living fish species and a carp called Raspberry, who lived in Redmire Pool in Herefordshire, was reputed to be

around eighty years old at the time of her death.

In May 2007 newspapers reported that British angler Graham Slaughter had caught a record-breaking 88.6-pound carp – the same weight as Kylie Minogue.

Graham's achievement was slightly eclipsed just three months later when a Thai fisherman landed a 256-pound carp. This 18-stone monster, weighing as much as Kylie and a couple of her backing singers put together, was, however, a Siamese giant carp and thus a different species to those found in Europe.

Graham Slaughter with his record-breaking carp (which looks nothing like Kylie Minogue).

"Just a minute," I interrupted Jonny. "So the carp has been through the whole hideous experience already?"

"Hideous for him, I suppose." I could see Jonny was upset by my choice of words. "We're very gentle with them." He gestured to his kit. "We have antiseptic to treat any cuts or bruises."

The rules of the pond were strict about how long the fish could be held in the keep net and what sort of hooks could be used. The carp were the real priestesses in this place, not the fishermen. The anglers were only the supplicants. I think Jonny rather wanted to believe that the carp shared his spiritual quest, hunter and prey bound in one mystical bond.

"They're so beautiful, Griff."

I nodded. I had seen the pictures of grown men hugging these bloated piscine sumo wrestlers and they were certainly big. If you liked big, these were the biggest.

We carried our boilies down to the water. I had volunteered to try eating one. They were sweet. "They love these." Gary got lyrical again. "Perhaps it reminds them of a ripe peach that has fallen into the water."

Gary was pretty much the country's leading boilie maker. It was his life's work to make appetising dumplings for fish. The batch he had just made tasted a little like a warm, sweet dog biscuit. Now we had to get the boilies out to the carp, and for me the mystery of this business deepened.

The carp were somewhere out in the middle of the gravel pit. This was hardly surprising. I imagined them hiding as far away as possible from the tents, folding chairs, cooking apparatus and excitable but determined fisher-folk on the bank. So we had to get the boilies out to them. There were several methods. The one I tried was a shooter.

It was a length of hollow tube, bent slightly at one end and with a handle at the other. You slipped the boilies down inside the tube and then, gripping the handle, swung it out over your shoulder to launch the little biscuits a hundred yards or more. Gary was devastatingly accurate. I put mine straight into the water three feet from the shore. There was a knack, apparently. You had to cut the arc short.

It was soon mastered. We launched enough fruity pie into the middle of the lake to feed a medium-sized pig. If we had been lazy we might have commandeered a little black radio-controlled boat instead. This was based on the far shore. It regularly headed out to our dropping area and deposited someone else's secret mixture, like miniature depth charges.

I didn't get it, though. Was this to lure the carp out of the depths? Was it to build up a carply appetite? Was it to fatten up the prey, or what? Surely, if the carp was hungry, it would be better to offer nothing more than your bait? This was an onslaught. The whole lake was force-feeding these sacred fish.

I suppose the fishermen hoped that their fat quarry would become inveterate bingers. They would grow so ravenous that they would finally take even their bait. But Jonny told me that they were getting more difficult to catch. What happened? The grotesquely obese daddy carp, having sworn never to eat anything ever again, especially those tasty, apricot-flavoured sweets that floated down from heaven (because he still had an aching mouth from the last time) finally couldn't resist it any more and ... oops, up he went.

Jonny laughed, but I could see I would never make a carp fisherman. I was failing to get into the proper "psychological mindset" of the carp.

We launched our casts far out in the darkening waters then Jonny set his electric alarms and we settled back in two purpose-built armchairs.

"This is it, Griff. This is what it's really about. This is better than sitting around watching television, isn't it?"

I had to agree. I had nothing as comfortable as this in my TV room. Fly-fishing seems to be about cane rods and retro tweeds, but the carp game owes a lot to the SAS. The radio-controlled black stealth boat was a pointer. Jonny was wearing camouflage fatigues. The tackle was set down on natty silver and black stands. They had little blue flashing alarms with trip wires out of *Mission Impossible* to let us know if the wily carp was nibbling our bait. We had twin aluminium easy chairs with easi-dri khaki backs and behind us a slinky bivouac with fully raised bed and super-lightweight camouflage sleeping bag. The carp was clearly the Blofeld of the pit. He was worthy of every hi-tech piece of kit and subterfuge.

Night fell. I lay in the bunk and read about the last sturgeon caught in the Trent. Fishing on the river has declined. Apparently the water runs too cleanly these days. The weed and the murky depths have gone and pollution has done for the rest. More than thirty species carry on, but the last sturgeon was caught in the late nineteenth century. It weighed in at 200 pounds. If that had been a carp I was sure that someone on the bank near me would have wanted it bigger.

TRENT. THE GRAVEL BARGE

We could only fish for carp because there was a hole in the ground where gravel had been. There are gravel pits along the side of the Trent because the river courses through a gigantic flood plain. At the end of the last glaciation when the North melted, a massive torrent ran out of the hills and reordered the landscape. Rock in the Highlands was carved by glaciers and then redistributed by diluvian catastrophe. That huge gout of water formed banks that can still be found on either side of the current Trent, some six miles to the north and south. Tons of gravel were deposited in the bed between.

We still take the gravel for building purposes, or rather Alan Codding and John Gifford do. They were loading near Newark. I followed a gantry alongside a travelator, which was in the process of trundling a heap of gravel towards the river and vomiting 300 tons into the holds of the *Valiant*. She was 180 feet long and capable of taking much more – but not today, because she would sit too low in the water and ground on the sandbanks. I thought it had been raining a lot, but there were fine judgments to be made on the way to Castleford.

"So is this a boat or a ship?" I asked, conscious that there were nice distinctions.

"It's a barge," Alan laughed.

He handed me a tangerine jacket. His own was split to the waist. He was bare-chested and a couple of medallions rattled in his chest hair.

We were loading gravel for concrete or roads. It cost £3,000 in fuel alone to get to the distribution site. Alan and John were part of a shuttle service. They had to do a solid week, end to end, making repeated trips along the Trent, down the Humber and up the Aire & Calder Navigation, sleeping on board and working straight through, before they were allowed a stretch ashore. Once aboard it was a full-time job. Today they had to get to our destination near York and then they were due home.

Alan moved the gravel chute up the hold making sure that the gravel was evenly distributed and then he handed me a brush and a massive hose. I started slewing the loose stuff off the decks and into the Trent, washing it over, getting the boat tiddly, pushing the stones out of awkward corners with a colossal jet of water. It buggered the paintwork.

As we finished loading, another barge swung up and came alongside with an immense bell-like "dong". Another 180 feet of empty space, waiting to tie up to the rudimentary piles of the jetty. As soon as we had gone she would take over the endless spew of gravel. It was a constant turnaround, and like every work station on the river it was a temporary arrangement. Sooner or later this gravel pit would be exhausted and the gantries and the belt would move to a different part of the Trent (if the lorries didn't take over first).

There used to be hundreds of barges on the Trent, carrying tonnes of goods, but now the gravel boys had it pretty much to themselves. There were pubs where they drank together, but there were not many to drink with these days. For the most part they rumbled on, as we did now, between green featureless banks, watched by languid cows, the odd thorn bush standing up against a white sky. Sometimes there was a distant farm, sometimes a landing place, but it was mostly crumbled banks and nothing much else. I lay down on the foredeck on a coil of tarry rope and fell asleep for a while. Andy filmed propellers and washes.

I sat up to watch Megawatt Alley roll by, with its phalanx of giant cooling towers.

"They're all finished now," Alan said. "But they use the jetty for a skiing competition. They do speed records here."

The Trent seemed remorselessly functional even in its leisure use. No sign of any converted narrow boats here; just one industrial function after the other and most of them dead. The power stations had sucked the water out, used it to cool their systems and pumped it straight back in again. Nearly six million gallons a day are still abstracted from this river in the Nottingham area alone. We were passing massive and uncompromising equipment. No one was going to rush to open a boutique selling tea cosies in this used industrial building. Engineers may lament the way that the harmless steam from cooling towers is used as a symbol of industrial pollution, but the power stations, despite their shapely grandeur, were forbidding, alien, blank, inhuman structures.

I made tea with John and chatted with Alan in his cabin as he steered the barge with his tiny control stick. Ironically, it was only after he had finished our recorded interview and the camera crew had left to get into a RIB to meet us later on the Humber that he started to expatiate on his work. "Fifteen," he said suddenly.

"Fifteen what?"

"Well, I've just been thinking about what you asked about the danger of the job and I reckon I've known about fifteen men die on these barges."

We had talked about the freezing winter. A heavily loaded barge sometimes had to punch against a steep chop in the Humber when the tide was ebbing and a strong northeasterly gale was blowing in.

"If the hatches are tied down you should be alright, but one barge coming up couldn't take the continuous waves and eventually they smashed through a loose hatch cover." He paused and pushed his lever twice to the right to give him a little more rudder as he came to the bend. "Then there was one lad who fell as the barge was coming alongside. That's quite common. You can imagine: the weight can crush you pretty quickly."

He drifted through an inventory of disasters: the parting cables that sliced deck-hands in half, the shifting loads that buried them and the dead weight of barges that crushed and maimed. He pointed to his control stick. "Before we had these things, there used to be a chain system to the rudder and that could be dangerous. One skipper just touched his barge on the shallow edge of a spit, on a bend, and the rudder grounded and twisted. That sudden flick on the wheel threw him right against the side of the wheel-house and killed him."

Overhead, the helicopter clattered up as we surged down the empty river towards the confluence with the Humber. To the east the land was rising up. The hill was comforting. For the first time in ages we could see farms and trees. This was the north edge of Lincolnshire, and beyond it was the sea.

We had passed a series of rudimentary jetties; not the sort of place you would consider landing unless you were on business and in a big boat. They were wodged a few yards out into the mud, made of thick weathered piles and rusting iron. Between the piles there were names, some of visiting ships but mostly of home ports: Riga, Hamburg, Gdansk, Gothenburg. We were nearing the end of the river and the beginning of a new junction, the route to a northern world that this waterway had served for thousands of years.

THE HUMBER ESTUARY

The last fifty-two miles of the Trent are tidal. We came out in fresh geography. The great escarpments to the east and north provided a majestic self-importance, but it was with a customary lack of fanfare that the Trent merged with the Ouse at Trent Falls to form the Humber

Estuary. A fifth of the water in England drained into the great swathe of muddy tide ahead. We swung around to our port and crossed the estuary, to squeal and bump against a massive wooden ship jetty and wait for my next lift onwards.

I climbed a short ladder and stepped for a little while on to the limbo of this vast podium built above the water, cut off from the land by locked gates. The 180-foot barge looked puny against it.

First the rescue boat came in, packed with men in orange suits, and then Ian Dobson arrived from the Solent with his personalised hovercraft. It was a mini hoover. We had to balance our weight carefully. We rose up and started the massive fan at the back. Ian let me steer. It was like a rolling marshmallow travelling at thirty miles an hour. There were acres of grey shore mud and I took her up on the bank a little.

"It would be better to stay on the foreshore in the water," Ian said. "There might be gullies running off the land. They can go quite deep and while we can get over most different land formations we can't leap ditches, so if the nose goes down…"

But I had already got his point and was turning the hovercraft with infinitesimal twitches on the controls. Ludicrously, I leaned into the turn, physically tensing up, as if riding a bolshy horse. Just swinging the prop didn't stop the forward motion at all. It simply added a bit of sideways motion too, and we skidded on air into the shallows. As we did so, a gulley such as Ian had mentioned flashed past on our left. It was completely hidden from view from ahead.

"We would have come a bit of a cropper in that, I suppose," I murmured.

The rescue boys had taken the camera crew away from us. They were crashing downriver in a white flurry. They had not been impressed by "the hairdryer" when it came alongside the barge, but now we could dart across the mud banks in the middle of the estuary like a nuclear-powered inflatable armchair, while they had to wander away up to the north, staying in deep water, and following the strange channel marker buoys. These looked like boats. They were each in their own miniature high-prowed hull, to survive the ripping tides in this great, wide, shallow slab of water.

But everything was scaling down as we charged up to the Humber Bridge. It was the longest single-span suspension bridge in the world when it was built. It may only be the fifth in line to the throne now (it would need a couple of hurricanes and a few major earthquakes to regain its title), but it is still big enough to throw its weight around. What's to compete? The featureless gulf, the blank farming landscape, the bare hills? It is the main attraction.

The bridge was originally going to cost £28 million. This soon rose to £98 million. It actually cost £151 million by the time it opened in 1981 (almost six times the estimate). They think the loan will be paid off by 2032, nearly halfway through its projected existence. The Humber Bridge has been given a finite life. Unlike poor Swarkestone, but like most of the rest of the river infrastructure, it will become redundant in time. I walked down from the toll area to the car park underneath. The trees they had planted there to disguise the car park are already full grown. They will probably outlast the bridge.

BRIDGE OVER THE RIVER HUMBER

When it opened in 1981, the Humber Bridge was the world's longest single-span suspension bridge. It held this record for the next sixteen years until the opening of the Great Belt Bridge in Denmark. Today the Humber is the fifth-longest single-span suspension bridge, although its span is still 512 feet longer than the Golden Gate Bridge in San Francisco.

The bridge contains enough steel cable to go 1.7 times round the circumference of the Earth. It also has 80 acres (that's 44.4 football pitches) of painted steelwork.

Because of its vast size its vertical towers are not parallel with one another. As a result of the curvature of the Earth, they are 1.4 inches further apart at the top than they are at the bottom.

A total of 480,000 tonnes of concrete were used in its construction, along with 16,500 tonnes of steel and 11,000 tonnes of cables. That makes a total weight of 507,500 tonnes, which is about the same as 7,250,000 people (at an average of 11 stone per person). This means that the Humber Bridge weighs about the same as the entire population of Switzerland.

The Humber Bridge: strong enough to carry John Prescott out of Hull.

SAILING *IERNE*

We had one last call to make. It was back across the estuary, half a mile along the foreshore, and tucked behind Barton-upon-Humber. The doors of a large shed gaped a little and I walked into Joe Irving's repair and restoration shop, past the spoon-shaped gleaming hull of a racing boat varnished so beautifully that I could see the reflection of the camera crew in the background. Inside, the familiar whine of power tools wasn't enough to break the zen of the place. The floor was littered with mahogany shavings. The smell of sawdust was in the air. The sun shot slabs of light through a filthy upper window.

Joe was working on the hull of a thirty-foot cabin cruiser, which had originally been built in the 1930s. He was painstakingly removing and resetting most of her planks. The paint had been burnt off, so I could see the layers of alterations in the structure. Essentially the boat, being made of wood, could be utterly rebuilt and restructured. It was endlessly renewable. Each plank would take about a day to prepare and set. Joe was using vices to anchor them in place. He would shave and mould them to the curved shape of the boat, then secure them, caulk them to prevent leaks and hone them to a perfect smooth finish. When it went back in the water the wood would absorb enough moisture to swell and seal the joint. There were elements of new technology involved but the boat he was making here, at the end of my trip, was not so different to two that had been discovered on the north shore at Ferriby in the 1930s. They were sewn together with withies but had been caulked and planked in a very similar way. They had built-in cleats and were some forty-three feet long. And they were dated to about 1750 BC.

"Yes, I am the last of a dying breed, I suppose," Joe said. But I think he said it because I prompted him. He had a full order book. There was another wooden boat, from the Norfolk Broads, awaiting his attention in the yard. He was more a symbol of renewal than redundancy.

I ventured out onto the river for the last time in a boat called *Ierne* that Joe had restored after she had been in a barn in Portugal for sixteen years. She may have been over forty-foot long but, apart from her lines, there was nothing very easy about her: low in the water, only seven-foot wide, sporting a tall mast and an extremely long and heavy boom. She had a heavy deep keel and had been built in 1914 by the Scottish designer William Fife III to carry a great balloon of sail aloft.

As we left the lock and headed along the shore trying to find enough water to pass over the sand bar and gain the channel, I helped pull up her heavy main. She took the wind and heeled radically, dipping her edge and surging on. No guard rails here – just a sliver of wood on the planked deck that you had to get your toe onto in order to stay aboard.

Her owner Huw Jones had specified that she was to stay pure. There were no modern winches. There were billy-hauls and a big crew. We were eight, heaving and hanking in two cockpits. We shot out into the river, picking up speed all the way, with a brisk force four and a bit of lee helm to cope with. It was exhilarating stuff. The land now rose up on either side as if England was taking a final throw. The mouth of the Humber would widen to eight miles.

As the low docksides of Hull, now mainly dominated by supermarket developments, rushed past on our port-hand side, a large tug saluted us by firing off all her fire engines and hoses. Apart from her we were alone on eighty square miles of rippled brown expanse, and yet this is one of Britain's major working waterways with 40,000 commercial shipping movements a year. The Humber was big enough to absorb it all.

Detail from "Plan of Shrewsbury", 1540.

Chapter Three

THE SEVERN
AND WYE

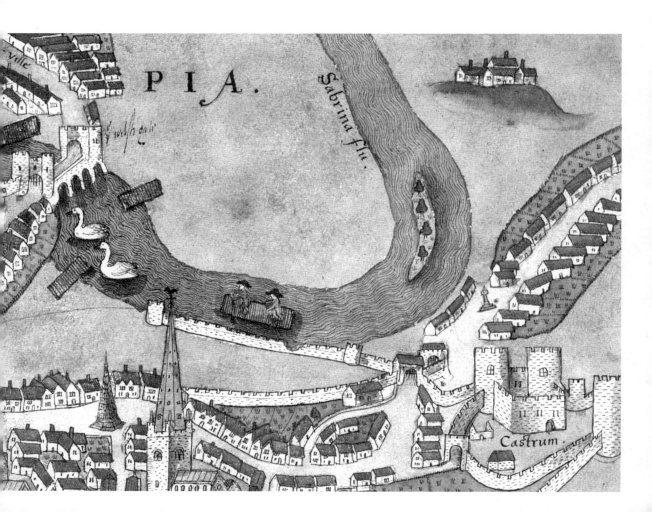

A WATER TANK IN THE ATTIC OF BRITAIN

The road between Aberystwyth and England rises out of the Welsh coast and keeps going up. When you think it's gone up enough, it goes up some more. And when the lorries start to roar and rumble ahead of you and slow to five miles an hour, you can imagine you are on your way to a Himalayan pass and these monster trucks are transporting food to a lost village of raven-haired maidens, but there are only sheep farms up here on the A44 to the Plynlimon Mountains and the lorries are probably going to Tesco's.

It was a brisk day with a high wind. Big mauve clouds were scudding up from the Irish Channel. Simon Bennett Evans and his sons farm about 5,000 acres up on bare sheep-cropped hills. We left our cars in front of some bow-roofed corrugated sheds and dark mysterious barns and wedged ourselves into a convoy of farmers' Land Rovers – with hard seats and baling twine handles and a satisfying disregard for health and safety fuss. You hung on or fell out.

After a series of gates, and on over a great swelling green hump of a mountain, we got to Plynlimon – a rounded, windy place of five peaks, and the source of five rivers and more tributaries. There had once been lead mines up here. Simon told me how the miners had lit fiery beacons on two of the summits in honour of Victoria's Jubilee and had then run into the valley in between for a good punch-up. "Afterwards they turned the horses in the landowner's carriage around so that when he tried to drive away in the dark there was utter chaos." He laughed at the folk memory.

Today there were a few bare outcrops of stone, nature's bald patches, glinting with quartz, on the very tops and a soggy pasture over everything else.

We trudged over one ridge then another and finally came to a more pronounced crease in a crumpled landscape of folds, then kneeling down and creeping forward we came to a definite cleft. A fingernail-sized frog crawled out of the moss. There was a glimpse of rock in the peat, a tiny fern and, hanging from a bright green plant, a single drop of water. I transferred this pearl to my forefinger. That was it. The smear of moisture was all there was to the beginning of the Wye. We looked down at the bed of what must be an occasional torrent carving its way into the mountain in front of us. Dry now, it sloped out of sight.

But this wasn't the only water we were hoping to find up here. The Severn began about one and a half miles away, across the ridge. This river, the longest in Britain at 220 miles, takes a different route down from the hill, crossing into England to link the great market towns of Shrewsbury, Worcester and Gloucester until it eventually joins the Wye again in the estuary below Chepstow.

We were in a water tank in the attic of Britain, with an annual rainfall of 85 inches. This was the dumping ground for weather systems that romped in from the Atlantic. As they rose up over Plynlimon the weight of water that they carried crystallised into ice and it fell in heavy drops that soaked into these peaty sponges. The Severn began in a bog somewhere. We weren't really looking for a trickle so much as an ooze.

We walked on, heading north and west, with the camera crew trailing behind, and paused on the brow of the hill to gaze into a tremendous landscape of green and blue bounding away to the horizon. The skies were clear in patches and sent huge blocks of light chasing each other across the hills towards England.

"You can see the Black Mountains over there towards the Brecons," Simon told me. "And that way," he rotated taking in the entire vista for a moment and pointed west, "That's out into Montgomeryshire and, yes, the Wrekin." If that was optimism I was for it.

As I clambered through the wet tussocks and occasionally plunged a boot into stagnant wet slop, I began to dispute this whole source thing. The Severn has a catchment area that covers 4,410 square miles. Even today I could only see a fraction of it. The water works its way to the river through a million capillaries and threads. What were we seeking but the top-most twig of a giant tree?

Most early travellers were unimpressed. The Reverend J. Freeman in 1826 called it "a long and continuous bed of boggy vegetable earth". He was right. It was pocked and hummocky, but a welcome relief after the green uniformity of the hill. It had been dug in the past for fuel, hence the uneven levels. There were tussocks of high ground, crowned with cotton grass. Creeks of stagnant peaty mud wallowed in between. Cadbury jumped in and floundered about in black ooze. On the far side of a particularly wet morass there was a little island sporting a weathered wooden post. It marked the official source of the Severn and the beginning of the Severn Way.

With a yattering helicopter filming us overhead, we trudged down a satisfying path. The Severn drops over 1,700 feet in its first twelve miles and then only a further 500 feet in the remaining 200 miles. The burn gurgled through a deep rock- and grass-covered scoop in the hills, plunging over little falls and into deep miniature pools that had, until fifty years ago, even at this advanced height, been the spawning grounds for fish. And then a shadow appeared. It was a dark and heavy, blank and flat-sided wall of sitka spruce. This was the Hafren Forest.

THE RAIN FALLS
MAINLY ON THE HILL

In the Plynlimon area the average annual rainfall is 85.06 inches, compared with only about 20 inches in the Thames estuary.

The wettest year on record was 2000 when 124 inches fell and the driest was 1976 with just 57.9 inches.

The measurement of one inch of rainfall translates roughly as follows:

▶ over a square yard one inch equates to about 4.7 gallons of rain – that's about two average-sized buckets of water;

▶ over an acre an inch of rainfall would mean around 22,651 – or about 500 bath-tubs full;

▶ and over a square mile it would mean approximately 14.5 million gallons of water – enough to fill 26 Olympic-sized swimming pools.

So Plynlimon's average annual rainfall of 85.06 inches over its 62.5 square mile catchment area represents about 77 billion gallons of water every year (slightly over one Lake Windermere's worth) while the 124 inches that fell in 2000 would represent over 112 billion gallons! You can see where the waters of the Severn and Wye come from.

Despite their higher than average rainfall, the people of Wales still manage to get out and enjoy themselves.

HAFREN FOREST

Forest has always been "a'ccurst". I suspect that wrinkled crones told fairy stories to try and stop children wandering away into those damned woods, where old witches lurked, where paths disappeared, where robbers and wolves hung out and where black bristly things happened.

This place I entered was hardly evil. In fact it was glistening with sharp sunlight and dancing with motes. Except ... no, they weren't motes. I see. Mosquitoes. The river settled into a long sluggish stretch and several million biting insects rose up, dancing prettily in the sun, to eat me and my dog while the camera crew filmed us on a usefully long lens.

Fairy stories never warned about the midges, but they missed a few other things too. Written in Bohemia, on the edge of great primeval thickets full of horrors, fairy stories had never encountered the Forestry Commission.

Hafren has the bureaucratic spookiness of a single-minded institution. It's not easy to turn left at the holly bush or watch out for the hollow oak when the pines are planted like a grain crop, so thick they defy entrance and so uniform that wildlife is banished.

I had the river to follow. I felt like an original inhabitant of these islands. I didn't need a map. These rivers must have been sacred natural causeways. Eventually the river would lead me out of this dark and gloomy place, if the mosquitoes didn't get me first.

My voyages across Britain often started in uplands. I had once naively expected to find them wild or remote, but our great British hills are dominated by a monoculture mania – geometric block plantings of commercial forestry disfigure peaks shorn bare by sheep.

I walked past sudden clearings, where whole slopes had been attacked by mad mowers. The shaven dirty brown areas were already being replanted with pine seedlings. Are we so impatient for British chipboard? Sitka spruce is a science-fiction planting – an organic blank mould of growth, pushed up out of the earth in the quickest possible time to be felled, stripped and pulped into composite solid goo for building purposes.

Some say that the life and vitality of the Severn River itself has been affected.

The Hafren Forest was originally planted in a series of specially ploughed irrigation channels, which drained run-off into the river. This water rushed down and washed out the gravel from the riverbeds. Salmon need gravel to make nests.

Some claim that, as they grew, the trees made the soil more acidic. The water draining off added a new acid component to the river. (To be strictly correct forestation alone does not cause the acidity. The acidity comes from sulphur dioxide in the atmosphere from industrial emissions when it rains. Forestation just concentrates it.) This also apparently deterred the salmon. The Severn had been one of the great salmon rivers of Britain. There is no doubt that sea netting is partly to blame, but salmon still spawn in the upper reaches of the Tay and the Tweed. The Severn, by contrast, has declined disastrously. Salmon in the Severn reached their highest numbers in the 1970s. Now the numbers are minuscule. They are supposed to be coming back. Apparently we shouldn't blame the spruce. But no plans are in hand to reverse the deadening visual blight of a policy introduced after the First World War to satisfy a mis-judged crisis. Whatever the truth, we have the means to make big changes with the best of intentions. And a 3,000-year relationship with the Severn is in flux.

THE FIRST WET

It was time to stop walking and get on the river. Paul brought the canoes around with the car and trailer. I drove, while he sat in the passenger seat with his short-wave radio and a map.

"They want us to get to a place somewhere up river."

"Straight ahead?"

"I think so." Paul blinked at the map. "They've found a bank where they can film you going in and paddling down to a bridge."

"But this doesn't feel right." I stopped. We were facing a narrow paved path that ran through closely mown grass. "This is a public park."

"That's where they are."

I drove gingerly over the kerb and along the path. There were a few upright half-buried cannons to negotiate and a set of swings to drive around.

Paul looked around. "We're definitely in a park."

"I told you that."

Paul gazed at the map and back at the passers-by, the in-line skaters and the benches, and then back at the map in a concentrated way, but it was too late to turn around now. It was, actually, impossible to turn around at all with sixteen feet of canoe behind us.

"You might be able to get down that way," he said, pointing.

Skirting some flowerbeds we tipped down a grassy slope. And then we couldn't get any further. That was it. There was a ditch in front of us and a little wooden footbridge over it.

Paul leaned around and peered beyond the trailer and the trees now brushing against the side of the SUV. "Oh, hang on!" he said brightly.

Siobhan, our production assistant, was walking across the bridge. "How on earth did you get along here?" she called.

"How did you?"

"We came by the public road. We're all on the other side of the bridge there."

I looked at Paul.

He looked at the trailer and squinted. "You're not going to be able to turn around," he said. "You'll never get the car out. You'll have to reverse about a mile up there."

I shrugged. "Me? I'm going on the river, on the canoe."

"Right."

"You're the driver. I'll meet you back beyond the bridge. Be careful, though. There are kiddies in the park."

The camera arrived and set up. We unstrapped.

There are two convenient handles at the bow and stern of the canoe. Now that it was sitting on the ground, a little more physical effort was required. We took a handle each in one hand and counterbalanced the other with a slightly camp, open-palmed gesture, as people do when lifting a heavy bucket or suitcase.

"Hup." Now we had it.

My equipment was loaded into the body of the canoe: paddles, boathook, rucksack, maps, bottle of reviving water, peanuts and tent. We had to carry it bodily about twenty yards, really not a great effort. Leading the way I took a solid stride on to the bridge. Paul followed. We jammed the entire boat into the gap between the handrails.

One of the virtues of the canoe is its stability, achieved by a fattening in the middle. This meant that it would not easily pass through a narrow gap.

"Couldn't you see that it wasn't going to get through?"

"I was just following you."

"Push it back."

We popped it out, hauled it up to shoulder height and teetered across the footbridge.

Exhausted, we dumped the canoe on the grass and found ourselves looking at a six-foot drop to the water.

Taking hold of the long rope tied to the stern I kicked the canoe over the side. It dipped forward at an alarming angle but when the bow made contact with the river it obligingly floated up and the thing bounced onto the stream. Paul took the rope while I slid down through the nettles and grappled with the side of the boat.

"Now give me the dog's lead."

"He won't come."

"Yes, he will. He'll be fine. Come on. There's a good boy. Behave!" I turned to Paul. "See that handle on the back of the life-jacket? Pick him up by it."

Cadbury is a fully grown chocolate Labrador. He has no enveloping curly fur. He is all dog. Paul lifted him up with one hand, staggered about, went red in the face and lowered him down to me. I took him, put my back out and dropped him in the canoe. Then I stepped up to my knee in the water, filled a trainer and slipped on a stone. I clambered into the back of the canoe and finally sat on the little woven seat in the stern, palpitating.

Konrad the director was peering down at me over the crushed nettles. "We just need you to paddle down the river a bit."

"Do you? Frankly, Konrad, I'm exhausted."

But the camera was running. I reached for the paddle, pushed off from the side and promptly went aground. We were in about two inches of water.

This was a pleasant spot. The Severn flowed down over the bedrock and through a series of pools. But it took me about half an hour to get a hundred yards down to the bridge. I needed a shallower form of transport.

WEAVING A BOAT

"Skin boats" were once found all over Britain and until relatively recently were common working boats on the Severn – a functioning link with the ancient past of the river. Pliny reported the ancient Britons using them. Julius Caesar was so impressed with their portability that he borrowed the idea for his wars in Spain. They are little more than a wicker basket woven out of willow fronds and supports, which is then covered with a hide. The size of the coracle was originally determined by the size of an ox skin. But they make a man-sized container.

To construct them, you stick hazel wands into the earth and work upside down. The seat (no more than a board across the boat which holds the whole thing together) is put in place first and tied to the uprights. Then you get to work weaving the willow strands one over the other.

It all came back. I distinctly remembered making a misshapen basket when I was at kindergarten. It ended up as a "wine holder". It had to, because it had grown too long and crooked to be anything else. But now, even if my folk dancing and finger-painting skills had deserted me, my weaving skills had returned.

When I was six we soaked the long lengths of pale wicker in a basin until they were supple. It was the same arrangement here. The willow had to be wet to make the coracle, though cunningly it wasn't necessary to weave the entire basket. Once a certain width of side had been built up to provide the tensile strength we needed, we looped the strands over, slotted them in amongst each other and then tied all the crossing points together.

What am I talking about? This was TV. Obviously we did some of it and then went and got one Helen and Pippa, our coracle experts, had made earlier.

The finished hull was an open weave. Each strand seemed individually weak and incapable of supporting the structure, but together they helped to pull each other into shape. It was "learned" engineering, and what we would call sustainable too. To our ancestors it was making use of what God and the river provided.

Willow is said to grow a terrifying one and a half inches a day in season. The trees provide a new crop of wands every year and willows along rivers used to be harvested for them. They still coppice willows in parts of the Somerset levels, but post-industrial Britain largely abandoned the practice. This is one of the reasons why willows now grow unmanageable branches, which crack under their own weight and fall across rivers.

We picked up a finished coracle and set off to the river. I have spent half my adult life heaving small boats in and out of rivers, but I had never experienced a fairy barque like this one. Rubber dinghies are lumpen compared to it. Surfboards feel ungainly. You can hold a coracle in one hand. You can balance it on one finger. It is the size of an ox because of that skin (or the size of an ox-sized piece of tarred fabric, because the oxen had heard us weaving and scarpered), but it is super-light.

In reality, that big round shape makes it difficult to carry on one finger, but they invented another way. You sling a piece of rope around your shoulders and over your neck and let the weight of the seating board rest against your back so that you resemble a large black beetle with two legs. As long as the wind doesn't get under your carapace and fling you back in the river, you can happily walk along balancing the coracle and carrying your freshly poached salmon and paddle in the other hand. It was so dandy that it was tempting to break out into a little dance. And if it rained, a slight adjustment was all that was required to turn the thing into an effective umbrella.

The coracle was considered an essential tool for poachers. The local mid-Welsh coracle owner would have launched himself onto a shallow stretch of the Hafren (as the Severn is known until it gets out of Wales) and drifted down a fair distance catching fish all the way. Then he would have landed and walked all those miles back. So it was handy that it was so light.

It had a huge capacity too. Apparently a "coracler" could carry a hundredweight. Sometimes they were loaded so much and sank so low that "a sparrow could drink from the side".

I was completely sold on this vessel. It was miraculous. It was an organic dinghy.

Then I tried to get in it.

First of all, imagine a bowl with a rounded bottom floating in your bath. Just push the edge. It tips. Now imagine getting into that bowl. Remember, it is only partially made. The floor is like a roof space with very thin rafters. You dare not put your foot into the gaps between the strands of willow because it would pierce the skin. So you have to put all your weight on a tiny cross tree, and then somehow get the rest of your body into the bowl. I did it. And then I sat there in a sort of petrified state, conscious that the merest twitch of a buttock would have upsetting consequences. I floated free but in a suspended immobility, only capable of the tiniest graceful manoeuvres, like the Mekon adrift.

Helen handed me the paddle. You paddle from the front, so you scull the boat away from you. It is curious, as if you are sweeping the water from in front of the boat so that it can advance forwards. This felt ancient. It felt wholly primitive. It enabled me to have my other hand free to lay out my net and catch my salmon.

I didn't have a net. Pippa came with me in her coracle and I floated around a bit. I would like to say that I paddled around, but I merely whisked my way about, as if by accident. The coracle moved, but mysteriously, as if it were following my paddle on an elastic band. And then the stream suddenly caught us and we began to float downriver. This was hilarious. I did paddle, but I felt as though I had a spoon in my hand and was trying to control a wayward duck. I was at the mercy of the Severn.

Rocking ludicrously from side to side, I got through the rapids. I have no idea how. I just bounced down the white water. I swivelled and saw that Pippa had not been so lucky. This was probably because she was in a less dream-like state than I was. With experience on her side she no doubt tried to do something sensible, like direct her coracle through the rough water, and over she went. The crash was spectacular. In a coracle you don't sink – you bounce over and roll like a ball. You whip straight from upright to upside down. In deeper waters the old boys used to go down and surface underneath their coracle, with their head in the hull. The secret was to do nothing until you felt something solid beneath your feet. There were no Eskimo rolls for this vessel. Sometimes they were carried miles downstream, with just the black beetle's back bobbing on the surface. Luckily it was shallow where Pippa fell. But it was cold too.

I found this out for myself when a few minutes later I fell in too.

A NATURAL RIVER?

I dried off and took stock in the safety of a nature reserve five miles west of Newtown. The Severn had become a wide stream, a well-defined river now, and this seven-mile stretch of it was being left to itself, for natural purposes. It ran loose over the floor of the valley, through bleached stone banks.

I had come on the Severn to follow "a natural river", but already this was a relative term. If the reserve I was in could be allowed to revert to its natural state, the banks would grow thick with deciduous forest. That wasn't planned. They were putting the clock back to a more nature-friendly form of farming, allowing pasture to seed with wild flowers that liked the silt and the damp and the poor soil but abhorred nutrient-rich modern fertilisers. It would be grazed and maintained at some expense. This was "nature" from a specific historical agricultural period, one that we were in danger of losing.

But even if these fields were free of nitrates, it was a tiny patch in a massive catchment area. Nearby agricultural land was still being "improved" and the alien fertilisers still leached into the river all around. An average of forty "drainage licences" a year are still granted on the upper levels of the Wye. It is much the same on the Severn. These drains sluice water out of the wet boggy upland straight into the river.

Water is also removed. I had already passed plenty of places where abstraction licences would be in operation, for irrigation or to run sewage systems or for industrial purposes. The Clywedog and Vyrnwy tributaries that ran into the Severn nearby had been dammed to make huge reservoirs up in the hills. The authorities sometimes released water to ensure that the flow was kept up, partly so that these abstractions could take place. The quiet stream gurgling past the alders in the dark already had a complicated and fragile relationship with the surrounding countryside.

SHREWSBURY (OR SHROWSBURY)

Konrad, the director, wanted to film me canoeing around the outskirts of Shrewsbury, or "Shrowsbury" as I had diligently taught myself to call it since doing another television programme in an ex-girls' school in the outskirts of the town. That's the received English pronunciation, while the Welsh go for "shrew".

The ancient border fortress sits inside a giant meander where the Severn loops around from the English Bridge to the Welsh Bridge. We met the camera crew, who wanted to spend an hour or so trying to get afloat, and bumped into an unexpected boat shop. So while they sorted themselves I went in.

I always feel secure in a chandler's. As a boy, my father couldn't pass one without making me hang around, while he spent an hour or so looking at shackles. Today I mooched amongst the orange mooring buoys, gas canisters and old-fashioned life-jackets until I found something I didn't already have. It was a shiny, black, electric outboard motor and a dapper little thing if it hadn't been attached to a massive car battery. But what an ideal river propulsion for a camera crew in their rubber dinghy: it was small, ecologically sound and utterly noiseless. I would be able to blather on to camera without endless stopping and starting.

We made a strange convoy when filming. Me paddling ahead in the canoe, with the dog (sometimes sitting and nosing the breeze, sometimes lying down out of sight so I was forced to kick him to show himself for the camera). And trailing behind us; the crew, in a dangerous-looking boat from a nursery rhyme. Whenever I appeared at my most placid on the river, drifting through calm waters and limpid currents, there was an Edward Lear boat just out of shot, with three men in a rubber ring, juggling equipment, a heavy camera and a long boom pole, fussing, twittering and bobbing in my wake, trying desperately to keep up with me and point themselves in the right direction for thirty seconds in succession. Passers-by stopped and stared. I had thought the electric motor would be a film-maker's dream. What could be better than this floating camera dolly? Apparently it was totally unmanoeuvrable.

It was still early in the pleasure-boating season. Shrewsbury was busy with its standard provincial town morning. The Welsh farm carts, which used to drive to the market across the Welsh Bridge, had been replaced by open trucks. We glimpsed the morning rush hour, noisily charging up medieval streets, while we drifted idly on the river. There didn't seem to be any other traffic on this waterway that had once linked the inland centre with Worcester, Gloucester and the sea. It had once been common to take a passenger ferry boat down river. The captain of one of Nelson's fleet made the entire trip by fast two-man skiff in twenty-four hours. But my over-laden outrider, my dog and I were taking our time.

The meander had acted as a natural moat for the original settlement. The Severn was a natural border. A conference of ninth-century bishops decided that those called Britons would live on the other side of the river. *Wal,* the root of the word Wales, simply meant "foreigner" in Anglo-Saxon.

I felt like an invader myself, easing round the back of the town and its splendid parks. We passed under a green metal pedestrian bridge as a teacher led a crocodile of children overhead. They stopped in the middle and started jumping up and down to see it wobble. Even the children were at work, experiencing engineering. There were magnificent Victorian boat houses on the right bank, but they seemed shuttered. Nobody was taking a pleasure cruise today except us.

Ahead of the Welsh Bridge, the river widened and there were quays. The railway station squatted down over the water and beyond that we were going to get swept away, so, skirting round a massive willow that had broken its back and fallen into the water, I crossed over to a set of steps on the left bank. I turned in neatly against the current and brought the side of the canoe up to a dirty little flat landing stage.

Now let us praise Plynlimon, a water tank in the attic of Britain.

Fast-growing chipboard in the gloom of Hafren Forest.

Weaving a coracle or possibly a bottle holder.

Beetle mania sets in.

Shrewsbury and its defensive meander.

Iron will float, as long as the plug is left in.

Ironbridge. Revolutionary in its time.

Druids take me to the river for a ritual dunking.

The Severn loops in the bed of an ice age lake north of Ironbridge.

Worcester Cathedral and the River Severn by Turner.

Cadbury had clearly had enough. But he was cautious. He wasn't going to leap. He stood up. "No! Down! Sit." He is eleven. He ignored the instruction of a superior intelligence, much as he has done for at least ten years. He put his forelegs on the stone jetty and pushed. The canoe moved out and the dog fell in. He didn't look particularly surprised and started swimming. He would have easily floated anyway but the life-jacket had other uses. I reached down and hauled him up on the jetty, like a wriggling wet suitcase.

Then I ran. But I wasn't quite quick enough. He shook himself violently.

Brushing myself down I turned to the dinghy.

"Did you get any of that?"

"Er, no, we had swung round to face the wrong way."

Silent but underpowered these electric motors, if you ask me.

ANY OLD IRON

Every man must hammer a rivet at some time in his life. I put it amongst the fifty things to do before you die. It may not be as widely touted as being in bed with two women at once, but it is probably a lot more satisfying.

You begin with a piece of metal shaped like a mushroom. Stick it into a burning hot set of coals and pump the bellows until the thing gets white hot. (You can make your own mushroom-shaped bit of metal too, if you are handy.)

After it is white hot you have to take it out. This is not as easy as it sounds, because in order for the metal to really heat up you have to bury it in amongst the coals and the coals get white hot too. Take your tongs and fork about a bit. (If you do all this at Blists Hill Victorian Town there will be a number of men on hand to explain that you have missed it, or knocked it on the floor, or pushed it right down to the bottom, where you are never going to get hold of it.) But let's just say you get your tongs on your mushroom, now shining brighter than a lightbulb filament and reminding you that we are, after all, made of stardust.

With some difficulty and minimum cockiness, given that it could burn a hole right through your arm, insert the stalk of your white-hot mushroom through a hole in two plates of wrought iron. Lay over an anvil and start beating the hell out of it. The stalk end of the mushroom is like a very hard bit of toffee. It flattens out, but only after prolonged beating, during which the rivet goes red and black. It takes on a slightly flaky, scaly appearance like a hot coal. And that is that.

As the rivet cools it contracts. We all knew that, didn't we? That contraction does the simple job of pulling the two plates of metal more firmly together than any amount of beating could ever achieve, and effectively seals them together. This is how iron boats came to be built.

Both the Severn and the Wye run into iron-making country about halfway down their length. The Severn almost seemed to have created the ingredients for an iron age. Above Ironbridge Gorge the river runs through a great plain, which was once the bottom of a huge lake. As the ice age unfroze, it burst through the hills and cut a way through the gorge. By doing so, the river itself brought ore and coal to the surface. It was the river that provided the power to run the works and the means to transport the finished metal products away.

The day before my riveting I canoed through this plain.

It was a long stretch of paddling, largely undertaken for one shot. The crew parked up on a hill overlooking the valley. I went two or three miles up river and canoed down to meet them. It took hours. We were all remarkably patient. I sat in my canoe muttering at the dog and assuming that every bend would bring me within sight of the hill. They sat up on the hill, in their van, eating sandwiches, listening to their iPods, phoning their loved ones, reading the newspapers and scratching their flabby bottoms. I was paddling on, and on and on. Eventually they thrust their papers aside and rushed to their cameras, shouting "Christ! That's him, isn't it?" and managed to get a shot of me diligently paddling around the notable meanders in the former lake bottom.

I would have got to them more quickly if I had landed my canoe and pulled it over the short neck of land that separated one stretch of river from another. This is exactly what travellers used to do in the past. The plain is so flat in places that the river has worked itself sideways. As the water speeds around a bend it cuts away at the outside bank, where it flows faster. Conversely it drops silt on the inside bank, where it flows more slowly and so builds that bank up in a spit. If left to its own devices a river will wander around all over the shop, just like a camera crew.

They had been working metal along the steeper parts of these rivers for thousands of years, but in the eighteenth century a man named Abraham Darby came up with a casting process that he had apparently "borrowed" from the Dutch. He made a powerful smelting furnace using cooked coal that made that casting easier and cheaper. The entrepreneurs of Coalbrookedale were able to work with a molten metal, which could be poured and shaped at will. The entire valley became metal mad. They made window frames out of metal, kerbstones out of metal, gravestones out of metal; they even, crazily, made a metal bridge – as extraordinary in its day as a load of cobblers thinking they'd try making a bridge out of leather, except that, incredibly, it worked. It was Abraham Darby's grandson, Abraham Darby III, who did it.

Thomas Telford saw the advantages and made an even lighter metal bridge further up the river. It became a metal race. This new smelting process seemed to indicate that metal had limitless applications.

If you ever clamber onto a big ship, as I have done frequently on this trip, and stand on the unadorned metal platform of a working vessel, then you have to stop and ponder what a peculiar substance it is – strong enough, when solid, to make our biggest objects, yet quite capable, when viscous, of being shaped as we want it. And we have loads of it. Much of the planet we live on is made of iron. Without it we would have had difficulty becoming industrialised beings. Furthermore, whatever has already been mined and refined still exists, somewhere. It may oxidise into rust but it can be recovered and reused.

In much the same spirit that the people of the valley experimented with their bridge, "Iron Mad" John Wilkinson made the first metal boat and launched it on the Severn. His great demonstration was attended by an incredulous crowd. They were so convinced that it was impossible for an iron boat to float that they took the day off work to come and watch him sink.

There were a few spectators standing around when we launched our metal boat. I hadn't made it out of wrought iron, alas. There wasn't time. We used a bath instead. It was cast iron and very heavy, so I clambered in and was lowered into the water by crane. As I reached the water I realised almost immediately that our own boat had more in common with a coracle than a barge. It lacked ballast. Even with my weight evenly distributed in a "Hang on, I've lost the soap!" kneeling posture, the bath seemed utterly unsuited to the water. I could see that our audience were untroubled by our buoyancy but credulous of our stability. I didn't want

JOHN "IRON MAD" WILKINSON

John "Iron Mad" Wilkinson (1728–1808) was an extraordinary man with an extraordinary nickname, who by 1796 was producing one-eighth of all Britain's cast iron. He paid his workers using his own coinage that depicted his own regal features and even had a pair of iron shoes made for himself (although he did admit he found these unworkable).

Wilkinson's success came after he devised a method of making cannons from iron rather than the traditional more expensive bronze. He had also developed a new type of borer that proved vital for the production of James Watt's steam engines, and had cast and made 40 miles of iron pipes for the Paris waterworks.

And then in 1787 Wilkinson astounded the world again when he produced the first-ever iron boat, a narrow barge named *The Trial*, which was 70 feet long and 8 tons in weight. When it was launched on 6 July 1787, a large crowd assembled in full expectation that the vessel would sink the moment it hit the Severn. In fact, when the boat was empty the water rose a mere 8 or 9 inches up its side while in deep water it was capable of holding a load of 32 tons.

Wilkinson died in July 1808 and left detailed instructions that he should be buried in an iron coffin in a crag at his estaate. When his coffin arrived, the grave turned out to be too shallow and the rock had to be blasted with explosives.

Wilkinson had threatened his workers that he would return seven years to the day after his death to check up on his beloved furnaces. Seven years later in July 1815 press reports record that several thousand people turned out in the hope of witnessing his promised return.

Portrait of the Squire John Wilkinson by Gainsborough, 1775. He looks worn out after a morning trying to break in a new pair of iron shoes.

to fall in the water and have half a ton of cast-iron bath roll over on top of me, so I kept very still and propelled myself to the nearest bank. The audience cheered but I think they were disappointed.

Wilkinson was less circumspect. He fired off a salute from a set of cannons made in his own foundry. He was saluting the launch of an idea that would change the world, certainly the world of shipping, though it would be another seventy years before metal boats became commonplace.

HOLY WATERS

We arranged to film on a country estate just upstream from Bridgnorth. The river looked magisterial, running through green fields under a sandstone cliff. I had come there to meet what I had been promised were practising Druids: some real living people who still worshipped water. I was, frankly, expecting something just a wee bit bogus.

Nobody knows much about the real ancient Druids. They were the priests of a society that hadn't got round to inventing writing. Some like to believe that meant they invented a lot of more useful things instead, like ley lines and ancient magic. But if they had only used some of their ancient magic to invent writing then we might have known how it all worked; instead their followers have to make up their incantations and basic nature worship. All that guff about moons and mistletoe is based on a couple of sentences in a second-hand account in Pliny of something that might have happened in some islands or other far to the north. If you want to think it means they worshipped the heavens in these islands, then feel free.

As I walked out of a spinney of those colossal trees that only grow on old-fashioned estates and saw four Druids looking rather fetching in their white robes and winsomely innocent in their oak garlands, I swallowed my misgivings and chatted inanely about trees and woods and flowers.

Yes, I was a coward. I was too polite to be scabrous. Chris Park the high priest was pretty earnest and the others were trusting and everybody seemed to be reasonably aware that there was a bit of play-acting going on. So I just play-acted along.

If I had said, "Stop just a minute. We don't know whether they worshipped acorns or bowed down in front of golden water voles or murdered whales and dolphins, and you have made most of this pagan stuff up," I think Konrad, the director, would have beaned me with the cauldron in which their herbs and grasses were boiling away. So I apologise to all you rationalists; I went with the flow. The flow was quite a lot of perfectly innocent stuff about how the earth and all her wonders have been neglected and it could have come straight from page ten of yesterday's *Guardian*. I put on a shining robe and I was taken to the waters to be cleansed.

I suspect that most religions are drawn to the water at some time or another. Christ himself spent a lot of time ritually bathing his followers. And there is something soothing about being bathed. In fact I had forgotten what it felt like to have water trickled all over me.

But what came first: the river or the magic? Did the original shaman clap eyes on the river and think "That's a useful prop", or did the river and all its fresh, renewing, clean, healthy water imbue the most primitive and basic of humanoids with a sense of wonder and mystery? I like to think the latter.

It was in that spirit that I allowed myself to be taken to the water's edge to repeat, with the others, a few words of benediction. My commitment, however, was severely tested by the dog. As we stood reciting blessings, he decided to walk into the water alongside us and he kept splashing about while we offered the river petals and jewellery. It rather undermined the solemnity. When we sacrificed a bowl of milk in the water, he simply waded forward and drank it. I felt awful. They took their ceremony as seriously as the Bishop of Worcester took his evensong. I tried to breathe out steadily but I started quaking. I had to explain, completely unconvincingly, that it was the dog. It *was* the dog.

I take my garland off to the Druids. They laughed too and praised Cadbury, but I think it may have affected what followed. When they dipped me into the freezing waters for my sins, they decided it should be done twice.

I cleansed myself of the burdens of the media world and felt bucked, because the water was fresh. The dog enjoyed the milk. Paul enjoyed the fact that everybody plunged in and the girls' robes became see-through. It felt more like *O Brother, Where Art Thou?* than *Asterix and Obelix*.

After we dried ourselves, and the Druids went back to being mountain guides or small builders or whatever they were, we went up river by a convoluted route. Konrad wanted to grab an improbable piece of camera trickery. The boat had to be seen from the cliffs as it approached some caves, coming round the bend in a stately fashion. "It's our helicopter shot," he explained. Though he lacked a helicopter, the cliff would provide the height.

Paul and I had to carry the canoe through the gorge, over the fields, through several locked gates, across a suspension bridge, up a track, over a stile, down past some startled bullocks and sling it in by a shallow bend in order to paddle down the route for ten minutes, with Steve hidden in the bushes to tell them I was coming and a walkie-talkie coughing my arrival. Then we turned around and did it again with the cameraman on board.

Cadbury lay down to order and salivated at the ducks passing by. We drifted down the dark, syrupy water in the fading light, with the mayflies dancing over the black eddies. I pointed out a heron by the bank. It was, in fact, a stick on a mat of weed. I think Kevin the cameraman was too polite to tell me. I kept explaining that it would take off spectacularly when we got close, but, being a stick, it ignored us and stayed where it was.

We finally drifted down to the yellow cliff and I nosed in under bleached fallen trees, sucked to the edge by floods. I could see the remains of dried reeds deposited along the lower branches of the alder that hung above me over the bank. Clearly, the water was sometimes higher and faster than it was that evening.

I needed to haul the canoe up a bit and the bank was steeper than I reckoned. I pulled Cadbury after me, his paws scrabbling at the soft wet terracotta incline as I carried him by his life-jacket strap. We reached a plateau overlooking the darkening river with the over-grown cliff ahead.

It was pocked with yellow caves. They weren't deep. Two in front of me were low dank holes but the space to my left was open and airy, carved into a spur, with twin arches to the front and side and a sort of pillar of sandstone between. The original caves had been dug out of the rock by early hunter-gatherers but in later times these shelters were used by hermits.

We have become far too sophisticated in Britain for holy men. These medieval hermits had apparently followed the example of a Dark Age king who was reputed to have camped out here while on the run from his enemies, but the hermits were not mythical. This was a river crossing, a ford, and those holy men living in the caves were here to guide travellers. If the water rose to the level I had spotted earlier then they offered shelter too. Like all drop-outs, they were the focus of unfounded rumours. It was said they saved children who fell in the river and raised them as their own.

The legends and the hermits somehow acknowledged that these caves in the wood, by the stream, were sacred. It seemed inherently mystical and very un-English – or at least the Protestant post-Reformation England we know. The river was a link to hermits, pagans, monks and modern Druids. It's a spiritual thing, flowing water.

BOG-SNORKELLING SUMMER

It was a thundering hot day. We had left the Severn and driven over to see how the Wye was faring some fifty miles further west. The sky was hazy, and not a mid-Welsh blank white but a smoking hot blue. "We've never seen the like," the little crowd told me. This was a phenomenon; a day Geoffrey of Monmouth or Gerald of Wales or any other medieval commentator would have noted in their histories. After months of rain the Welsh hills were verdant, baking and plump and I was going to jump into a line of bog cut in a field. The sun was shining just for me. The heat was up and I was getting into a wetsuit.

This usually makes me fractious. There is too much yanking and twanging involved, dragging sticky rubber over sweaty flab. The hood bit tears at the little hairs in front of the ears.

I glanced at my reflection in the car window. It wasn't quite the Dark Knight. Like some all-enveloping corset it had stretched me into the shape of an Antony Gormley cast-iron man. Then I breathed out and a black ovoid tube popped out beneath my ribcage: my Pirelli-ridged, black and glistening spare tyre.

Joanne Pitchforth of Heckmondwike, the reigning world bog-snorkelling champion with a time of one minute and thirty-five seconds, explained the rules. "Keep your head down and swim to one end and then turn and swim back. You're not supposed to look up and see where you are going."

"Are there obstructions?"

"There are eels."

"OK." I went over to the edge and sat for a moment above the murk and then I lowered myself in.

I assumed I would do all right. I am a strong enough swimmer. I did not spend my entire childhood "bombing" Harlow public pool for nothing. I may waddle on the land but I am The Human Fish in the water.

I pulled down the mask and powered off. It was like swimming in the washing up. The water was murky brown and full of bits. I could see it, swirling and opaque, but nothing else except, sometimes, a horrible white flappy thing which turned out to be my hand.

I thumped the flippers up and down and tried not to drag my head out. "Don't look where you are going." The instruction had been perfectly straightforward. So I stuck my hands forward and wiggled my fingers a little as a sort of protective early warning device. But it saps the confidence to be jiggling on with no idea what you are getting into. It was like doing the back stroke facing forwards. You involuntarily slow down. You become agitated in case you bang your head on the end of the pool. I was dragging breath out of my snorkel and tiring quickly. This must be the end. I must be there now. This is the end, surely?

It wasn't the end. I had another twelve or so yards to go before I found the white post, and turned, rather less stylishly than I had planned, and flapped back.

Several times I got bobbles of water down my pipe. I knew what to do. I blew powerfully and the water shot away. Except that some little bits of water didn't evacuate the pipe. They trickled back down just as I was heaving a particularly huge breath to fill my exhausted lungs and so I sucked them straight down my own windpipe, choked, stuck my head up too far, filled my snorkel with water, inhaled a pint of ditch and swallowed the rest. I stood up, coughing, wheezing and drowning. The dog who had been running alongside barking encouragement went crazy and I lost about thirty seconds. If I hadn't done that I would quite honestly have been within several minutes of the record. Probably.

Luckily I wasn't just there for the swim. I was there to examine the bog and to record the diversity of plants and mosses. I got dressed and Ray Woods took me to explore. He carried a six-foot aluminium pole with a rotating handle at the top. This was a soil sampler. By pushing it deep into the earth and swivelling, we effectively sliced a core of material from the depths and pulled out a long sausage of deep brown and interesting material.

Here was a record of layers of organic matter dating back for thousands of years. This was peat – quite simply pickled vegetation, packed down over centuries. We could see climate changes in the different stripes. We could note when the vegetation had altered its make-up. There were little bits of burnt areas where forest fires might have occurred. Everything settled and stayed, adding to the richness of the swamp, which was all the time growing. Ray estimated that the original peat area would have once been ten feet higher than it is now. The fields around had been improved many years ago and the water had steadily drained out of this bog, lowering it in the process.

At the very bottom of the core we picked out a lump of tree, probably birch, and quite possibly a remnant of first growth after the last glaciation. The wood crumbled to the touch. I was sorry to crush something that had stayed intact and preserved for so many thousands of years.

So much of this habitat had gone. On wet uplands, in order to provide more sheep pasture, it is still going. Land drains take away the water. Nutrients "improve" the soil. We are losing more than crumbling chocolate-coloured repositories of biological history. We are losing natural reservoirs. These unimproved wetlands are sponges. They control the release of water into the rivers. Instead of being absorbed into a bog, the river sends its spate charging down to flood the lower valleys of the Severn and Wye. Improvements in the high hills of mid Wales can affect the citizens of Tewkesbury.

And finally there was another role that all this water once played in this fertile pre-industrial landscape. Ray explained that these bogs had provided fuel. It certainly wasn't always sunny in the Welsh hills. The winters were cold. Peat had been an essential source of energy to the population. That resource was unlikely to return, but it showed once again that the water in the landscape was not just part of bio-diversity; it had also been part of human diversity. Historically the river had run through the lives of mankind in a hundred subtle ways. Today we seem to be channelling it all in one direction. Literally so, as far as floods are concerned.

SHOOTING THE RAPIDS

Ross sits on a meander in the Wye, high above the river. It seems to have been built with a certain respect for the waywardness of its neighbour. I canoed around a bend on a brown sluggish stream and pulled in next to a car park and a pub where Graham, Regional Access Officer of the British Canoe Union, introduced me to my first kayak. This was essentially a large orange plastic beach shoe. After a short lesson in its capabilities, I clambered into it by the side of a little jetty smeared with the droppings of a parliament of ducks and swans that occasionally hissed at me.

To begin with, I had to learn to capsize the thing. Apparently, it wasn't difficult. I paddled up towards the rubber dinghy. Graham floated nearby and I leant sideways. Plop. I was in. The kayak effectively sat on its back and dangled me underneath as a counterweight. I was stuck. I knew the skill. It had all been laboriously explained. I was supposed to pull off the waterproof cover that sealed me in and then tip out of the boat while upside down, disorientated and remembering to hold my breath.

Rivers never seem to be fresh flowing silver streams except in shampoo commercials. The Wye was brown and dark. I thrashed about a bit, dragged the elastic rim of the skirt off its lip, yanked my feet out of the footrests and my thighs out of the boat and eventually surfaced, spluttering and mawing.

"Well done," said Graham.

I thought so too and prepared to strike out for the bank. But he wasn't finished. "Now climb back in."

This was ridiculous. The kayak was a slippery and unstable plastic toy bobbing in a river. The hole I had to get into was tiny, but with a gigantic heave and a medium-sized bruise I managed it. I was feeling pretty pleased with myself.

"Good. Let's do it again for another angle," the director Konrad announced from the camera boat.

We did it three more times. After that I could probably have got out of a kayak in a force six wind in the middle of the night while carrying a sack of potatoes.

Graham and I finally set off down the river towards Symonds Yat on a great long paddle, side by side, like Tweedledum and Tweedledee, bolt upright and sociably paired.

Ross was a good starting point for our jaunt. In 1745 the local vicar Dr John Egerton started taking friends downstream to show them the wonders of the Wye and, inadvertently I am sure, started the British Tourist Industry. By 1808 there were eight excursion boats operating on the river. Half a century later, more than twenty breathless accounts of the trip had been published.

None proved more influential than William Gilpin's. He sought a proper, eighteenth-century, rational explanation for his agreeable experience and urged his readers to examine "the face of a country by the rules of picturesque beauty". He encouraged tourists to carry a little convex black mirror called a Claude Glass, which smudged the detail, so that they could arrange the scenery into a neatly ordered, carefully framed picture and thus "improve" the landscape. His "artificiality" was attacked by later generations, particularly Wordsworth, who came to be horrified by "picturesque" tourists in the Lake District. Today we want something more "natural". We crave a sort of organic authenticity.

But how can we mock poor William Gilpin and his landscape bossiness? What were we doing, nearly two hundred years later, except drifting about in hot debate, framing shots, closing off the unsightly bits, trying to influence the viewer, and editing and cutting the vistas for the camera?

Gilpin was keen to impress on his audience that the dramatic scenery of the Wye, with its ruined abbeys like Tintern and its beetling cliffs like Symonds Yat, were quite the equal of any Italian scenery on the Grand Tour. But as we paddled on it wasn't Italy that came to mind. It wasn't Britain either. The slight low mist in the air heightened the experience of drifting into a wild North American landscape. It began to rain in a lazy way: the drops widely spaced across the river, sending concentric ripples across the flat, oily, slow-moving surface. It became a day when a paddle seemed an intrusion and the blade slithered into the water like a spoon in dark mixture.

"We stopped much further up," I told Graham, "and went to try and get on the river with my canoe, but there were notices telling us that the 'owners of the river' restricted access to certain times of the year."

"You're only allowed to canoe on certain parts of the Wye," Graham replied sadly. "We're actually quite lucky here. The Wye was used by bow-hauliers for much of its early life so that essentially meant we have a right to navigation up as far as Gaslin, but beyond that everything is restricted. You are not allowed to canoe on the vast majority of rivers in England. There is no right to paddle. The owner of the land on either side owns the bed of the river right to the mid-point."

"And they exercise this?"

"Oh yes. I've been warned off. But we try to negotiate where we can."

RIGHTS OF ACCESS TO RIVERS

Put a foot in any river in England or Wales and chances are you are trespassing.

Surprisingly, there is no automatic public right of access to the vast majority of England and Wales's rivers. By contrast, in Scotland the Land Reform Act of 2003 provided statutory outdoor access rights covering rivers.

The banks and beds of English and Welsh rivers are technically owned from source to estuary by the people who own the land on either side. If the opposite banks are owned by different people, the mid-point of the river is taken as their boundary.

The British Canoe Union has recently highlighted the fact that only about 3.2 per cent of the 42,693 miles of rivers in England and Wales have access rights. If you swim, sail or throw a stick for your dog anywhere in the other 96.8 per cent without the owner's permission you are theoretically committing a crime.

The private owners of rivers do not, however, own the water flowing through them but instead hold limited rights to its abstraction. They are usually allowed to take out 700 cubic feet a day (that's about two milk tankers-worth, in case you're thinking of marketing the contents of the muddy stream at the bottom of your garden as mineral water).

A Family of Anglers, by Arthur Devis, 1749. Two steps closer to the river and they'd have been trespassing.

Of three hundred rivers in Wales suitable for kayaking, only eight have any legal right of access. The situation is the same in England but less strict in Scotland.

We stopped to clamber up the bank and wade across a mud track in a chestnut wood to look at an eighteenth-century monument. It sat alone in dripping trees to commemorate a boy who drowned swimming. He would have been trespassing. The water that took him belongs to anyone, but the land beneath the water is someone's property.

It was angling associations that organised themselves to prevent rights of access. They feared that passing canoes would disturb the fish. Now, I have never struck a fish with my paddle. It is a difficult feat to achieve. I suspect that a fish would rather take his chances with a paddle than be hauled out of the water by a metal hook and half-asphyxiated while a man in a check shirt hugs him for a photograph.

On the challenging long bend that would take us round into the deep gorge, with the rock towering almost 400 feet above, a swan rose up from far ahead on the shining river. It struggled off the surface towards us, flapping up, rising inch by inch, its wing tips dipping to the water, honking upwards to pass just overhead and pulse the air with its beating wings.

The loop brought us back close to where we had been an hour before. There were houses now amongst the trees on either side and ahead of us the river gave up being slinky and languid and started to froth. Graham intended to lead me through the rapids.

The rapids below Symonds Yat are described as "harmless" in one guide and "easy, even for beginners" in another. They certainly don't disappear over a foaming lip like something out of *The Last of the Mohicans* but there is a certain intensity in the air at any white water. The noise increases. The river starts to speed up perceptibly. What has been a leisurely glide gradually becomes a matter of urgent control. It is not helped by having a film crew who want to tie two canoes together and go down the rapids backwards in front of you, filming as they go.

This is irritating behaviour. The director wanted me to look terrified and roll my eyes. (I do this anyway. My eyes have a built-in pop and swivel effect.) But how could I begin to feign dignified alarm when the three of them were floating down in front of me at the caprice of the rapids, making no attempt to look out for their own safety and running camera equipment at the same time? It makes a mockery of all my televisual derring-do.

In the event the white water was utterly harmless. The main danger proved to be the camera catamaran, which lumbered ahead of us. I was convinced I was going to smash straight into it at any moment.

"Aim for where the water looks clearest," Graham shouted. I aimed for the glistening smooth lip of the fall.

"Now paddle forward to maintain the momentum."

I took a couple of strokes and noticed that Graham had already turned and was nudging in behind a spot of rocks on the eastern bank, because that was it. The rapids were, as one might expect, quick. I had successfully shot them.

"We just need to go over to the other bank now, so we can get out and come down again for another run," Graham said. "Follow me."

I followed him and promptly toppled sideways into the river. It figures. The kayak exposes itself to the pressure of the full stream as it turns and you need to counterbalance. I became aware that I had forgotten to do this from an upside-down position, under water. It happened so quickly that I needed a second or so to work out that this was the very thing I had trained for. Now … what was it I was supposed to do exactly?

Ah yes. Eventually I pulled the skirt off, got myself out of the kayak and surfaced, blowing like a whale. Unlike the practice, we hadn't come to a halt. We were still charging down the river: me, the capsized canoe and my paddle. There was nothing except water under my feet. Graham came and canoed alongside and we both sped down the river together until we made it to the bank.

"I'm glad I rehearsed," I said.

PUTCHERS

A putcher is a fish trap. It is traditionally made from hazel sticks arranged like a giant funnel and woven together with osiers, or strips of willow, a design that dates back to prehistoric times. It is smaller than a putt, which is equally old but seemed to have existed in a single form. Putchers were arranged in ranks tied to posts in the river and acted as a form of permanent net, and they struck me as a highly satisfactory way of catching fish.

We had parked up in the yard of John Powell's house, perched on a low cliff overlooking a great sandy bend in the tidal Severn before it is joined by the Wye. After admiring his collection of traditional Severn boats, including one with twenty-foot oars, we walked down through the village, carrying six of these fish baskets to his friend Eric Jackson's cottage.

We went through a picket gate, negotiated a garden path under pear trees, edged past his shed and came to a heap of flotsam that Eric gathered from the river: buoys, driftwood, old benches, bits of boat and chairs.

"Fridge freezers and things go up and down on the tide," John explained. "They become like old friends."

We had reached the end of the garden and the path abruptly descended to the muddy foreshore. "But the big floods bring huge things floating down. That's the problem. Take the rope there."

There was a length of rope, which was thick with mud. I lifted the putcher onto my back (it was light but cumbersome) and took the rope to lower myself down through the grass to the water's edge.

John had a licence for his trap. These were issued in the 1860s. In 1865 the authorities banned all "fixed engines" being used to catch salmon unless under the right of "immemorial usage", which implied that John's traps had been around for a bit. In the 1920s there were 2,400 baskets on this stretch of the river alone. Now we were approaching one of the last ranks, maintained as much for tradition as for food.

We plodded out into the stream. Cadbury followed, up to his jowls. In a few hours the tide would rise and completely cover the putchers. They were ranged ahead of us, facing upstream, to catch the salmon on the ebb tide. They would be sucked into the funnel and stranded in the basket. As we got closer I could see that there was a fish there, doing exactly that.

"It's not a salmon though."

"No, it's a bass."

I took Eric by the arm. "Now, you knew we were filming today. Promise me you didn't come down here a few hours ago and stick that sea bass in there for the camera. That's come from Waitrose, hasn't it?"

"Ah, you know me well, Griff," he said. "No. Of course not."

After I had retrieved the fish and helped Eric and John tie their putchers on to the posts, one above the other, squeezed tightly to create a closely fitting web, I began to realise that the fish weir had its demands. "You have to come down every tide then?"

"Should do, yes."

"In all weathers?"

"Ought to, yes."

We would have been lucky to catch a salmon. John wanted to see more fishing by traditional methods, but there are currently strict restrictions in force. He was worried that the old customs would die out. He and Eric were facing a new ten-year ban on traditional methods of fishing, which was going to stop anybody learning the craft. And this wasn't the only fishing skill on this stretch of the river that was under threat.

CHASING SALMON ON FOOT

Mike Evans felt the same way as John. He was seventy. He had been lave fishing since he was a boy, when he used to sit on the side and watch the old men on the sandbanks until one of them let him have a go.

If I wanted to get a taste of this ancient art I needed to get out with Mike before the tide came back in. We carried his net, the oars and his "knocker" (some call it a "priest" because it's used to administer the "last rites") down to a concrete launching ramp a little further upstream. The ramp cut through a reed bank to give a long view of the sweeping bend of the river by Black Rock, with Newnham away on the cliff to the west, and in front of us a wide shallow curve of water. We slithered over the mud to his tin boat.

Mike knew he wasn't going to catch a salmon for us today. The conditions were wrong. It was too windy and too sunny. Or perhaps not sunny enough. Too cold or maybe a little too warm. The tide was definitely wrong. There could be as few as ten days in a month with the right conditions.

As he and the small remaining number of lave fishermen have long argued, they are hardly any threat to the salmon population, whatever size it is. But he offered to show me what he did and how he did it. I took his splintery-handled unpainted oars and rowed him across the swingeing channel to an eddy under a sandbank, dropped him into three feet of water and rowed back to pick up Konrad and the crew. It was tough work, getting the chicken and the fox across the river, and I needed to pull hard against the tide.

Once we were all in the middle of the river, on the edge of the far spit of sand at the top of the great bend, with the boat anchored, Mike unfolded his equipment. The lave was like a big shrimping net, made from a natural fork of wood. He stalked the salmon as they came up around the bend.

"How do you spot them?"

"I can see them coming," he said. "They're like a shadow. I see the brown mark in the water. Or sometimes I see little ripples on the surface." He needed the right light conditions to do this.

"And then you have to stop him."

"I have to work out which route he's likely to take. But I can say that if I do spot him he has very little chance of getting by."

The tidal river was surging and tugging around our legs, already threatening to tumble us over. Disconcertingly, whenever I stood still for a few seconds, I could feel the sand giving way almost instantaneously, sucked out from underneath my boots.

Mike zoomed off through the waist-high water. "They're dangerous tides, though. You have to be careful," he said.

Last year, in the Black Rock area, the lave net catch totalled six fish. The season is restricted now to June, July and August. But the Severn once teemed with salmon. Poachers used oil to set fire to the water and collected them with spears. In the late nineteenth century when catches fell, fierce regulation was imposed and the river filled with fish again. The largest salmon caught on the Wye was in 1923. It weighed fifty-three pounds.

"The best total I ever had," Mike told me "was in the 1970s. I caught a hundred fish in one season."

The 1970s; that's when I was at university. This river had been at its most fecund only thirty-five years ago. And now a disaster has happened. The salmon population has almost gone.

In the 1970s the secret feeding grounds of the Atlantic salmon were discovered off the Faroes and Greenland. Immediately, man tried to fish them to extinction. At around the same time, intensive farming methods and massive changes to land use in the upper reaches of the river altered the nature of the water itself and destroyed the salmon's breeding grounds. Climate change did the rest. Now we are trying to limit a tradition of fishing that is prehistoric in origin and that has managed to exist on the banks of the river, on a much larger scale, for thousands of years.

Some sort of deal with the Environment Agency has recently been made, but it is not the depredations of Mike and a few remaining lave fishermen in their dangerous occupation that have done the damage. It's not the putchers. It's not even the anglers. It is simply greed and stupidity of scale. We collectively are to blame, but collective blame is hard to attribute. In the meantime we make small bureaucratic restitutions.

The River Wye with the Black Mountains in the distance.

Bog snorkelling in a wetsuit with a spare tyre in supagrip.

Scene near the New Weir, Symonds Yat, by Thomas Girtin.

Tintern, a Cistercian abbey founded in 1131 in the Wye Valley.

Symonds Yat looking Picturesque but not Romantic.

Putchers, the non-anglers' preferred fishing experience.

Later that day I caught a man and a dog. Lave fishing.

I took the Severn Bore lying down.

THE DIURNAL CHOCOLATE MILKSHAKE

I lay awake at 5 a.m. in a hotel room covered in signs. The management informed me it was saving the universe by leaving me with dirty towels; that the lavatory was a special small-bore plumbing system which guaranteed, in writing, to keep me awake at night; and that I wasn't allowed to escape to the garden (where the paths, incidentally, were "uneven and slippery") because of the security arrangements. My door gave detailed instructions about how the responsibility for telling anyone I wanted to get out after eleven rested with me.

I should have stayed on Steve Hyslop's mud barge. That was the original idea. It had been built to transport silt dredged from channels, and he was building an ever-extending garden hut on top of it. The previous evening we had sat amidst the geraniums at the back with a cup of Earl Grey tea and discussed the sad urges of surfers, while a Californian sunset played on the hulks lodged in the dock like abandoned submarines. How some come from other countries, how some live by the river, how some go out in winter, when the ice freezes their long dude locks, wearing puffa jackets and wetsuit long-johns, to catch the perfect bore.

This Steve had stood on his board and done about two miles, but the other Steve, Steve King my Druid friend, had stood on the wave for seven miles. It was the unofficial record.

"The best time is in winter. Effectively there is a bore every tide but not every one is much good for surfing. By living by the river we can get out if the conditions are right."

"At any time of year?"

"It can be best in, say, March."

Coldest too, I imagined.

A bore is quite simply the sea tide coming up a river. As the incoming tide marches up the shallow estuary, it picks up pace and pressure. By the time it hits the more confined space at Sharpness, where the river has contracted to a mere mile wide, it has begun to lift up. The Severn fills like a saucer and the tide rises with incredible rapidity.

"There it is." The two Steves were practised at spotting it.

Standing with them high above the river in the dusk I could see the bore coming. It was a line of white, crossing from bank to bank and dragging a carpet of muddy water behind it. The tide appeared to clamber up the wall towards us. It only took an hour for the boats to float. I had never seen such a huge space fill with water so quickly.

A following wind and a full moon help.

The largest recorded bore was on 15 October 1966 downstream of Stonebench, when the water lifted itself up to a height of nine and a quarter feet. But it is visible twice a day for 130 days a year and strong on about twenty-five days. I got up early in the morning because it was going to be a strong day.

We started near Newnham. We were going to do this the professional surfer way. We had a powerful speedboat and the idea was to chase the bore up the river.

I got into a wetsuit. Steve took me away to a corner of field behind the sea wall while they loaded the camera equipment.

Surfing is like playing the violin. It takes a long time to learn, when you do nothing creditable at all except irritate other people. Beyond the age of six that period gets longer. It had never seemed worth it to me. "Body boarding is all I'm good for and I'm not very good at that," I explained.

SPECTACULAR BORES

It is difficult to calculate the number of bores in the world. I have read that there are sixty but also that there are "over a hundred". Both accounts concurred, however, on one matter. The Chinese may have the most spectacular, with a wave 20 feet high on the Hang Chou Fe River, but Britain has the biggest number: eight in one account and twenty in the other. I suppose it depends whether the oncoming wave counts as a notable phenomenon.

The Severn has the largest of the UK's tidal bores. According to folk tradition the Severn Bore occurs once a year on Good Friday – but folk were wrong because in fact there are two bores a day on 130 days of the year with the largest occurring around the equinox.

The factors that cause the Severn Bore begin far out at sea when the Atlantic Ocean hits the shallower waters of the continental shelf.

The shelf slows the incoming tide and forces the waves up.

This tide then passes through the Severn estuary and into the river itself, where the width and depth of the channel decrease rapidly. This funnels the water into a truncated wave, which can travel up the river for over 25 miles at average speeds of between 8 and 12 mph.

The bore itself regularly attracts spectators but even this can be a dangerous activity. Once the bore passes by, those watching from the banks can enjoy two spectacles. First, the entire river will flow in the opposite direction to the way it should be going. Second, the river level will rise for about an hour afterwards forcing spectators to run – or perhaps paddle – for the hills.

Surfers riding the Severn Bore in January 2006.

"You just need to get yourself aboard," Steve said. He laid the surfboard on the grass and showed me how to get the weight forward. "Then paddle and you'll lift up and ride it."

This was familiar. Kayaks, canoes, abseiling and mountain climbing. I was supposed to learn a skill in the gap between "roll the camera" and "action" and then get filmed falling off, so that hobby magazines could write about how I betrayed an entire sporting fraternity by not doing it properly.

It was another slither down a safety line to get into the speedboat. We gunned downriver in early sunshine and for a while kept going aground. It was, after all, the very bottom of the tide. Finally, we came into a long shallow stretch. We got out and stood up to our thighs in the water. My board was tied around my ankle with a bit of Velcro. Steve demonstrated again how I should launch myself onto the water.

"There it is," he said casually, "so we'd better get ready." He pointed behind me. It was coming already. It was a low garden wall of white froth and it was about a hundred yards away. I had expected more notice. It seemed rather precipitate and oddly demanding. And very ... singular.

"Er..." I thought, "stand, throw myself on the middle bit and paddle. It's much closer, isn't it? How am I supposed to tell when it's actually time?" It was actually time.

It washed past. I threw myself on. I missed. I toppled sideways and found myself sitting in a chocolate milkshake surrounded by eddies and another foot of water. The bore is not just a single wave, like a wave on the beach; it is the front of a slab of water which instantly fills up the riverbed. I stood up and turned around to talk to Steve, but he had gone. He was fifty yards away, standing on his surfboard and disappearing up the river with the bore that I had completely failed to ride even for a few seconds.

"Griff! Come on."

They were shouting at me from the boat. I waded across, fell in and we roared away. Ahead of us, just on the bend, Steve jumped off his board and we caught up with him. He got in and we shot forward again. Then we caught up with the tide. There was a sort of grinding surge and we dipped and lunged through the bore.

We were back in the shallow water. Steve was looking earnestly ahead. They had done all this before. We zoomed around another bend and they slewed to a halt.

"Out! Out, Griff."

It was like *Groundhog Day*. My failure was wiped clean. Another part of the river, another few seconds of preparation and another distant roaring. We had cheated time. Here was the very same wave coming to catch us again.

Steve wanted me to perform. "Look, Griff, try this." He gave me his own board, one that he had had made specifically to ride the Severn Bore. It was lighter and slightly difficult. I threw myself down as before, only this time I surged forward. Yes! I was riding the Severn Bore. On my stomach, obviously, but surging forward at a good eight miles an hour. It was like body-boarding on a beach except that the wave didn't peter out. It just kept going.

Steve was beside me, standing and waving at the passers-by. I was surprised that he wasn't smoking a fag and reading the newspaper. I looked to my right and there were other people on the wave: blokes in wetsuits and one man in a dress. And then I went the wrong way and while everybody else surfed off into the main channel, I collapsed in a heap on a sandbank.

But I was content. I had felt the power of the tide. It was swirling around me.

"Griff! Come on." The boat caught up with me again. "A little camera glitch. Jump in." And we were off again.

I forget how many times we chased the bore. Rushing up the river, it rolls great logs onto the shore. Trees and branches wiggle and undulate in the froth. There are whirlpools and rips. We surged on through the lot. Sometimes crowds gathered on the bank to watch the natural phenomenon roll by. Other times several surfers were waiting in the foam, and I would roll helplessly while they mounted up and whooped away.

At some point we were joined by another speedboat doing much the same as us except their passengers were a Norse god and his paramour, who had clearly travelled from Bali or Hawaii for a once-in-a-lifetime gig. They flicked great manes of bleached hair back over their shoulders and soared away up the increasingly narrow river like surf gods. Only my local Druid and guide, Steve, was on hand to overtake them every time and continue up under the willow trees when they had fallen off; until the first bridge appeared and even Steve finally stepped down and gave up.

Afterwards, we motored back down a different river. The tide had filled in behind us. There was no danger of going aground now and I absorbed the meandering grey-green beauties of the Severn. We had travelled about fifteen miles and broken no records, although we had probably broken a few bye-laws. The Gloucester Harbour authorities officially discourage surfing the Severn Bore.

CATCHING THE TIDE

The bore, a wonder of the natural world, may thunder up to Gloucester but once there it hovers for a bit and turns around to sluice out of the Severn with the full power of the river at its back. The discharge further up at Apperley in Gloucestershire has been measured as 3,780 cubic feet a second, more than two Olympic swimming pools a minute. This is now joined by the tide. Only the Bay of Fundy in Canada boasts a greater tidal range. The estuarine Severn can rise as high as fifty foot. That is a lot of water to gurgle away. A few days previously the boat we were now in had taken part in a miserable search for the body of a child carried away by the tide. He and his family had been out on one of the great sandy spits in the tidal river.

"It overwhelms you. A man can't stand in it. What chance did this kid have?"

Duncan Milne, our skipper, had built this boat himself. He showed me the joystick control of his jet engines in the wheelhouse, which enabled the boat to sit still in almost any conditions in any moving water in virtually no depth at all, and map the bottom. He had paid for his investment in a few years, charting entrances for marinas or port developments. "We do a lot of planning applications," he said.

He was also on hand to note the shifting sands of the estuaries where the Wye and the Severn came together after their separate 200-mile journeys from Plynlimon. They churned up the bottom. The channels altered month by month, sandbanks shifted, and navigation buoys had to be realigned. We were sitting in a wide stretch of water. England was a low long lump, far to the East, and the tide was charging out across a shallow expanse. Peter's jet engines were delivering eight knots of power but we were sitting stock still.

Ever since I sat off the Cherbourg peninsula trying to make five miles against a flood tide, with fourteen and half tons of boat totally incapable of any forward motion at all (despite her engine pushing as hard as it could), I have been in awe of tidal power. Tidal power is mammoth and unrelenting. Tons and tons of water charge around the world in unstoppable rushes. The tide lifts massive weights and can destroy bridges or crush ships with its energy. This river, on its trip to the sea, may have turned the odd waterwheel, but here, at the mouth, the quantity of water and the shallowness of the entrance seemed to offer a superfluity of natural, moon-driven oomph.

There is a plan to stick a monstrous great dam across the mouth of the river, let the water pour in every day and then harvest the turbo power on the way out. This is probably the cleanest electricity from the most reliable source human beings could ever devise. Here is a renewable power, which has worked as regularly as day and night without fail for millions of years. It would have a low and unobtrusive profile compared with wind farms. It might ultimately produce five per cent of Britain's electricity from seven per cent of her estuarine capabilities, but the whole idea is opposed by an impressive number of sage and reputable bodies.

Did you lose sleep over the Hadron collider? Natural England, Natural Wales, Greenpeace and the RSPB see the barrage as a doomsday machine. Nobody suggests that the thing will explode and start a chain reaction that will eat every atom in the entire universe, but they worry for the Severn. The dam would put a stopper in the flow. Instead of the great daily flush-out, there would be a giant lagoon stretching from Weston-super-Mare to Gloucester. It would completely alter the habitat and probably finish off the salmon. What these protestors really fear is not the end of nature, but the end of the rivers Wye and Severn.

As I stood there on the foredeck of the survey boat, bathed in the silvery light of the estuary, I struggled to define what they were worried about, because it was roughly what I was worried about as well. Many define it as biodiversity. I would go a bit further and call it bio-historo-agri-fisho diversity.

These great rivers are far more than a stream of water in a ditch. They support wildlife, drain the farm land, provide amenities and character; they have created towns and directed the history of the countryside as they flow past, and have done so hand in hand with the people who live on their banks for thousands of years. There has always been change. Not much of what I had seen could be described as truly "natural", but over the last fifty years we have begun to lose our ancient connections with the river and in pursuit of big ambitions we are in danger of sweeping away the stuff that makes it thrive. Overweening intrusions like forests and drainage and fertilisers have had unexpected consequences. And nothing was more overweening than the proposed barrage.

I like estuaries. As we drifted down through the muddy churning water there wasn't much to see except the no-man's land of salt flats to our west and the huge bridges and giant gantries that spanned the distances that the river now commanded way to the east. Nonetheless, this was the remotest place I had been on my trip. After all the high forests, the cathedral cities, the mud banks and sandstone cliffs and the quiet tree-lined valleys, this place, this empty vastness, felt remote and wild and unexplored. The rivers were losing their individuality. In a few short miles they would be absorbed into the vast anonymity of the sea. It seemed wrong to tamper too radically with the spirit of the place.

"I was brought up on this river," Duncan said. "I've loved it all my life, but the most overwhelming feeling I have for it is one of caution. Whatever happens, the Severn should be treated with respect."

Detail from "Map of the River Lea from Cheshunt to the edge of London", c. 1594.

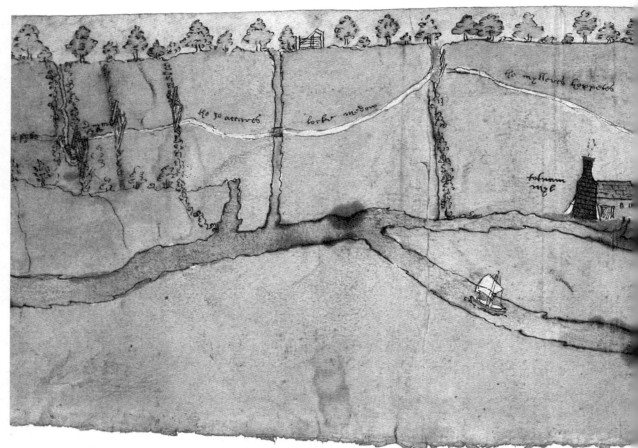

Chapter Four

THE RIVER LEA

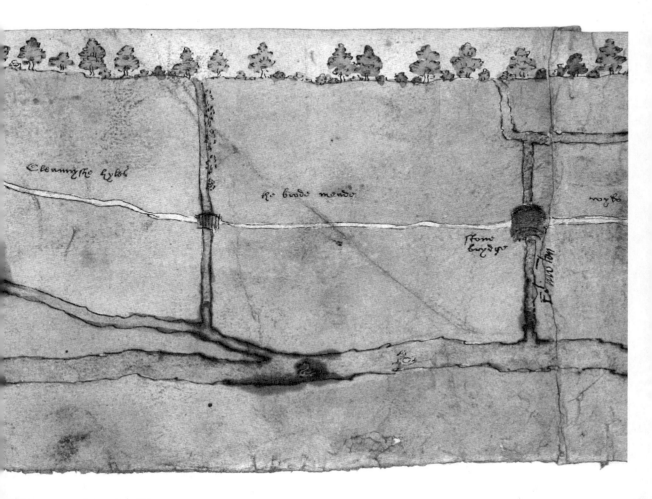

A WET PATCH IN LUTON

On an early autumn day in 2008 I got in a taxi and rumbled thirty-odd miles out of London to Luton, home of straw hats, Vauxhall cars and Lorraine Chase. (You might remember that famous 1970s advert which established Luton as the place to fly away from.) I arrived at the edge of a bare common fringed by expressways and roundabouts, only thirty-six minutes from the centre of London by reasonably fast and overcrowded train (though quite a bit more by taxi), and Cadbury and I walked along a path across a yellowing hill in search of the source of the Lea, or the Lee. You can take your pick. It used to be called the Ley, the Leygan, the Luye and the Lyan. Over twenty-five different ways of spelling it have been discovered, but they all mean something like "place of the God of light". (Ironically, for those who recall the advert, this really was "paradise" after all.)

Passers-by knew exactly what I was looking for. "In that clump of trees," a woman walking her dog told me, pointing towards the stump of a 1960s tower block fringed by a small section of wood, and I marched on.

People have been living around Leagrave Common for 5,000 years. I was near the site of Waulud's Bank, a henge at the foot of the Chilterns, which was built in 3000 BC to be close to a sacred spot on a sacred river: finally I found it. I had come to a concrete shelf, a metal balustrade and a balcony overlooking a clearly obvious trickle of water, running out from a rusty culvert below me.

Cadbury clambered down and did what he does when he reaches any sacred source – he got thigh-high in the mud and started snapping at duckweed – and I stood and marvelled and waited for Trevor Tween to arrive. Trevor was the environmental officer for Luton. This was his patch. He joined me, said hello, laughed at the dog and told me that I was looking at the run-off from a car park round the back of a tower block.

"The Lea proper emerges at a place called the Five Springs," Trevor said. "It's up this way." And we tramped off, through willows, down thistle banks, past areas of marsh, over bicycle wheels, sweet wrappers, bottles, tins and condoms.

"I've often hoped that we might come across a Bronze Age sword thrown in to propitiate the gods, but it's usually household rubbish and fly tipping," Trevor murmured and paused.

We had come to the middle of a swamp overhung by dense willow. It was difficult to imagine some siren or ancient goddess inhabiting this brown and putrid bog. Nonetheless the springs were still identifiable. "There are only four of them now," Trevor explained. "The fifth dried up in Victorian times."

It was a modest beginning for a modest river. The Lea is not celebrated in many odes. It is only a tributary of a far grander, more famous brother, the Thames, and it joins it after travelling through some of the most forbidding urban territory in Britain, but it has played a major part in the history of a great city, London, and also in the story of the people who lived along its banks – even though here in Luton it seemed to be largely ignored. It was one ditch among many. Trevor, Cadbury and I walked on into the town itself, following the river past the faint and forgotten remains of old swimming pools and the sites of fish ponds.

We crossed a footbridge, where Trevor's department had had to stop local people harvesting watercress from the brooks because of the danger of liver fluke. The river ran through a park. It temporarily turned into a lake. And then seemed to get embarrassed for itself as it neared the centre of town. In front of a concrete pub by a railway bridge, in a bleak central square, we came to an oblong gap full of startling green weeds. It was the last appearance of the Lea before it gave up on Luton altogether and headed underground.

Trevor explained that there were plans to uncover it again and make "a water feature", but I didn't bother trying to trace any further. Instead we bundled back into the cars and joined it again at the eastern edge of Luton amongst tall willows and kudzu by a little footbridge. It had become a wide stream. It was gushing over a weir. Trevor stopped me.

"This is as far as I go," he announced dramatically. "This is the edge of my territory."

Like an Apache guide reaching the beginning of Navaho land, he shook my hand and wished me well. Ahead lay six miles of mills, weirs and dams. Ahead lay Hatfield. I was on my own in uncharted territory. I needed a map.

THE HATFIELD HOUSE MAP

If you want to hire Hatfield House for a day's filming you require £5,000. We weren't up for that sort of extravagance, so we covered the

camera and scurried across the entrance hall, ignoring the breastplates
and crossed halberds, the black oak furniture and the crew making
Harry Potter and the Wealthy Location Manager of Azkaban.

We went down into the basement to meet Robin the archivist.
He took us to a low-ceilinged office. Slightly disappointingly, there
weren't any rows of yellowing records. There was a long wooden table
and several severe desks. Encouragingly, there was also a map.

Robin Harcourt Williams laid a long, folded piece of paper on the
table without much of a flourish. (I guessed he wasn't a man given to
flourishes.) This, however, was an absorbing document. It was only a
few inches from top to bottom but, when unfolded, it stretched several
feet along the table.

This beautiful, hand-drawn strip of a map had been created in about
1594 to settle a dispute. Lord Burleigh (sometimes spelt Burghley) was
a senior minister to Queen Elizabeth I. The map covered the entire
river from his palace in Cheshunt (on the main road between Ware and
London) to the edge of the city.

At first sight, it seemed oddly modern because there was so little
detail on it. The banks on either side were painted a uniform ochre
yellow, still highly coloured for something made in the sixteenth century.
The river itself had been left a blank white. The map showed hardly any
evidence of roads and no real field boundaries. There were a number
of enchanting little cartographers' details: a swan here, fish traps there,
three men pulling a boat on the bank. Some houses were drawn in great
detail, but not all of them.

Robin himself admitted that he didn't know entirely what it was
meant to show, or perhaps settle, except that he could see that a section
had been added in Lord Burleigh's own hand. This was on the far right
(northern) end, next to his palace: "Theobalds".

William Cecil, Lord Burleigh, was proud of Theobalds, which he had partly modelled on a French château. (His son eventually swapped it with the King for Hatfield House, where his descendants still live.) An extra bit of paper had been pasted onto the relevant section of the map to show the road up to his house, a stand of trees and, in some detail, a heronry with birds flapping their wings in the branches.

Perhaps the heronry was valuable. Or perhaps the senior minister of the crown had grabbed the map and immediately said, "Look, you haven't got it right here at all. Give me that pen." But whatever the reason, it demonstrated a considerable personal interest.

Robin knew his Lordship's amendments because he recognised the handwriting. We leaned in and studied this wonderful document. The course of the main river was perfectly easy to understand. It clearly showed a series of other streams running off and alongside it. These took long dog-legs out to mills, themselves drawn with windows and chimneys. I guessed that they were leats, or man-made trenches to power the machinery, and that the map had been drawn to establish where water could be abstracted or diverted: an age-old problem on any river and one that is still jealously guarded today.

There was clearly a weir halfway down, which might have made progress for the hauliers difficult. I assumed that a series of other marks were either some form of primitive lock or gate, possibly a flash lock or "staunch", but leaving aside his rather neat drawing of the herons, I guessed that Lord Burleigh had probably had the map made to establish the navigation rights on the River Lea.

In this, he was only heralding a long struggle between centralised authority and local interests. For five centuries the crown had been passing legislation to prevent the blocking of waterways. Edward III had passed laws ordering that all weirs, dams and fish traps were to be cleared from rivers across the country. The right to river navigation is enshrined in the Magna Carta. Sea levels were higher in the early Middle Ages, the climate was wetter and rivers were deeper. The roads were truly terrible. It was far cheaper to carry goods by water. Rivers were important.

The Lea was one of the earliest rivers to be kept navigable by law. The first act to order the improvement of any river in England for the purposes of trade was made for the Lea in 1424. There was another act in 1430. The commissioners of the Lea navigation were established in that era. A few years after Lord Burleigh's intervention, people who wanted to carry goods to London by road threw obstacles in the way of barges and cut down bridges to block the river. The matter was taken to the Star Chamber, the superior court of the land. It decided in favour of river transport and the boatmen.

What I was looking at, in the bowels of Hatfield House, was the authority of London reaching out to Essex and beyond. Here was Elizabeth's first minister himself, adding a few doodled herons, probably for his own purposes, but otherwise representing the interests of the City and the Crown. He wanted the River Lea kept clear of obstruction, to work for him. The map detailed exactly where mills were allowed to extract water, what obstructions were permitted and where the towpath went. With bright unfaded clarity, it showed a clear route for the men pulling their heavy boat along.

Notably they were going in the direction of London.

PADDLING THROUGH HERTFORD

It was time for me to do the same and to get afloat. Leaving the house and crossing the park, Paul and I drove the canoes down to the river, past copses, through rustic gates and over fields (where they had tested tanks in the First World War, and we now tested our four-wheel drive in a big puddle) to where the Lea glided through an eighteenth-century fantasy. Massive trees drooped down to water that flowed under a brick bridge as placidly as a lake.

It soon became a sort of combined industrial ditch and canal. At Hatfield House it had been organised to look like a sylvan idyll. A little further down it was controlled and channelled for running mills. It wasn't until Hertford itself that the Lea became what Lord Burleigh had envisaged: a goods-way into London. This was marked by a splendid pond wide enough to turn a barge around, some robust warehouses and a towpath. I was canoeing into a new form of "improved" river.

I like creeping about on a waterway in a busy town. A great network of brooks and run-offs snakes through the middle of Hertford. The main road went over my head. The smell of curry drifted down from somewhere above. Cars were beeping, traffic was roaring and I was slipping out of a warren of little tunnels into an empty backwater.

I paddled past the back of the pub. A rather dingy parking space overlooked the river. A couple of guys with bright red faces, in bobble hats and too many pullovers, were hanging about by the edge of the water.

As I canoed past them, they snorted and giggled in my direction. "We saw you there," one of them said. "Where are you going then?"

I drifted over to them. "Just canoeing through the town. What about you?" I asked.

"We're trying to catch some crayfish."

Under my prompting, they pulled up their net. A red creature was snapping away in what looked suspiciously like a converted Tesco shopping basket. I picked him up behind his head and he snapped his claws. He was handsome, but the American Signal crayfish is an illegal immigrant. I have no idea who introduced it, but the Yank crustacean has started to dominate the waterways of Britain, driving out the much less aggressive and slightly less colourful British crayfish. As a result the nature experts and regulatory bodies are keen that we catch and eat as many of the American invaders as possible.

The men were there to help. They reckoned that they would get seventy or eighty by morning; enough to sell to a Chinese restaurant. While they waited for the crayfish to nibble their bacon bait, they were going to sit in the pub and talk up their nature conservancy business.

For my part, I paddled on to where a dignified, black-tarred, weather-boarded warehouse with a malting tower overlooked an assortment of rusting rings, old posts and restructured walls around an open stretch of water. An old lady was sitting in the garden of her converted flat. I asked her which of the two streams ahead I should follow to London. She told me that either of them would eventually lead me through the town, but one was an overspill taking the back route. It was completely overgrown. She didn't recommend it. So I went right, down an eerily deserted canalised river running just a block away from the main street. A row of workmen's cottages with miniature front gardens filled with hollyhocks and roses faced the water. Opposite them was the arse end of the Hertford Waitrose.

The architect of the supermarket had clearly decided that this was an industrial ditch, so he had dumped a great slab of backyard, containing all his goods' entrances, his rubbish disposal and his noisy air-conditioning there. It hummed and rattled at me as I paddled past in the midday stillness. Sometimes the Lea was beautiful and sometimes bleak. And sometimes it was both at the same time.

Beyond a stretch of well-walked towpath, I came to another open area of water, crammed with narrow boats: a great fleet of pleasure vessels, hovering thirty miles north of London, on the edge of a route that could lead them down to the Limehouse docks and thence, I suppose, to almost anywhere in the country.

These were largely canal boats, but this was not a canal. It may have been hemmed in with wharves and straightened out with piles but it still accepted tributary streams and the water of the Chilterns. To my left ran a great length of weir, topped with a magnificent gantry bridge. This artificial waterfall allowed any water that built up in the navigable stretch to drop harmlessly over a fall and join the river further down. To my right, the river hit a lock. That was the route to London, but I wasn't going to take the safe way. I was meeting up with Andy Morley from Herts Canoe Club. We were going off-piste. We were going to join up with the old lady's overflow. I transferred the dog into the care of my sturdy dog-handler, Paul, and set off to shoot some homemade rapids.

AN OBSTACLE FOR FUN

Andy led me down a dark brown peaty river, past the park and under overhanging willows, leaving the town instantly behind. We were beginning to pick up speed and he leant backwards to explain that we were about to come to a weir. It was a relatively new weir. In fact, the club had had it built on this backwater for their sport. Meanwhile, the main river continued away to our south and dropped down through a pound lock, which was the first major obstruction of the navigable River Lea.

We most often see pound locks on canals. The boat goes in, the water goes down, the gate opens and the boat floats through. The first pound locks in Britain were built not on canals but on rivers and one of the earliest is further down the Lea at Waltham Abbey.

Natural rivers have an irritating habit of finding their own level. They can silt up. They can run too quickly. They can spread out, spill all over the landscape and become too shallow for transportation. If Lord Burleigh and all those who followed him wanted to bring ships up the River Lea, they needed to ensure a reasonable constant depth all along its length. So as well as improving the banks, clearing the rights for a towpath, cutting passages to bypass long meanders, and tearing down inconvenient fish traps and mill races, they introduced a locking system. Most of the technology and engineering skills that were later to be employed on canals had their origins in these early improved rivers. But the pound lock was far from being the first idea. Before them mill weirs were sometimes equipped with opening gates. These were called "flash locks".

I was about to experience what early boats were expected to do at flash locks. There was no gate on the two-step weir at Hertford. Instead there was a notch or gulley through which the river gushed. It was a slope, like a log-flume. The principle was the same. I was going to rush down with the overflow.

In a flash lock, the mill owner temporarily opened the gate in his dam and the bargee went over and took his chances. I wouldn't have been keen on going through in anything big, laden to the gunwales with barley or jesters' hats. I wasn't entirely keen on going through it in a canoe. But Andy didn't hesitate. He went up to the edge, straightened himself up and popped over in a sudden rush. Floop, and he was gone.

I paddled cautiously forward and peered over. He was waving at me from the other side, in the pool at the bottom where the water boiled about a bit.

I knew what to do. I had seen him do it. I got off my little perch and knelt on the floor of the canoe, my knees akimbo for balance and to get my centre of gravity down as low as possible, and then I paddled up towards the drop.

I'm sorry. It looks almost nothing on the television. It's hardly a waterfall. I don't think the last of the Mohicans would have hesitated. But it was pretty excellent. There seems to be no onward rush at the top at all. The water that is not going through the gully appears to stop altogether. It all brims at the brink. There's a classic false sense of security involved. Plenty of time to get yourself straight and ready for that "floop". You hover for a millisecond and then immediately you're sluicing over the top and down in a sudden rush.

Tudor was drifting about in the pool below in the camera boat.

"Did you get that, Tudor?" I asked.

"Pretty much, yeah."

"Oh. You don't want us to go again?"

"Well…"

"Don't worry. It's fine. We'll go straight back up."

I don't suppose the skippers of medieval barges went round the flash locks six or seven times. But I thought we had better, just to be safe.

WORKING LOCKS

In past centuries rivers became battlegrounds between those who needed the water for different purposes. Some needed a clear route along the river to travel or transport goods. Others needed to dam their rivers in order to build up a head of water sufficient to power a mill.

Weirs and flash locks were a compromise that allowed both uses of the river – but both caused problems.

Flash locks were an early form of lock found widely on British rivers. They involved little more than a row of paddles in a weir. In order to let vessels pass, the paddles could, for a small fee payable to the mill owner, be opened, creating a flash of water on which the vessel would be washed through.

In truth the ancient boatmen suffered from unscrupulous mill owners who would open the gate in their dam, let the boat go through and almost immediately shut it again. The boat would ground in the shallows and the bargee would have to pay a second time to get the miller to let enough water through to float them on to the next bit of deep water. Opening the flash lock also caused a huge amount of water to be washed through which was then lost to the miller, as well as potentially causing flooding to any adjacent land.

You can see why the idea of pound locks began to catch on. They solved this problem by creating a chamber with gates at both ends that controlled the level of water in the pound. Mill owners were happier, but boat owners found them a fiddle.

A pound lock in the Lea Valley. If you turn the lock handles the wrong way, the house in the background fills with water.

WHAT MADE
STANSTEAD ABBOTTS FAMOUS

By 1772 the Lee Navigation was acknowledged as the best in the country. Following the lead set by Lord Burleigh, Parliament had intervened to make it so. As I paddled on through these valleys, the reason for this lay in the fields all around me. It was probably barley that Lord Burleigh wanted to get downstream. The Lea was the beer route to London. By the end of the eighteenth century some 5,000 quarters of corn and malt were brought by barge from Ware to London every week – largely for the brewing industry.

I drifted into a cut that must originally have been made for these barges. There were still two or three moored up at the entrance, now turned into houseboats. The confluence of the river was marked by a gigantic boat store. Hundreds of cabin cruisers and motorboats were laid up in a field above me. I paddled on into a gradually narrowing canal behind the back gardens of Hertfordshire.

I loved these interludes, where the river stilled and I became like a water-borne cat burglar, drifting past faded landing stages, barbecues, picket fences, half-sunk rowing boats, crumbling walls, neat back gardens, neglected back gardens, gardens loaded with boats and gardens that ignored the river altogether. The blank remorselessness of the wider river was left behind for an endlessly detailed cul-de-sac. There was seldom anyone to acknowledge me, especially now when the damp

An aerial view of the sprawl of the Lea Valley, as it enters the sprawl of London.

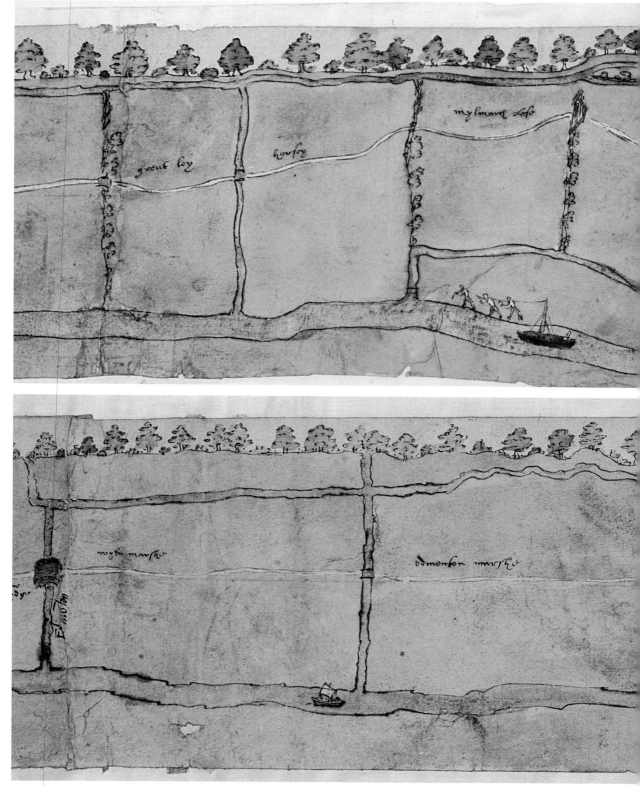

great ley

house

my smanes lose

nyto marshe

edmonton marshe

Two sections of Lord Burleigh's hand-finished map of the Lea, c. 1594. The original is several feet long.

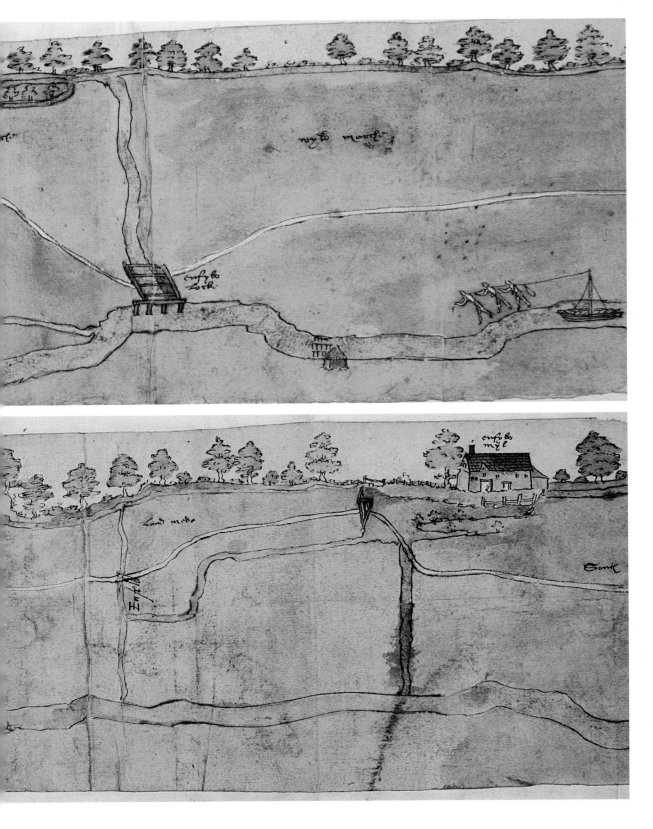

The Lady of the Lea.

Canoeing over the two-step weir in Hertford.

New Gauge House, where water is diverted from the Lea for North Londoners to drink.

Up river into the Royal Gunpowder Mills, Waltham Abbey.

The Prince Consort: steam-driven magnificence.

Abbey Mills, Bazalgette's cathedral of sewage.

Prescott Lock. Named for a pre-war Civil Engineer, not because it is big and shallow.

leaves were beginning to drop. I was only ever accompanied by slightly aggressive swans or furtive mallards, and the camera dinghy. The paddle dipped into cold black water and the canoe became a satisfyingly pliable form of transport, dancing around to order.

I was round the back of Stanstead Abbotts when I first smelled it, a waft of burnt toast. The conical tower of a malting chimney drifted up above me. I went ashore on a ramp and crossed over a metal bridge straight into the grounds of French and Jupp's, the last working maltsters on the river.

They used to have 200,000 square foot of malt floors. The buildings were still there, made into industrial units. This was pretty clever in itself. Maltings are difficult to convert because the floors were laid out tightly, one above the other, with only four foot of headroom between them. The barley was spread out on all this floor space to germinate, kept damp but not wet, and then turned regularly with big wooden shovels by workers creeping about in the cramped spaces.

I went in and immediately banged my head on the ceiling. My guide Mark North wanted to hurry me on into the new factory. The modern, up-to-date system was based on gravity, just like the ancient, out-of-date systems, so first we clambered about sixty feet up into the roof to take a look at a gargantuan funnel.

"It should be here any minute," said Mark. He tapped his fingers on the railings and I peered down at the rest of the crew scuttling about three stories below us.

There was a rumbling in a galvanised pipe and a huge cascade of water crashed into the funnel.

"There we are," said Mark. I leaned over to look but almost immediately there was more rumbling and another huge gush. It was the barley. We were making mixtures in gigantic quantities.

The stuff was led off into mammoth drums ranged in a row to the right below us. Seventy tonnes each, they revolved very slowly, turning with a stately gravity appropriate to their vast size. They allowed the barley to germinate and put armies of shovellers out of work. When it had sprouted, the barley was gathered up and roasted in furnaces, which were now roaring away at the far end of the shed.

French and Jupp's specialises in porters or black beers. They are experts at dark roasts. Mark pulled out a gizmo from the heart of the oven, like a coffee scoop from an old-fashioned grocer's. It was full of crumbly brown toasty malt. It was much the same principle as coffee roasting, on a mammoth scale. They even had a straightforward electric coffee grinder on hand, to test the quality. Depending on the length of time that they roasted the malt they could vary the colour and the flavour to match the brewer's requirements.

I hindered the process of bagging up sacks of crystal malt which were on their way to Korea, holding the sack under the funnel, pressing one lever with my foot to clamp it, another to release a sackload into the bag with a great whump, letting it fall back on the conveyer and then guiding the top through a vicious-looking sewing machine that sealed the freshness in. I left the freshness out a couple of times, desperate not to sew my thumbs together.

"Why Korea?"

"We send it all over the world."

Stanstead Abbotts malt goes everywhere. Brewers make a basic ale but they buy their flavouring and their colour from French and Jupp's. So if you buy a specialised beer in the American Midwest, whatever made Milwaukee famous, it will probably have been flavoured with malt roasted on this disused cut of the Lea. There were once hundreds of maltings. You see them all over East Anglia, particularly at the

MINE'S A PINT!

In the eighteenth century Londoners considered beer safer to drink than water and with good reason. Alcohol is toxic to most pathogens and boiling the water during the brewing process also helps to kill bugs.

In medieval times Londoners used the Thames as their main street and their main source of drinking water. Unfortunately the Thames also became the main drain for the city's population and its industries, which made sensible folk think twice before downing a tankard of the stuff.

Beer soon became the principal method of hydration used by both adults and children in the capital and was regarded as a wholesome, healthy drink. And clearly Londoners used this as a good excuse to down copious quantities of the stuff.

In the 1724 Benjamin Franklin visited a printer's in London and he noted in his diary: "My companion at the press drank every day a pint before breakfast, a pint at breakfast with his bread and cheese, a pint between breakfast and dinner, a pint at dinner, a pint in the afternoon about six o'clock, and another when he had done his day's work." Admittedly this was "small beer" with a lower alcoholic content than porter or stout, otherwise I doubt whether much of the printer's output would have been readable.

Small beer was made by a second or third mashing of the malt that was

"Beer Street", an engraving by Hogarth, 1751.

used for stronger beers. But small beer would still have been around 3.5 per cent alcohol and therefore not particularly weak by today's standards. Maybe that explains why the spellings can be a bit funny in eighteenth-century books.

head of rivers. There were once many more on the Lea but they made white malt. Only French and Jupp's, with their specialised stuff – from low-colour caramalt to highly coloured roasted barley – survives. I asked why.

"These fields produce the best barley in the world. It's as simple as that," said Mark.

London was a beer city. Beer was a much safer drink than the water from its wells. Man, however, cannot live by beer alone and the Lea was also to play an important role in providing London with "sweet" drinking water. A few miles further on, I would encounter the beginning of that story.

AMWELL AND THE NEW RIVER

Just to the east of Hertford, the Lea takes a big bend round a long low plain crossed by road bridges, railways and pylons. Negotiating a flock of Canada geese and a couple of agitated swans we slipped down towards an isolated building standing on the southern bank. Plainly built, in early Victorian, yellow London stock brick, this was the New Gauge House. It was built to extract water from the Lea.

We filmed me knocking and entering. Just inside there was a peeling corridor and a door that led into a noisy cellar, floored with metal grids and overlooking an enclosed weir. I was greeted by John Liddard, who was there to help me to steal a quantity of water. It was a disarmingly simple operation. We got a bent metal hook, inserted it into a hole and lifted a metal plate out of a dam. Each single plate could release about a million gallons. It felt absurd. The thing was the size of a tea tray. The water that surged directly under us into a pool below our feet seemed little more than a medium-sized brook. It flowed away under an arch into a wide arrow-straight canal. This was the beginning of a new route to London.

To the right of where we stood, on a grating above this simple mechanism, there was a gauge on the wall to measure the amount being taken from the Lea. John took me upstairs and showed me round the empty, flyblown flat, where an employee of the water board and his family had once lived, keeping constant watch on that gauge. Today the system is controlled and measured by machine and computer, but there is still a strict limitation. The river is a politically controlled resource. Nobody, not even London, can just have what it wants. The river has to remain a working river as well as an open mains water pipe. London can take no more than 22 million gallons a day.

The New Gauge House was built in 1856 to add river water to a much older network. This was an aqueduct first mooted in the reign of Queen Elizabeth I and then actually constructed (with the backing of James I) by a Welsh gold miner called Thomas Myddleton: the original New River.

In the very early years of the 1600s, the City of London had come to Hertford not in search of water from the River Lea, but from fresh springs at nearby Amwell. Cadbury and I and the camera crew trudged across the mysterious Hertford flood plain, past cows grazing under motorway bridges, to have a look at these wonders.

Most sources, including the Lea, are muddy bogs. This one was a sacred spring. It was a perfect round pool some thirty feet deep. On a sunny day with high white clouds it reflected the light with a deep and mysterious aquamarine blue. A single carved stone stood guard, commemorating the construction of the canal that exited from its southern end, and from there the New River progressed, in a stately arabesque, to distant Islington. There were only two weirs to control it and, apart from some straightening, it essentially fulfils the same function today, taking water from the River Lea whenever a computer decides it is necessary.

Amwell answered some riddles for me. I have lived in Clerkenwell, just below Sadler's Wells, so I know "Amwell Street". It runs along the side of the Lloyd Baker Estate in the heart of London. In front of the old Thames Water Authority buildings there is a round Victorian bedded garden, which I also know well. This was where the original canal debouched, having flowed thirty-nine miles. This was where, in 1613, in a magnificent ceremony celebrated in verse and song, twelve labourers in matching green outfits and green hats, carrying shovels on their shoulders, came to welcome King James, who financially supported the venture when Myddleton ran out of money, having only got as far as Enfield. James I never seemed to make any profit from the project. His share, known as the "King's Moiety", was bought out, and was only eventually repaid in 1956.

Fresh water is a long-term investment.

BUILDING A NEW RIVER

equivalent of four pence a day to dig the river channel.

As it was not possible to pump water over long distances, the channel had to follow a route that would take it downhill to London. This meant that it had to follow the 100-foot contour line from Ware into London, dropping just five inches per mile. The total drop along the entire original 39-mile route was a mere 23 feet. The New River was eventually opened in an official ceremony on Michaelmas Day, 29 September 1613.

Water from the New River was supplied to customers via hollowed out sections of elm trees. Fish were sometimes found in the pipes and a dozen two-foot-long eels were once reported in Pall Mall. The water supply was also extremely limited and at first ran for perhaps only an hour or so on two or three days each week.

The New River is still bringing water to Londoners but now stops at a reservoir in Stoke Newington. It was only from 1904 that a constant water supply was guaranteed in London. Today the New River continues to supply about eight per cent of London's drinking water.

Monument on the New River at Amwell.

Supplying water to London's ever-increasing population was a problem. For this reason the New River was constructed in the early seventeenth century to bring in clean water, bypassing the polluting industries that had developed along the lower reaches of the Lea.

The scheme did not go down well with landowners along the route. The project soon ran into financial difficulties and had to be bailed out by King James I in return for half the expected profits. Two hundred labourers were employed for the

THE INCOMPLETE ANGLER

The last salmon was caught in the Thames in 1833. In 1828 the Royal Commission on the Water Supply of the Metropolis noted the "entire destruction of the fisherman's trade between Putney Bridge and Greenwich". They estimated that the number of fishermen had halved since 1800. The river was becoming polluted. The creeping growth of London effectively meant that the rivers, far from being providers, were becoming its poisoners. The fish were like canaries in a coal mine. They were the first indicators of the water catastrophe that was about to hit London.

I walked across a field of cut barley towards an overgrown hedge. They were the only directions I had for the Amwell Magna Fishing Club, founded in 1841 by the sculptor Sir Francis Chantrey and nineteen other "Gentlemen from London", who had no doubt grown tired of fruitless casting into the putrid waters of the Thames.

I let myself through a little gate and walked straight over a wooden bridge to a shed and bench by the side of a fast-running stretch of the river. It has always been a good spot for fishing. The Lea runs down through "holms" or marshy valleys around Stanstead Abbotts, at the junction of the Chiltern chalk bed with the Reading bed of clay and gravel. The surface soil produces clear streams of such value that the Old Testament of angling, the original fishing manual, Izaak Walton's *The Compleat Angler* begins not on the Tay or an expensive chalk stream in Hampshire, but with a walk across the fields in unassuming Hertfordshire, to catch chub.

Walton was born in Stafford and became a businessman of London, with an ironmonger's shop in Fleet Street. Perhaps the reason his work has never been out of print (and is commonly said to be the third most-read book in the English language after the Bible and Shakespeare) is because he effectively invented the self-help manual. His stated purpose was to help gentlemen find diversion and amuse themselves by adopting the "contemplative life".

The Amwell Magna Club (the oldest fishing club in Britain) is now the closest place to London to catch a rising trout. The membership has doubled from the founding twenty. Jeremy Paxman is president. Feargal Sharkey was flitting about in the rushes the day I was there. But I was after lesser fish.

When I finally arrived at the little clubhouse shed they kitted me out with a proper vest with the requisite three or four hundred pockets and a good pair of waders and I sat down opposite Bob Dear to be taught to tie a fly.

I could see that this was part of the contemplative life in itself. Bob, by his own admission, made at least a thousand of these a year for his own use (and, I suspected, his own amusement). It was a fiddly business. He had invented a few of the things himself, but he wanted to teach me to make one from the 1950s, an Elvis-era fly. So we began.

Pay attention, now. I had to.

I fixed a minute hook in a tiny vice, with the hole at the end of it, the bit where the line attaches, pointing in my direction. Then I had to tie a bit of thin line to the hole and lay a length of "hackles" alongside the haft, which was only about half an inch long.

Hackles are black cockerel feathers. They look as if they have been plucked from an old lady's hat on the set of *My Fair Lady*. Ours were delightfully long and lustrously black, but I was staggered to find someone reared these chickens just to make flies. An entire agricultural industry had grown up to service the needs of gentlemen seeking a contemplative life by winding feathers onto hooks.

God knows who first discovered that if you tie a couple of these hackle feathers onto a metal shaft and wind a thread round them, the edges stand out, but I had to admit that this was inspired. Close to, we had made what looked like a particularly furry fly's abdomen.

We used another bit of the feather in a different way. We plucked it out, stripped most of it and then, in a variation of the earlier winding technique, we wound the shaft of the feather itself around the shaft of the hook.

Now here was the miraculous part. The feathery bits of this feather, the blades, suddenly stood out in a startled Mohican fashion. If you squinted at it sideways these barbed bits, standing on end, now resembled the legs, wings and appendages of a proper, black, round-the-lights-in-circles housefly. And there you have it.

There followed a half-hour interlude while I tried to twist the end of the minute line around three mammoth fingers and a gigantic thumb and turn my wrist over itself, to create a half-hitch knot.

All I had left to do was to transfer a bee's nose-dribble of glue onto the tip to hold everything in place. But I managed a dollop where I needed a smidgeon and ruined everything.

We held Bob's up next to mine. His fly looked like an insect ready to bash its head against a lampshade and mine like the sort of fly that had recently met its end via a rolled-up *Daily Telegraph*. Or at least this was the opinion of the trout because we then all walked over to a shady bank by the stream – me, Bob, the chairman, Feargal, the dog and my bedraggled fly – and I plunged into the water to try a few casts. They resolutely ignored it.

I could cast alright. I got the fly into the pond and began to get some idea of the skill involved. Then Bob lent me his Polaroid spectacles, which put me one-up on Izaak Walton, and to my astonishment, once the glare had been banished, I could suddenly see the trout themselves. There were three or four monsters just out of reach amongst the weed. After several fruitless casts, I managed to get my fly to drop right by one of the fattest fish in Hertfordshire. It fell in front of its beak and drifted enticingly an inch in front of its eyes.

That bloody fish. It ignored it completely. My creation was clearly nothing like a fly. It looked like a bunch of feathers tied on to a bit of metal. How the trout knew, I have no idea.

I left feeling discontented, frustrated and in a foul temper. But fishing does that to me. It's the contemplative life. I simply don't like contemplating fish that avoid me.

GUNPOWDER TREASON
AND ALLOTMENT PLOT

We were on the outskirts of Waltham Abbey now. The road ran steeply down into the valley of the Lea. While the crew set up on the river, Paul and I went in search of coffee. Parking the canoes under the amused eyes of resting traffic wardens we sneaked between a pub garden and a Korean holistic healer's into the pedestrianised, medieval high street.

Waltham Abbey seemed a little wan. It was Essex on its uppers. The pubs were old-fashioned enough to be called "ye olde pubbes". For the first time I felt we were on the edge of the East End of London, perhaps even in the bit where the East End deposited its runaways. Beyond

Waltham Abbey was the M25 and beyond that London collapsed into chaotic North Circular country.

The monks of the Abbey had mills around here. They first ground corn and then, from the seventeenth century, they used the same mechanisms to grind sulphur, charcoal and saltpetre together to make gunpowder. We know this because local people turn up in the registry of deaths as "blown to bits". For the following three centuries, the principal industry of this now-depressed town became the manufacture of high explosives, quickly considered the best explosives in Britain.

I would certainly have been far more excited about visits to Waltham Abbey as a boy if I had known about any of this. Now I had permission to canoe my way into what had been a top-secret place – all 170 acres of it – via the old service canal that ran off the Lea, formerly called the "Barge River", which was built in 1806. In doing so I probably became the first boat to pass that way for half a century.

Not that we passed easily. It was a still morning and I was far from any current, paddling into limpid black water, pushing back the low branches of Canadian maples, with the cameraman Tudor balanced in the front of the canoe and Cadbury getting in the way in the middle. I marooned myself on half-submerged branches as we crept into our own undiscovered Peruvian jungle. Huge buildings – no, not buildings, more like improvised pyramids – loomed up on the banks: geometric, fifty-foot-high loaves of brick. Beyond them, almost disappointingly mundane after these Inca monuments, were blockhouses and abandoned one-storey factory sheds with covered porches that led directly on to the river.

Water had performed two functions here. First, it was the power source. The six-foot-high Mill Head Stream had driven the watermills that engaged in the deadly process of grinding the ingredients of gunpowder. Secondly, it was the ideal transport system for high explosives: smooth, steady and slow. As a result the entire site was riddled with cuts and channels.

The canal I was on emerged from the jungle and met a T-junction. A metal, hemispherical, bow footbridge crossed the river to my left. It had been built to allow headroom for bigger ships than mine, but the next bridge drove straight across the canal leaving so little room I had to duck to get underneath it. Sliding past silted edges full of rushes, I reached the bottom of a derelict pound lock, built in 1879 to link the two separate water systems that had grown up in the huge factory. I drifted between the half-shut and rotted gates and into a choked canal stretching away through the trees.

After centuries of milling black powder, making the explosive charges that kept the army going through the Napoleonic and Crimean wars, cordite had been developed here; so had gun cotton. Waltham Abbey had made TNT and supplied the needs of the First World War and met the huge demand for explosives from the private sector, blasting their way into mines and railway viaducts across the world. But then with the coming of the threat of air power, the whole factory system had moved further west and left the empty places to the advancing forest and a few dedicated research scientists. What had been secretive work became secure, top-secret work. The woods closed in.

I paddled into a perfectly circular pool, at least fifty yards wide, ringed with trees and damp forest, where they had tested underwater explosives and perfected the Bouncing Bomb during the Second World War. It was deathly quiet. The occasional conker plopped into the water. I felt uneasy sitting in a canoe on top of a hole where boffins had tossed their half-tested bombs. What if one finally stirred in the mud at the bottom of this lugubrious pond?

The place was steeped in danger. I had assumed that the big shapes were some form of peculiar chimney, but most of them were simply extremely fat walls. On one side of these revetments the grinding process took place, and on the other the unfortunate workers, waiting for some malfunction, huddled together, praying that the massive blast protection wall would be big enough to save them from the effects of whatever fiendish new explosive the scientists had developed.

You might have expected that these would be the richest families in the land – the blaster men, the danger-money mechanics – but, naturally enough, the more dangerous the work, the less they were paid. During the First World War more than 5,000 local people had worked in the mills until the factory moved away. When the top-secret stuff was finally abandoned in the 1990s, the government decided to scrap the lot and build a brand new metro-land on top of the burnt-out fireworks.

Except that English Heritage did what I was doing. They came exploring in the jungle and found wonders. This was one of the earliest organised factories in the world. There were twenty-one important historic buildings hidden away on the site. Natural Heritage was even more excited. Parts of the forest had been abandoned for centuries and were full of rare species. Lord Burleigh might have been interested to know that the largest heronry in Essex is hidden away in its dank woods. It has theatres, exhibitions, tours and – perhaps best of all, given that we were so close to London – prohibited areas where the top-secret work of nature can continue undisturbed.

You can visit and explore the Royal Gunpowder Mills if you want to, but I wouldn't necessarily take your canoe.

THE GUNPOWDER BARGE

I was going to travel on down the river aboard the *Lady of the Lea*, built in Rotherhithe for the War Department in 1931 and one of the last working wooden sailing barges on the river. She was specifically made to carry armaments down to Woolwich because she could transport the gunpowder without fear of a spark from her engine blowing her into splinters.

As we joined the towpath above Walthamstow, there she was, still in all her glory. She was easily spotted, towering over the water, with her tan sails up for our benefit. They were luckily hanging lifeless in the still air. She wasn't really designed to sail in the river. She was built to "canal barge plans". An inch under seventy-two feet long, she would have been towed by a horse down the Lea and then sailed the rest of the way down the Thames.

These barges are rigged with a sprit. This is a massive spar that runs from the deck level at an acute angle to the mast and carries one huge main sail. It leaves a soft trailing bottom, so there is no danger of a colossal piece of timber swinging across the cargo deck and knocking everyone off. The canvas can be wound up on brails, like a festoon curtain, taking in a little bit at a time, and reducing the amount that the captain has to have out hanging to the wind in a big blow.

A barge like this used to be handled by one man and a boy, but there were a lot more members of crew crawling about the *Lady of the Lea* – useful, because she was stuck.

Her owner, retired headmaster Brian Pain, having brought her up from the big river, exactly as he was supposed to, now wanted to turn her round in the little river, exactly as he was supposed to, in a specially designed space just above the Walthamstow lock, exactly as he was supposed to.

He gunned the engine. Great gouts of water eddied at her stern. He set her massive rudder hard to port. She went around alright; seventy-two feet fitted the available space exactly. Alas, she was jammed right into the gap. She went aground at both ends. Owing to disuse, the river had silted up.

It was four o'clock in the afternoon. We swiftly became a local attraction. Walthamstow was on its way home for tea, or out walking the dog, or going for a jog. People stopped and made calculations.

"Are you needing to get anywhere in particular?" a fat lady asked me.

Some crossed the bridge at the lock and tried to estimate whether the captain was simply trying it on. A party of old geezers in soft shirts and caps took their time to walk a few yards back up the path to get a good view of the whole affair from a safe distance.

Brian disappeared below deck and came back a few seconds later with a giant spanner. He started to dismantle the tiller mechanism.

"He's taking the rudder to pieces now," said a man who was standing next to me lining up a photograph.

Further up the channel a narrow boat chugged round the bend and began to slow, as if taking a few moments to realise that the entire river was blocked from side to side.

I ran across the bridge. "Throw me a rope," I offered.

There was a discussion, it was agreed that it might help and a length of bristly warp the thickness of my arm appeared. We ran it back as far as we could. There was at least a hundred foot of it. I wrapped it round my back and started pulling. This was ineffectual on its own, but I only intended it as an advertisement. A couple of school kids ran over. A man put down his bike. Two of the old codgers ambled up.

At the stern, Brian now had the rudder on board. Twelve of us started heaving on the warp again. The engine began churning. The big black bow began to slide in the bay; fitting it completely, swinging like a ball in a socket. The stern started to carry away from the other bank, and with a steady, graceful motion *Lady of the Lea* came away from the banks and stood facing down river.

The riverbank cheered.

It was river patience. We had spent an hour at work and moved three yards. Before these boats had engines, they could take days to get anywhere at all. Further up the coast, on the River Alde, it was not uncommon for a Thames sailing barge to take a month to journey twenty miles up to Snape, drifting a little with each tide in a narrow river, with almost no ability to head into unfavourable winds, but a lot of time to consider options.

Now, as the crowd dispersed like a chorus in a musical, we motored forward into the lock. Again, the *Lady* was made to fit this exactly. There was hardly a foot of space available. In front of us, however, was the bridge I had been using to cross back and forth. We were sinking down, but the masts were fifty-foot high. We weren't going to squeeze under that. The skipper had his spanner out again.

The mizzen mast at the back was lowered in seconds. I was invited to climb up the ratlings to help at the cross trees. I clambered up, sticking the arches of my feet into wobbling rope steps.

"You'll see a fid just above a metal loop at the top of the lower mast," someone shouted from below. "Take that out now!"

I did.

The top mast began to slide down alongside the lower mast. I monkeyed down in an ungainly manner. Somebody released the forestays and the entire rig was lowered down onto the cargo hatches. Like a ship entering a bottle we slid forward under the bridge, a flat slab of a boat now, and out into the Lea again.

Ahead were several railway bridges, a road bridge, the M25 and the beginnings of reservoir alley.

DROPS TO DRINK

From the air, the Lea becomes a thread and the valley, which once provided hay for London's horses, becomes a patchwork of reservoirs. These were the great flat areas of swamp: Tottenham Marshes, Hackney Marshes, Walthamstow Marshes. The river was seeping into the land, through the Dagenham Brook and the Ching Brook, creating a boggy plain, which was first partly drained by King Alfred to get at a Viking stronghold. It became football fields where Tottenham Hotspurs had originally played as an amateur team, and A.V. Roe found enough space to experiment with flight and founded the AVRO aeroplane company. But from the perspective of the river itself, it all seemed a confusing horizontal line of protecting banks and walls.

Tamsin Davies took me round the Middlesex Filter Beds. This was converted from a former Victorian filtration plant and tucked in behind the Lea Bridge. It had been abandoned when the major waterworks moved away to Coppermills and became a nature reserve.

At Coppermills today it takes twenty-four hours for water to pass through their purification systems. The Filter Beds had been a primitive precursor. I was there for a demonstration of how it had been done.

Tamsin leapt over the hedge and clambered down to a murky pond under some willows by a great trumpet-shaped pipe. She scooped up a plastic beaker of water, thick with interesting biological diversity, and held up another beaker full of a descending layer of gravel and sand. She poured the dirty water into the gravel and we watched as it soaked through the sand and plopped out of the bottom into a cup: bright, transparent and seemingly clean. The sand picks up the dirt. In large quantities it also breeds microbes and fungi that further the cleansing process, via the zoogleal level called the Schmutzdecke, a layer of health-giving cleansing slime.

I refrained from drinking the unsoiled water. It had been water from these very filtration beds that had caused the last great outbreak of cholera in London in 1866, and 1.8 million people around the world still die every year from bad water. The most obvious "particulate" matter had been removed from the water I was holding. Even parasites had probably been sucked out. It looked clear and bright, but how lucky did I feel?

London's search for "sweet water" had continued for hundreds of years beyond the reign of James I. The New River was still gurgling away into Stoke Newington reservoir to the west of me but by the 1850s the river water in the reservoirs of East London had been added to the total. It was taken from the Lea by privately owned water companies, which were offering supplies of drinking water to the crowded city. The Walthamstow Water Company, owner of the Middlesex Filter Beds, used scientific filtration methods but these were disguising the reality, a reality that few were initially prepared to accept: that the rivers were not merely quenching the thirst of the population – they were killing it too.

With historian Stephen Halliday, I went to Bow Cemetery to look for graves that might contain victims of the 1866 cholera outbreak. Like so many of London's graveyards, it was simultaneously beautiful and disgraceful. Ranks of faded and disintegrating gravestones were toppling into the undergrowth dominated by forest-sized trees. We passed a team of volunteers cheerfully clearing kudzu and brambles under a massive beech and, in the leaf mold, came upon the tiny stones of paupers' graves. These were a poignant image, but what frightened the Victorians about typhus and cholera was that they were no respecter of class. Unlike the diseases of want and neglect visited on the poverty-stricken slums (the "rookeries" with which Dickens was so familiar), the cholera epidemics cut down old and young, high and low, rich and poor. (Prince Albert was a notable victim of typhus.)

Over 5,000 had died in Whitechapel in a few short months in 1866. What made the outbreak significant was that it was used by statistician William Farr to prove that cholera was linked to water.

In June 1866 a labourer called Hedges had died of the disease. His toilet flushed directly into the River Lea. The East London Water Company vigorously denied that there could be any link with their reservoirs, but while the epidemic was raging two customers announced that they had found eels in their waterpipes. The eels and the water in the East London reservoirs came from the same source: the Lea.

We found no inscriptions declaring "Died of the Cholera" on the headstones, but even our cursory enquiry, though not up to Farr's standards, revealed a high number of monuments dating from the deadliest months. We struggled through the brambles and over broken flags examining gravestones, while Stephen told me that the main culprit, the instrument that had changed the relationship between London and its water, had been the flushing lavatory. "It was originally invented by a courtier in the sixteenth century but he only made two: one for himself and one for his godmother, Queen Elizabeth. They didn't really catch on then, but at the end of the eighteenth century, another man, a serial inventor, developed a system that really worked."

Until then people had night-soil closets, dry systems, that were emptied by highly paid night-soil men.

"The water closet was an absolute disaster," said Stephen.

The story of the flushable loo was a familiar tale. The "convenience" to the individual was an inconvenience to the world at large. It was fatal to many.

"London nearly doubled its population in the first twenty years of the nineteenth century," Stephen continued. "And then doubled it again in the next twenty years."

Nothing was more fashionable to new Londoners in their new houses than washing away their excretions with a big gush of water.

"There had actually been earlier laws to prevent human waste going into the sewers, but now it all sluiced away into the rivers where the drinking water came from."

So much for "sweet water". In 1858 things came to a crisis with "The Great Stink". The Thames, then a much broader, slower river, proved unable to carry London's effluent away. It was a simmeringly hot summer. Parliament could hardly vent its own hot air because of the stench. They hung curtains dipped in chloride of lime in the windows but finally had to adjourn. The city decided something had to be done.

"What is really interesting is that the water companies had a vested interest in persuading people that it was nothing to do with the water and tried to popularise the 'miasma' theory: that the outbreaks of disease were caused by 'germs' borne in the air, by the smell. And since it was pretty smelly during the Great Stink they had a credulous audience ready to believe them. It was the danger of the smell that partly prompted the great London sewage project."

It was to be another twenty years before German scientist Robert Koch identified the cholera bacillus, but by then Victorian pragmatism had triumphed. A massive underground sewage system essentially separated the cesspit from the waterhole.

During London's last cholera epidemic, caused directly by polluted water from the River Lea, Farr had written to Sir Joseph Bazalgette with his findings and suspicions. Bazalgette had written back, apologising that his great work was as yet unfinished. He had to install a temporary pump to clear the sewage, because his giant pumping house at Abbey Mills was not yet ready for the task. It appeared to work. The Lea would never kill in such numbers again.

THE CATHEDRAL OF SEWAGE

Leaving the river near Three Mills Island we went along the main Stratford road, turned right by some mammoth tower blocks and clumped over road bumps to a dirty wall and some beautiful wrought-iron gates covered with annoying yellow notices. They were there instructing delivery services and construction site traffic, because Abbey Mills is still a working station.

BAZALGETTE, ARCHITECT OF SEWERS

SIR JOSEPH BAZALGETTE, C.B.

HE IS GREAT AT DRAINAGE, AND WAS MADE A COMPANION OF THE BATH.

In 1858, the year of the Great Stink, at least 140 sewers discharged their contents directly into the Thames. The introduction of flush toilets during the 1830s and 1840s had helped make the situation even worse by increasing the amount that was pouring into cesspits and thus causing them to overflow.

In 1854 Dr John Snow demonstrated that of 500 people in the Soho area who had died of cholera, the great majority took their water from a single well in Broad Street. When this pump was sealed off, the outbreak subsided. William Farr made several statistical surveys that showed, among other things, that mortality was significantly increased for people who drew their water supply from the Old Ford Reservoir in East London.

Joseph Bazalgette, Chief Engineer of the Metropolitan Board of Works, was given the job of designing a new sewerage system for the city.

Bazalgette's scheme involved building 82 miles of intercepting sewers. These were fed by another 450 miles of main sewers, which received the contents of an incredible 13,000 miles worth of small local sewers. The whole system was designed to divert waste away from the main centre of population to the Thames Estuary.

Building Bazalgette's new sewer system demanded 318 million bricks, 880,000 cubic yards of concrete and mortar and the excavation of over 3.5 million tonnes of earth. Construction was finally completed in 1875, having reached a total cost of £6.5 million – equivalent to £422,500,000 today.

Caricature of Sir Joseph Bazalgette, published in *Punch* magazine.

Joseph Bazalgette built two massive pipes on either side of the Thames to carry away London's sewage. The Thames falls three inches for every mile. Bazalgette calculated that his pipes would need to fall two feet over the same distance in order to avoid blockages. The resultant enormous coagulate mass was then pumped upwards again, to drop harmlessly back into the Thames and be carried beyond danger by the tide. He needed powerful engines to do this.

Abbey Mills was built to house them and took the unlikely form of a Romanesque Byzantine cathedral. Cleanliness is next to godliness. Godliness can shift sewage. I would like to have seen it when the chimneys still stood. All that remains of them is a thirty-foot-high base, a pedestal the size of a house, built for a fake minaret complete with a muezzin turret that towered over the East End (until it was decided that the two of them were too useful as aiming markers for the Luftwaffe trying to bomb the London docks).

I walked Cadbury up under the shadow of the base and round the side of the massive building.

Wandering the asphalt surroundings on a bright autumnal afternoon, with the sun darting on the decorative brickwork and the vast, curling hinges of mighty be-knobbled doors at the top of granite steps, I felt like a pilgrim at the gates of some mythical citadel of sewage. It came from an age when public works were quite innocently given a public grandeur. You can shine shit after all.

Alas, the door was locked. I was told that inside, electric pumps had taken over the shovelling duties. It was a shell. But a twin building at Crossness, way down on the south bank, still had its original four engines, and I now possess a certificate telling me that I am one of a small select few who have been permitted to start the great beam engine, the Prince Consort.

I could tell I was privileged. The doors swung wide. I was greeted by an informal committee of wise men in boiler suits, clearly in a state of suppressed excitement. Their dormant beast, the Prince Consort, was to be woken again. There were four engines, all named for members of the royal family. The others, lying idle at the quadrants of the building, were Victoria, Albert Edward and Alexandra.

Simon Hodges showed me how to set a tiny steam engine in motion. This was used to turn a fifty-seven-ton flywheel, mounted on the wall of the building. With a spurt of kettle-hot water, it slowly revolved until the beam, a mere forty-seven tons but forty-two feet in length, was sitting in a position where momentum would help it when we started the main engine, which we now did with an impressive toot from a steam whistle.

In the early days of the twentieth century, the engines had been improved to carry heavier loads, but their essential form was unaltered and they were utterly magnificent: magnificent like something of majesty and proportion, like a great symphony. These were the Beethoven's Ninth of mechanical things. Once the power was applied, high above our heads, the enormous ovoid-ended beam began to rock up and down, sighing and rumbling like an animal. Simon led me upstairs, two flights, to the platform, through which the entire mechanism protruded as if breaking the surface of a lake.

This was the vantage point to understand the room, because a perforated floor ran from end to end of the attic space. The fully restored green-and-gold beam was echoed by three identical rusty corpses. Instead of bucking and swaying, they stood pale, unpainted and unmoving, as if waiting for blood to be restored and life to return.

Eleven times a minute the great beam swung. And eleven times, six tons of raw sewage would have been lifted thirty to forty feet up to the exit pipe. Today the suction pistons are disconnected, and the rods simply rise and fall, but I left the place fervently wanting to see the other engines operational, even if their function was strictly ceremonial, and solely existed to excite small boys like me.

LEA ROWING CLUB

For reasons to do with making television, I had to paddle around in the Lea opposite Springfield Marina. There were dignified barges moored on the bank. There was a towpath, a hill with park trees and a flaking boathouse, in front of which various elderly men swaggered up and down and offered advice.

"You've come in the wrong sort of boat, mate!"

"Are you aware you are going in the wrong direction?"

I was aware, but there is a vow of silence as the camera rolls. I continued my studied, vacant gaze into the nether distance as the badinage increased.

"You'll never get anywhere at that sort of speed."

"You ought to try rowing with seven other people."

I let the canoe turn my back to the camera.

"We're filming so if you continue to behave like twats the camera will pick up everything," I said. They laughed at me.

The banter and the frisky swagger came from several triangular-shaped men with frosty quiffs. They had shoulders like Mr Incredible in the amusing cartoon about the superhero family and spindly legs supporting big chests. They were all elderly and all wearing Lycra and just about getting away with it – much better than I would have done anyway.

These were the veterans of the Lea Rowing Club preparing for their row, in their eight, on the river.

Jimmy O'Neill, oarsman, official and club coach, was seventy-four and he still rowed every week. He had worked in a printer's and had joined the club in the days when rowing had been a segregated sport. He told me that he and his mates had not been allowed to row at Henley because they were working men. It was felt they had an unfair advantage because they engaged in manual labour and so they were not strictly speaking "amateurs".

He still came for sessions pretty much every week. He used to coach the younger teams and now took part in competitions with the veterans.

"So how often do you do that?" I asked.

"It's not really very often," he said and then listed a long series of regattas they had been at over the last few months. It sounded a lot to me.

A double scull was coming down the river. "Those two guys there," said Jimmy, "they're in their eighties. It keeps you fit."

I agreed. We watched as they brought their boat alongside and, unaided, lifted it up over their heads and carried it into the shed beneath us.

I had a rigorous training session with the team including a fast-paced two-mile run, in which I was beaten by a load of girls, and a circuit-training session that nearly made me weep, then the following morning I went out with the old guys in the "eight" – a sport I hadn't done since I was eleven. I made them shout out their ages as they called themselves off for the cox. I was the second-youngest (because one of the rowers was Jimmy's son and he was in his thirties) but the others were all past retirement age.

Joshingly, they ran through the basics: how to start with just the arms, feather the blade, row on one side and pull together, and then we rowed and ignored most of the niceties. I thought they were automatically starting with arms only, but they went straight for the sliding seats and we powered up the river.

After a while, exhausted, I could hear the cox yelling "finish", so I assumed we must be nearly there, but apparently he was shouting instructions about the way the oars came out on each stroke. The actual finish took a long time coming and I sat feeling weary, weak and old.

Jimmy, sitting behind me, congratulated me. It was sincere. I was chuffed. Then he gave me a little advice. "Don't try and drive the boat, just put the oar in the water, follow the stroke and the pace. You don't have to heave it."

So I didn't and I had a much better run back. Alas, I could never do it regularly. Maintaining the fitness level required would kill me.

PASSIVE SMOKING

We were now in the heart of the city, no more than three miles from St Paul's Cathedral. The sun was up and I was paddling slowly through a bare and deserted landscape. When I spotted anyone on the bank they looked suspiciously at me and I tried to look suspiciously back. People went down to the river for solitude or invisibility or possibly for creativity. The walls of the warehouses were decorated with mammoth swirls of graffiti, twenty yards long.

New developments were creeping in along the western bank. I wondered if they were building up for an Olympic sales fever. The towpath was deserted. I passed a row of decaying houseboats. Much less pampered than the ones further north, they were caked with dirt and the paint was flaking, but each was heaped with junk, stacked with old bicycles and cans, tarpaulins, or bits of fridge or prams, and they all had a pile of cut branches mounted carefully on their cabin roofs, like Russian dachas waiting for a hard frost. These were boat people, not barge dwellers. But nobody was around there either.

It might have been quiet, except that a network of railway bridges was undergoing extensive repair. The deep span, some forty feet of over-arching low-lying metal slab, was wrapped in protective cladding. Welding flashes emerged from the middle of this cocoon. The invisible thundering racket was made unbearable by trains rattling across.

I drifted on towards a lock and through a blanket of lime-green duckweed. "Bow Lock" the sign announced. That was Bow Bridge behind me, then. I was in the middle of Cockney territory, and this was once the only way out through the morass to the East. The original bowed stone bridge (reputedly the first in England) was commissioned in the early twelfth century by Queen Matilda after she almost lost her life in the ford there. It remains an important bridging point some 900 years later.

I had reached the lowest level of the marshes. This was the "Lea delta", I suppose, where the river mingles with the Thames and spreads out into myriad runnels.

I have a great map on my kitchen wall showing the extent of London in the 1870s and the Lea marks the start of no-man's land. This was the dirty end of town. The prevailing winds blew in this direction. The river flowed out to the sea to the east. Everything filthy and obnoxious was carried down to the East End. There may now be the odd pink edifice filled with city workers, housing estates may have smothered Docklands and Thamesmead is hoping to bring a bright future downriver, but it has been a long time coming and there are 700 years of historical prejudice to overcome.

In the nineteenth century the smelly and smoky industries, like tanning or dyeing, were exiled from the city and banished to the Eastern marshes. Some remain there today.

Lance Forman at H. Forman & Son would hardly thank me for calling their bright hygienic new factory dirty, but it was undoubtedly built on smoke. The Forman family started a salmon curing business in this area a hundred years ago. I drove up at dawn ready to join the early shift, pulling off the Stratford Bridge at the end of the Hackney approaches along Wix Road. I thought it was a feeder for the M11 but it took me into a grid-patterned industrial estate, tucked away in the hinterland between the river and the motorway. The sky itself was turning fishy-coloured as I slunk through the electric gates.

On the walls there were photographs of Forman grandfathers, wearing double-breasted suits, shaking hands in Billingsgate, in front of record-breaking salmon the size of wrestlers. They looked down on me as I put on a white coat and baseball cap and plastic overshoes and tramped out to the wet and freezing Preparation Hall to grapple with a tub filled with salmon. Two days previously this heap of fish had been in a river in Scotland.

After instruction, I slapped one on the table, chopped the head off, curving round with a vicious knife, and made a couple of nicks in the skin, just enough to let the smoke in. I got that bit right. My hands were already red and frozen. Next I had to slice down from the tail and make contact with the bone, come up and along in one sawing motion freeing the starboard side fillet from its moorings before turning and doing the same on the other side. The skill was to get that bone free with hardly any flesh attached, and sling it into the bin.

Lance extracted a clean white comb. I left a ragged bony disgrace.

"It'll all be recycled," Lance said. "Soups and stocks." But he was hurrying me on. The next phase was sprinkling with salt and I met with more approval here. I was a natural sprinkler.

The sides of salmon were hung on clothes racks and rattled into the smoke houses. No clean air act would be needed. The cabinets were shiny stainless steel. The doors had glass windows and the smoke stayed entirely within the system.

"It doesn't come from a heap of shavings any more." Lance was reaching down to the side of his magnificent machine. "Look." He opened a door and pulled out a three-foot length of four by four. It was like an oak table leg. It could have come from Habitat except that one end was blackened. "This is it," Lance explained. "This is the sawdust, automatically ground and burned to smoke. It's all highly efficient."

The factory is always experimenting. Beetroot-flavoured gravadlax is very popular. Sturgeon, tuna, crayfish and eel are all smoked in the factory.

It is the smoked salmon, however, that made the fortunes of the place. I took a long slender serrated knife and ran it down a freshly smoked side.

"You have to get it so thin you could read a paper through it," Lance instructed, "though quite why you would want to do that I have no idea."

I sawed away as best I could and laid three slices on the table.

"Not bad," said Lance. He was an exacting master. I was chuffed. "Here, have a taste." He leant forward and carefully chopped one of my rags into six separate small pieces. Then he offered us a sliver each: one for the cameraman Tudor, one for Brian on sound, one for Suzanne the director and Patrick the researcher.

It was fish bliss. Not simply because I had spent the last three hours working the morning shift, but because this was wild salmon, fresh salmon. It was smoked by a table leg, not treated with chemicals to get the "smoke effect", or painted pink to get the "wild effect". For an ambrosial moment I remembered what proper smoked salmon should taste like, not the fishy acrid jelly they serve with a wedge of lemon and a piece of flabby "brown" bread, but a dry and melting delicacy. Before the others could finish I reached out and snaffled the sixth piece.

Lance carefully pushed my other slices to one side and piled them one on top of the other.

"That's about forty pounds' worth there," he said.

I think he had seen enough waste for one morning.

FROM HACKNEY WITH LOVE

The British Waterways Board building site at Prescott Lock was modelled on a Ken Adams-era James Bond film set. There were heavies at the gate, who grunted suspiciously. We were escorted to the headquarters office, which bristled with fake panels and air-conditioning tunnels (though no LED countdown machine that I could see). There was even a glamorous blonde woman in a tight skirt who didn't really seem to know what was going on, but who watched us very carefully all the time (the press officer).

And I had to stand and nod with a single furrowed brow aloft while a crazed madman outlined an improbable scheme. "So, Mr Jones, nothing can stop us now. I will have total command of the tidal reaches of the lower Lea and Bow Creek."

Richard "Scaramanga" Rutter didn't have a white cat and there weren't any sharks in his pool, but he did take me to a cage that was picked up by a crane and lowered slowly into the bottom of a deep hole in the ground, while lots of men in hard hats marched around and talked into walkie-talkies. It was fab.

"This is the climax of ten years' work," he explained, clanking open the door and stepping straight out into the 200-foot puddle at the bottom of the lock. "You are here to witness history. This is the first time that we have actually taken a boat through." (The boat was to come later.) In the interim, I wondered whether Richard was going to chain me to the bottom when the gates opened. Because, clearly, if he was I would have to shoot him and shin up the mitre gates, laying out the staff as I went. But he was still outlining his scheme.

"Prior to this, the maximum size of barge that was capable of using the Lee Navigation was about 150 tons, but now we are talking about barges of 350 tons."

"You're mad."

"Silence! Tie him to the twenty-one-tonne fish belly gate!"

It was indeed a massive thing. The lock was 244 feet long and was built to take not one but two of these bigger barges at the same time. Until the end of the 1970s, the Lea had continued to function as an industrial waterway. Coasters and lighters lined the entire route. Derricks, gantries, chimneys, warehouses, wharves and junk dominated the river. They were horrible at the time but seem rather wonderful and prosperous these days. The end had come startlingly quickly and is generally blamed on Mrs Thatcher. But Richard was an enthusiast for a new, green resurgence.

"The immediate need is for the Olympic site," he said. "We can carry 6,000 tonnes of goods a day, in and out, and save 75,000 lorry journeys a year."

The thought of 75,000 lorries roaming around the daft street plan of the East End, asking people where they wanted the aggregate, gave a certain urgency to his plan. Richard was the King Canute of the Bow Rivers. His lock would stop the sea coming any further into the river and he rather fancied that the rising costs of fuel would at last bring the country back to his beloved canals.

British Waterways have had a brilliant restoration record. Men with pipes can putter improbable distances in their own floating caravans. Now they want to quadruple the commercial use. "It costs about a penny a mile. We can't transport bananas but there is no time limit on waste removal, for example," Richard said.

The ambition was to get Hackney's rubbish back on the canal instead of in it. Not bananas, perhaps, but certainly banana skins. So here we were, paddling through six inches of murky waters at the bottom of the latest pound lock in Britain – a historic tribute to the river, given that very early lock that had been built about twenty miles further upstream.

Richard summoned his lift. We were running out of time. The water to the south of us was tidal and he needed to get through the lock before Bow Creek ran away into the Thames, so we clanked up the cage, transferred to a RIB and made our approach, past noxious banks of glistening mud. We hovered in front of the new portal. The big shiny pistons pushed at the gates. We motored in carefully, feeling unnecessarily small. The waters surged, and we passed through and up river. We should have had a ceremonial sack of gravel aboard.

As in a Bond film, the men in hard hats carried on padding about as if nothing out of the ordinary had happened at all.

We approached the Olympic site from beneath Old Ford Lock, where the Lee Navigation comes down from the north past the original *Big Breakfast* house. A man with a key unlocked a chain of big yellow buoys linked with fierce sharp stars, like a bulldog's collar, straddling the entrance to a narrow cut and leading along a concrete culvert into the Olympic site. This was the way to arrive. This *will* be the way to arrive in 2012.

I instantly hatched a mad, *Goldfinger* plan of my own. I would rent disused Russian cruise ships and anchor them in the Thames. I would fill them with demented sports fans and then run fast ferryboats up this culvert straight into the heart of the Olympic Village. I could beat the traffic and make my fortune.

Obviously not, but I made a mental note to stand up at a public meeting and ask Boris the mayor whether he was going to use the river to prevent traffic congestion, because within seconds (a silly time), we were through the leafy channel and right in amongst the bulldozers. The banks were an earthquake. No part of the scenery was not on top of another part of the scenery. And we pootled serenely along in a bare concrete drain, calmly surveying the chaos all around.

I have driven over the slightly forbidding flood relief system many times and wondered what the horrible thing might be. After Stratford Market station disappeared under three feet of water in the 1930s, they built this massive concrete conduit. Smooth-sided and forty feet wide, but decidedly a drain. And made of concrete. Now they intend to prettify it and turn it into a tree-lined water feature. No ditch has ever had such a makeover. The Lea is about to enter its finest hour. I hope so, because this maze of waterways is a confusing warren.

The canals were originally cut to service ancient mills. During the recent building they found the wooden walls of an embankment dating from Roman times. In 1909 the *Morning* leader wrote: "None but the lightermen knew all the tortuous and casual channels into which the Lea breaks in its old age between Bromley and Tottenham." As it gets closer to the Thames the names themselves – "the Waterworks River", "the Pudding Mill River", "the Three Mills Cut" – indicate that they were all working waterways. We cruised past little blocks of allotments, under massive road bridges with feet of dripping clearance overhead, alongside patches of devastated waste ground and pylons and then beneath the Northern Outfall Sewer on its way to Abbey Mills. This underground pipe crossed over the river, above our heads because the water we were on was so low.

Two old wooden motorboats were stranded high on a patch of ground, paint peeling on their striated hulls. We were in the middle of a great urban wilderness of dead ends, culverts, islands and leats. The Olympics threatens to tidy it all up, but can it? Or will it simply deposit another twenty-first-century layer on top of the accumulated mess?

I had never been in such a dysfunctional urban environment. The slums of Rio have more cohesion. Nothing fits together in the Bow Marshes. The geography of the river, the low-lying bog and its myriad channels, have shaped the history and the look of this place. It is London's swampy heart of darkness. Even after studying all the maps and websites and cruising through the main channels, I remained completely disorientated, until after sliding down the muddy gut of the Bow Creek, past a redundant light ship, leaning drunkenly against a black wharf, I sluiced out of a channel. The horizons cleared and I faced an empty wide river. Tony Blair's folly, the Dome, crouched like a toad half a mile across turbulent grey water on the opposite side of the Thames.

I had reached the end of the Lea.

Detail from "A Chart of the Fens between Lynn Regis, Denver Sluice and Wisbich" by William Hayward, 1610.

Chapter Five

EAST ANGLIA

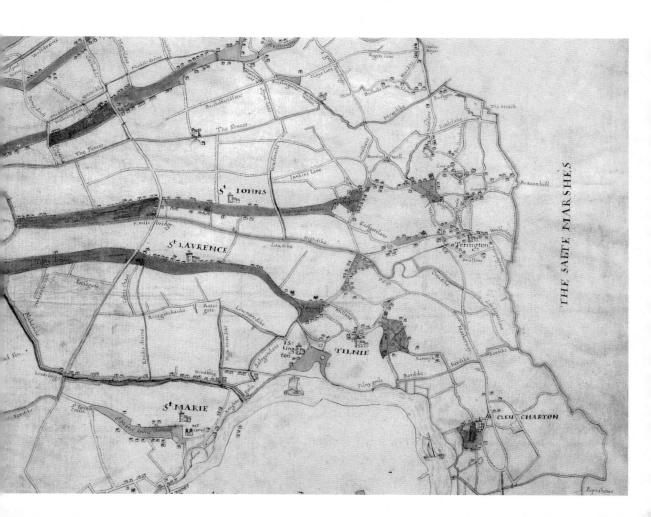

TAKING A PUNT

I like punting. It's a manly pursuit. The secret is to trail the pole. Let it lie on the water, lean the shaft against your hip and use it as a rudder. Make sure you have enough room to pull it up into the open air for the next stroke.

Don't bang it on the underside of a bridge. Don't let it drop on the passengers. Don't get it too wet or it will slip out of your hands. Don't push it out too far to the side. Don't plonk it down on the foundations of Major Works of British Architecture, which project into the river just below the surface at St John's College, Cambridge. Don't let go of it. Don't let go of it, even if it threatens to drag you in the water.

Ease it through and climb along it hand over hand. That's it. Effortless. That's cool. It's a tango, not a rumba. Anticipate the end of the stroke and swing it up, as it tips forward, with another little screw to clear it from the mud, and enough time to reassert your firm hold. Don't thrust it too heavily back in. It might dig right down. Just rest it gently on the bottom and let the forward motion of the punt carry you on, so that you can give any turbo thrust you want at exactly the right point.

Don't stand in the punt. Stand on the slippery varnished transom. You're not in Oxford. And as you slip down the river reflect what a pointless skill it is to have mastered anyway.

It was nice to be back in Cambridge and to be able to show off. The river was thronging with punts on this June day. After lounging just under

Magdalene Bridge, waiting for Peter the cameraman, Jamie the director and James the boat boy, I nonchalantly eased out into the traffic. Four years of wasted undergraduate life came back in a splash. My own skill at punting was hardly the issue anyway. It's no good turning twenty-one foot of varnished mahogany in a forty-foot river, using nothing but a long polished stick, if a party of drunken schoolteachers is going to veer over and smash directly into the side of you. Practise punting by all means, but practise smiling benignly too.

The river was crowded with new "punt charabancs" piloted by moonlighting undergraduate taxi drivers. Three athletic girls with big arms were poling flat, wide, big punts up towards King's. They had ten or so paying tourists on board and caused tailbacks under the Bridge of Sighs.

As I came up to them I trailed my pole to brake myself and the girl behind slammed into the back of my punt. I was jerked forward. I had nowhere to go. I quickly two-stepped out of my punt and onto the punt ahead.

The tourists looked startled. I looked startled. My punt was bobbing alongside with nobody in it. I recovered myself. I apologised, brushed myself down, and, still holding my pole, stepped back into my own boat. I assume they thought it was what everybody did. I thought it was pretty deft, myself.

And on I went past the artful gardens of Trinity, under exquisite Clare and along the back of King's where Wittgenstein once threatened Karl Popper with a poker.

King's choirboys, in their top hats and gowns, trooped across the bridge as if summoned by central documentary effect suppliers.

Does anybody punt outside Oxbridge? The very act seemed slightly shameful to any undergraduate of the 1970s. It was something for hoorays, or engineers who had finally finished all those exams. In fact, the punt is a distinguished workboat built on a ladder principle for fowling and angling in the shallow waters of the Fens.

Looked at through narrowed eyes you can almost see its dug-out canoe ancestry. It is the river boat *par excellence*.

TRAPPING EELS

Some days later, I paddled my canoe to the edge of Cambridgeshire where the village of Welle had been divided in two (Upwell and Outwell) to accommodate a county boundary. I was looking for one of the last working duck punts to take me hunting for eels.

The village was nearly four miles long and strung along the River Nene as if it were its high street, with neat red-brick houses and dinky passenger bridges. I met Peter Carter further up the river. We sat in the reeds under an open sky but every now and then we had to strain to hear each other as a vegetable lorry thundered past to Peterborough.

"This is the one area in Britain where you don't have to take a hill start as part of the test." Peter was proud of the Fens. "And when cars go for their MOT they often find that the handbrake has broken through lack of use."

We had left my canoe and were sliding up towards Peter's hunting grounds. He was dressed for the chase in a long, dark, full-bottomed waxed mackintosh and a slouch hat and was propelling us with a long ash pole. It still had its bark. There wasn't any varnish on his vessel.

Covered with layers of thick pale-grey paint, it was narrower than a University punt, and had canoe ends, which had been docked to make a blunt prow and stern.

"Mind you, you have to be careful because there are slopes," Peter carried on. "Some of them you wouldn't be aware of, but one woman left her car outside the post office a while back without the handbrake on and it rolled backwards into the river."

There were signs along the roads everywhere: "Think, don't sink".

We now passed a massive installation. Peter grabbed his paddles – spade-handled, short and round-ended, for use when lying down – and we crept under one bridge and over the next. Like a lot of the Fens, the sluice gates had a desperately utilitarian, engineered appearance. The bridge was made of lumpen grey concrete, with galvanised fences and institutional green metal fixings, hung with stern safety warnings – unattractive and unwelcoming. We were on the original river. And yet below us, in this ironing board of country, there was another, deeper level. The Nene was crossing over another waterway.

"That's the Middle Level Drain," Peter explained.

This whole region had originally been a deep soggy waste of marsh and fen. "Marsh" meaning land visited by the sea and "fen" referring to land mired in fresh water. It was Britain's Camargue. South of Lincolnshire and north of Cambridge, with nothing to prevent it, the sea crept miles inland and mingled with the waters of 6,042 square miles. This was more than a tenth of the area of England. It had been a sump, a silt bed, a sponge and a drain. The Great Ouse seeped into the landscape, wandering at will, and joined the Witham, the Glen, the Welland and the Nene spilling over the land. It was a place of mud and reeds and eels. Man had long tried to "improve" this place. The earliest dams, drains and dykes were put in place 6,000 years ago. What I was looking at was only a recent example of a series of schemes to organise the flood and separate land and sea and river.

Throughout all this the Fenland retained its ancient mysteries. Birds still flew here by instinct. Eels came back to breed in the safe murky shallows from distant grounds in the far Atlantic. Peter was one of the last of the eel catchers.

We were paddling up towards a reed bed. We leaned over and grabbed them to get us closer in.

Peter disdained a life-jacket and I had left mine behind.

"I can't swim," he told me. "None of the old boys could swim. They told me I was best to let myself sink, and crawl along the bottom till I got hold of some reeds and then use them to pull myself to the bank."

He stuck his pole into the mud, anchoring the punt against the reeds.

The plan was to set traps in the evening and come back to look and see if we had caught any of the long green fish with the tiny heads by morning. He had made the eel traps himself. They were woven out of willow – long thin baskets with a wide mouth and a narrowing neck like a wicker bottle.

The sun was dropping below the reeds out of an unaccustomedly fierce, empty blue. Clouds rise as they cross over this far eastern plain, but even without them the sky seemed higher. This wetland paradoxically has very low rainfall.

"I love the Fens," Peter said. "If I go away I feel claustrophobic, with hills and things around me. I don't know how people can stand them. I like a bit of space and big clouds."

He was pushing hazel rods into the reeds close to the bank, about ten feet apart. We were there to bait the traps with earthworms. It was my job to stick the worm on a piece of copper wire – a hateful task.

THE LIVES OF EELS

Ely was once effectively an island surrounded by wet Fenlands in which eels were extraordinarily plentiful. The Domesday Book noted that 52,000 eels were caught in the River Ouse in the course of one year. Eels were even used as currency, with villages during the Middle Ages expected to pay their taxes in eels. The village of Outwell, for example, had to provide the Abbot of Ely with 10,000 eels a year. And that was just one village, and just a small proportion of what they were actually catching.

The oiliness of their skins enables eels, unlike other fish, to survive out of water for as long as 48 hours. Eels can also survive in mud during dry periods and even, if they see fit, travel short distances over land.

Traditionally, European eels were thought to spawn in the Sargasso Sea between Bermuda and the Bahamas. More recently, it's believed it might be volcanic outlets in the continental shelf of South America. Females carry up to 10 million eggs and their larvae then travel thousands of miles back to Europe on the ocean current.

Here they turn into dark-skinned elvers and enter fresh water, where they attempt to migrate upstream to find a place where they can mature into eels. When faced with an obstacle such as a waterfall or weir, elvers are capable of climbing extraordinary heights of perhaps 80 to 100 feet to continue their journey upstream.

"An Eel-Catcher's Home in the Norfolk Broads", photograph by Peter Henry Emerson, 1887.

With the worm between a thumb and finger, I pushed the copper into the blind, coiled head that waved away from my probing needle. I stabbed it, feeling the rest of the body squirm in my palm, on and up in a squirt of blood and yellow intestine. I didn't want to look squeamish so I stabbed and threaded them all until they were a wet loop of meat, to be pushed into a gap in the wicker. Finally I twisted the copper ends on to each other.

After I tied each trap to a hazel wand with garden twine, Peter told me to plunge the stick into the mud, deep in the reeds, and launch the trap onto the water, where it sank slowly down.

Several times Peter made me drag it back up and push it closer to the bank. Then we turned and paddled back to Outwell.

Peter still caught eels. The Romans valued smoked eels. Chinese restaurants still gobble up his catch, but eel numbers have dropped catastrophically because of over-fishing at sea. Some say nutrients leaching from the intensively farmed land have changed the nature of the water, too.

The following morning we went to inspect the traps. Laboriously we pulled them all up: one after the other, dripping and slimy, some covered with thin green woolly weed which had to be scraped away so that I could put them to my eye and peer into the telescopic depths. I began cautiously, in case a big one shot out and caught me by the nose, but as we came to stick eight and then nine, I was resigned to the fact that there would be nothing in the dark recesses. But at number ten, I noticed there was something there. A grey shape was squirming down the dark end.

Peter held up an eel bucket like a galvanised miniature milk churn and I tipped a tiny eel into it. Black and silver (its freshwater colours), it was no more than six inches in length with butterfly fins just behind its head. It lay like a snake in geometrically perfect shapes. For a while I sat and marvelled and then we tipped the churn over the side and watched it slide away. It certainly deserved to grow fat and long and undisturbed in these waterways that once teemed with its forebears.

DUCK PUNTING

I found out later that the eel we caught was in a trap that Peter himself had set. I fear that we had brought him into the daylight as a living exhibit. He was our representative of the old ways of the Fens. The next day the sun shone again and the reeds clattered in the ditches. He took me off to show me what his punt was really for.

It was not built for eeling. It was built to hold a mammoth blunderbuss. This attached to the forward thwart with ropes and settled into a notch at the bow. It had no stock to speak of, a wide but not flared barrel and was as long as me. Peter was one of the few remaining slodgers licensed to use one. The principle was straightforward enough. The punt was low and silent. The gun was huge and deadly.

We tested it in the Welney Wetland Centre on a flight pond in front of some nervous wildfowl. We were firing blanks. The gun was reassuringly old-fashioned, loaded up with gunpowder and wadding. This would have taken a fair time in the past, because it needed a quantity of metal pellets – tin tacks were not uncommon. You prepared with care because you only got one shot.

It had a massive flintlock. We dragged it back and put a layer of black powder in a little groove. Then I lay down and they launched me on the pond. Peter's two intriguing stunted paddles were now put to use. I rested them against my forearms and, lying prone, propelled myself forward. In reality this might have taken most of a night. The hunter went with the moon behind him and paddled to a stretch of water where ducks, widgeon, woodcock or other birds were roosting. He got within range, aimed and pulled the trigger.

No ducks were harmed in the making of this television series. No presenters were harmed either. I was under instruction not to put my shoulder to the stock. We were firing nothing but powder – but, when the real thing went off, the recoil acted as jet propulsion and the punt would rocket backwards across the water. The shooter sometimes made a last-minute noise to get the birds rising. This was a ground-based fusillade. Once they were off, the moment would pass very quickly. I had none of that urgency.

I pretended to line up the end of the punt with an imaginary flock, stuck my own head under my wing and reached around and squeezed. There was a colossal roar. A jet of flame shot out of the muzzle. A thick cloud of smoke rose up and, yes, I did shoot backwards. The armourer chuckled. "We put a bit more powder in for the actual shot, Griff." I looked up with glazed eyes from inside the reed bank.

"Well done."

My neighbour in Suffolk is one of the last licensed duck punters on that estuary, but he doesn't go any more. I once asked him why.

"The wife wouldn't allow it," he said. "I'd be away all night."

That was because, after he had blasted off his gun and after he had picked himself up from whatever part of the mud he ended up on, he had to go into the darkness and start collecting any birds he had shot.

To the manner born. Punting in the Fens.

An aerial view of the Bedford Rivers showing the straightened flow to the sea and the Washes.

The Forty Foot Drain.

Sedge at Wicken. Sharp enough to draw blood.

Holme Fen. Straight again.

The ship of the Fens, Ely Cathedral with a Cambridge eight in the foreground.

The iron post that was originally sunk to its tip in the peat.

The blunderbuss fired a wide-ranging shower of deadly metal, which took out dozens of ducks in one blast. There was a hell of a lot of post-fusillade work to do. Then off to the London markets in the morning.

STILT-WALKING AT WICKEN FEN

In popular imagination the historic Fens were a wet, impenetrable wilderness, thronging with eels, reeds and wildfowl, all of which provided a harvest for a muddy, remote population half composed of romantic runaways like Hereward the Wake and half of web-footed retards.

Not much original fen has been preserved. An intimidating total of 99.9 per cent of land has gone over to modern agricultural methods. Quite frankly, that didn't seem to offer much left for me, but Wicken Fen promised a glimpse of the unimproved wetlands.

In the nineteenth century, Cambridge entomologists had become accustomed to collecting moths and butterflies from the boats that brought the reeds for thatching and had followed the source of this scientific bounty back to Wicken. When the thatching industry finished and the land was threatened with drainage, they encouraged the National Trust to get hold of Wicken Fen to preserve the natural environment. Now it was the oldest nature reserve in the country – but there was little entirely natural about the 1,500 acres. It was a mosaic of abandoned farming practices and drainage schemes that had provided a huge variety of different habitats.

I borrowed some stilts to try and walk about the reed beds, as the original inhabitants had done. I had to lace them around my shoes and knees. And when I had effectively cut off my circulation I essayed a few steps. It was quite easy but I fell over a few times for the camera, dropping theatrically backwards into the sedge.

This reed was tough and sharp. It could cut your hand. It was used for the more complicated weaving of thatched roofs: the top ridge, for example, where the beds of hollow reed had to be stitched together. For centuries these waterlogged fields were a lucrative source of this important building material. Far from being the remote and unsuccessful backwater of legend, Fenland was an almost ideal landscape for pre-industrial man. It was rich with annual free food, marvellous grazing and natural building materials and shot through with by far the best and most economic way of transporting goods at that time – water.

There is evidence that men started channelling in this region, building dams to keep the water on one side and the earth on the other, from earliest times. The Romans were particularly adept. Car Dyke, at eighty-five miles long, is still the biggest un-natural watercourse that the Fens have ever seen. The Romans' arrival corresponded with a lowering of sea levels and the first great age of drainage in the higher, silted land. Like all engineering work, maintenance was complicated. It lapsed after they left. The sea came back too. The population receded, but people returned towards the end of the first millennium and by the fourteenth century, far from being a land of muddy waste, Fenland was amongst the richest areas in Britain.

Travelling up and along the Ouse brought me to one of the largest and most magnificent cathedrals in England, at Ely. It stands on what I would call a bit of a hill. This is the "eel eye". The island of eels. Wherever a place name includes the Saxon word "eye" or "ey" we can usually identify an island, often in the middle of an area of wet or boggy land. There are dozens of such places in East Anglia, from Eye to Bawdsey.

But Ely is hardly a huddle in a marsh. There are offices, stables, outbuildings, palaces and high walls, all built of fine yellow stone imported from Northamptonshire. They dwarf the later building. This was power. This was wealth. This was the medieval bishop. Living out in the watery wastes of the region, he and his monks set about harvesting the real riches of this area, the wealth of the land. They concentrated on the partially inundated areas, the boggy edge lands. They built or restored the Roman Bank – sixty miles of massive earthworks – to protect more than a million acres from flood. Long before any Dutch engineers arrived on the scene, capable, largely unknown, clerical bureaucrats had made huge improvements to the Fens.

I approached Ely, with the Ship of the Fens, the Cathedral, looming over to my right. I was canoeing along the Great Ouse on a spectacular golden evening. The banks were thronged with geese. Swans negotiated menacing circles around Cadbury and me. A gorgeous girl swooped by in a single scull. The landing place was stiff with pleasure boats. They, more than anything, indicated that I was on a river rather than one of the artificial drains.

I paddled in under the railway bridge, brushing close around the stern of a mammoth white pleasure cruiser almost entirely covered with green mould. The mooring ropes were bleached by the sun. A canvas cover was blackened with goo dropping from a nearby tree. Perhaps a long-cherished project had been abandoned. Retirement beckoned. A life exploring Britain by the back ways called (until a doctor or a heart attack intervened). The rotting hulk was called *Moonraker*. Why was James Bond saddled with this sad, neglected backwater fantasy? I eased over towards the other bank. Better still: *Hot Gossip*. I turned to the camera and sniggered. "They'll be talking about us. Those loose dancing women, eh…" I was a little too loud. The owner came out on deck. I had thought they were unoccupied. Not at all. "Come in and have a drink, Griff."

Poking their heads out of cabins on *Pourquoi Pas* or *Sugar Daddy*, there were sociable people everywhere, in highly coloured knitwear.

I accepted an invitation from the live-aboard owner of a proper narrow boat. He had cashed up and taken to the water. He showed me around his carefully designed home, with its coal stove, its clever under-bed storage, its galley and bathroom. Running costs were low. He paid rent for his bank-side mooring. He kept a little car in the marina car park and a bicycle on deck. He didn't pay any rates ("but don't tell anyone or they'll all want to do it"). And if they did come after him he could untie himself and motor off. He had taken his boat right up the Regent Canal and spent time in London, but had tired of that. He would move on soon. Essentially he could settle anywhere from one end of England to the other and his £60,000 house went with him. John had no dependents. His children were grown up. He was a wanderer with a floating Recreational Vehicle, could pretty much guarantee tranquillity and he wondered why everybody else stayed on shore.

A RODDON RUNS THROUGH IT

After a week on the horizontal I was itching to get some height under me, so we went to a grass airstrip to take a lift in a microlight.

FEN FACTS

East Anglia was once joined to Europe and its rivers were tributaries of the Rhine. After the last glaciation the area's forests became flooded and its trees rotted into peat. In the eighth-century *Life of St Guthlac* the area around the Wash was described as "a hideous fen of bigness".

One thousand years later in the eighteenth century, Daniel Defoe called the area "the sink of thirteen counties", because a number of rivers from the Midlands drained through the Fens.

Here in the flat landscape the flowing waters of these rivers slowed down. This in turn caused them to drop any sediment they were carrying, which then caused the rivers to meander to the extent that they took twice as long to get to the sea as they strictly needed to. And so the Fens had become a vast, flat, soggy area.

- ▶ They now cover an area of about 1,500 square miles, or about 1 million acres.

- ▶ Defence against flooding in the Fens involves about 3,800 miles of watercourses.

- ▶ There are 286 pumping stations in the area, which can pump the equivalent of 16,500 Olympic swimming-pools' worth of water in 24 hours.

- ▶ There are 96 miles of fluvial embankments.

- ▶ The area is protected from the North Sea by 60 miles of coastal sea walls.

Drainage Mills in the Fens, by John Sell Cotman, c.1830–40.

I had imagined that I would be dangling from a flexible kite, but micro-technology has advanced and I clambered into a pair of desk chairs wrapped in polystyrene. It was a small plane really. It had seats that you could sit on and doors that shut you in. What made it micro was the engine. It could fly at well over a hundred miles an hour with a following wind, but was built to pootle at motorway speed, so we trundled over the grass, pootled upwards, pootled a bit higher and finally pootled along at about eighty.

There was another aircraft on the strip, built by Mary Poppins out of a newspaper and UHU, but Peter the cameraman got in that so that he could film us pootling. They wanted my pilot Ben Robinson and I to discuss what we saw.

What we saw was the Hundred Foot Drain.

On the map, and indeed to drive about in, the Fens appear ruler sharp. Fields are severe rectangles, roads run for miles and even the rivers are straight.

In the seventeenth century, the Fourth Duke of Bedford had brought over a useful bunch of immigrants to help drain the land that had remained sodden to that date. Dutch engineers were drainage experts, and they knew a bit about canal building as well. They straightened and embanked the rivers, taking out the natural meanders and the wayward creeks and encouraging the waters to run straight to the sea. The land on either side was neatly parcelled up and handed out to those who had helped fund the works. This deprived the locals of their common land and they fought back, calling themselves the Fen Tigers.

Looking down from our airborne capsule, we could clearly see two great open pipes running away across the landscape to the sea. One was the New Bedford River, the other the Old Bedford River. There was an area between the two called the washes, which regularly flooded. This was where the wildfowl came and where I had been for my mock duck shooting two days before. Cattle grazed in the marshy area. It is thought by countryside historians to continue to embody the spirit of the original Fen but Ben pointed out the ghosts of the landscape, the scars of the ancestral world that still showed through the new facelift.

"You see there," he said, "we can make out the old creek."

A faint outline of darker grass traced the creeping branches of an old waterway running across the middle of a fifteen-acre rectilinear field. It had been ploughed up several hundred times. Crop after crop of high-yielding wheat had been taken from it, but the original outline still remained.

"And over there, you can still see a roddon, or ghost river. That farm down there is probably an original settlement. It was on a bit of high ground that was effectively an island. The river deposited silt which alters the quality of the earth, and that shows up as a different colour. It can be much clearer at different times of year."

But it was clear enough. The sea had once reached all the way in here. Some of this was old tidal salt marsh, some swampy ground, some flooded by water that drained into the tide. The outlines of a hugely complex landscape could still be discerned. I grasped at metaphors. It was a palimpsest. But we've never seen a palimpsest, have we? It's a wallpaper pattern coming though a new paint job. It was a bra strap showing through a wet T-shirt. But, whatever it was, it was most certainly a glimpse at the shadows of a lost world.

Was it a world that was threatening to revive? Was the rising sea level once again going to reclaim this place? We can allow ourselves a certain Romantic frisson here. What if the sea broke through again, as we are told it eventually must? What if we decided to stop maintaining these ditches?

Ben was pretty frank. He came from a farming family. He recognised the value that had been extracted. This was still the bread basket of Britain, with what is indubitably some of the very best soil in the country. Two hundred and fifty million loaves of bread a year come from wheat from the Fens. Thirty seven per cent of all vegetables, bulbs and flowers grown in the open in Britain are grown here. Over 800 square miles of land had now been recovered by such fierce control of the water. This was prime farming land of great agricultural importance to the nation. Even at the height of the Second World War precious resources were set aside to improve the pumping systems. There was no turning back.

I was gradually becoming aware, talking to farmers, meeting locals and using my eyes, that the issue was more complex than the Dutch had originally envisaged. "No turning back." This was the phrase that hovered in the background. The whole system, once begun, needed constant refinement and improvement.

PUMP ACTION

After bumping back to earth, I took my canoe and paddled down the Forty Foot Drain. It was the sort of cloudless day that makes any British citizen worry about climate change. We passed down the cut, between high featureless banks, waiting for a break in the traffic. A crane was hammering home replacement piles further up the road and cars were trying to avoid a diversion. Each of them came through at high speed, crossed the bridge in front and shot off down a long straight track heading east. When they found out this was leading them in the wrong direction they came back, slightly faster, to make up for lost time. This happened with such regularity, roaring into our solitude and destroying our remoteness, that we cursed them for spoiling our film. But we could not be really lonely here. This felt like a remote area because of the big skies and the waving reeds. But it was a busy place. The Fens are crossed by ceaseless traffic feeding the great agricultural factory.

I was looking for enough time to explain to camera that the ditches were dug by seventeenth-century Dutch and Scottish prisoners of war wearing white woollen uniforms so that if they ran away they could be easily tracked across the big empty plains. As we waited to sort things out, I talked to the man who had been sent to look after us. We were standing by his pumps, which even today were thrumming away, emptying water from a ditch that ran through fields below us. He explained that the pumps were there to stop the water building up to unacceptable levels and flooding the fields. That's what the drain was: a drain. It took the water off to join the middle levels where it could be expected to flush out to the sea. But he freely admitted that it was all under strain. The water could easily prove too much for all the banks, drains, ditches and levels to hold, and then disaster would strike the region.

"When did that last happen?" I asked.

"Last Christmas," he said promptly.

His mobile phone alarm system had dragged him from his bed at three in the morning to come out and get all the systems working. There was a lot of power on hand. If all the pumps in the Fens were switched on at once they could shift a hundred million gallons a minute. But it all had to go somewhere. That was the point.

My canoe was floating on water that had been pumped up from fields below it and would be pumped up again to join the water of an original river. The river had silted up somewhat. That was part of the problem, but only a small one. Clearly it now ran some considerable height above the land that once surrounded it. It was enclosed in high walls and seemed to be getting higher. That was the purpose of the great system built by Cornelius Vermuyden, the chief of those Dutch engineers. Two long straight canals were built to take the old rivers. An area of land was left between them to allow them to flood. But on either side there had to be two massive banks to hold the whole construction in place. The new rivers were designed to be straight and fast to carry silt away. That was to prevent the rivers from getting higher. But nothing could prevent the fields on either side from getting lower. What was going on?

The peat that had been exposed by the drainage and put to work to grow crops had almost immediately started shrinking. The earth started dropping away. The water seeped out of it. The processes of rot that had been held up by the fresh water now began and the soil began to eat itself up. Worse than this, the cropping systems actually exposed the earth to the wind. Even today, when it gets dry, strong winds can whip up "fen blows" – great black clouds of peaty dust rip across the flat landscape and carry away more.

This was why there were so many pumps and so many bridges carrying one river across the top of another. Originally farmers had come up with ingenious methods of crop rotation that allowed some fields to stagnate under water for three years, to rebuild their silt and moisture content and expand again like a damp sponge. They had built windmills throughout the Fens to pump out the low-lying water. But the wind was unreliable and the windmills were horribly inefficient. They froze up in bad winters and big floods simply ran over the top of the scoop wheel. The engines of the industrial age were to solve all that with steam, electricity and the internal combustion engine, allowing the pumps to really get to work. And the land got to sinking seriously again.

In some parts, agriculture didn't last more than a couple of years. I drove across the baking plain to park in a green wood, called Holme Fen. They decided pretty quickly that this boggy place was unsuitable for crops, partly because it appeared to disappear straight into the earth.

I crossed a little wooden bridge over the obligatory arrow-straight ditch, plunged into head-high bracken and crossed a mature wood of high birches and tall oaks towards a green pillar standing solitary and incongruously like the lamppost in Narnia.

It was anchored to the ground by supports that had to be put there to hold the thing up, even though it had originally been sunk right into the ground. The earth had completely dropped away all around it. It had miraculously emerged by "the height of a man in the life of a man" (as one saying had it) so that it now towered above my head, well over twice my height at fourteen feet. I had to pull Cadbury away to stop him raising a leg to this significant monument.

By removing the water they had made this place the lowest point in England at the time, some nine feet below sea level. That record had been superseded now (subseded perhaps) by the place I went to next, which was deeper into the mere and still farmland – but only just.

Engine Farm was little more than an agricultural facility, with a great tin barn and a range of tractor sheds around a wide yard. Holme Fen wood stood along one horizon. Far to the north were a few trees. Otherwise these buildings stood in a bare level plain of soil, criss-crossed by ditches and planted with crops.

In front of me, Greg Bliss represented the puzzled voice of local farmers. There was a plan afoot to let the water return and turn all this area back into natural fen. The Great Fen Project aimed to link Holme Fen to Woodwalton Fen by buying up the farms between and returning them to nature. But Mike could not see what would be natural about it. This was his livelihood. We stood in the middle of prime productive agricultural land, threatened with extinction at a time of dire food shortages. His perplexity poured out in a stream of anguished statistics and opinions. How the compensation scheme was absurd. How they had worked the owners and forgotten the tenants. How the farms that had been bought up were now being abandoned and left worse than useless. How Prince Charles had visited and wanted to see the farms used properly. How it was impossible to re-flood the area without effectively re-flooding hundreds of square miles.

Ironically, Greg was as angry and frustrated on behalf of the tenanted land as the Fen Tigers must have been on behalf of the common land when the government had ignored local concerns 400 years ago and first licensed the Great Drainage Scheme. Once again someone far away in an office was deciding on the future and seemingly ignoring those who lived and worked locally. But this time it was to let the water flow in rather than keep it away.

SAILING IN THE BROADS

A day later and seventy miles further east Cadbury and I were looking for the film crew. As I entered the Norfolk village of Wroxham, the trailer nearly lifted off over a hump-backed bridge. Nicola and Paul were strung out along the High Street waving vaguely, but I still missed the turning and had to go around and swing my canoe-caboosh about in a yard where ranks of floating recreational vehicles, river motor homes, long low caravans of the Broads with sliding roofs, were laid out in a row waiting for the summer season. Appropriately for the complete British holiday experience, it was just beginning to rain.

There's an obvious clash of tourist cultures in Norfolk. It's a crossroads for the leisure-bound tribes of Britain. Coach-trip types and family-holiday bucket-and-spade people (or six-pack and barbecue blokes) mingle with the hunting and shooting set. Middle-class Barbour and Ugg women and books-in-the-lavatory folk are here for wet and windy holidays in little Arthur Ransome sailing boats. They vie for car parking space with genteel river dwellers and trimmed-front-hedge retirement-home owners.

But in Wroxham all this is subsumed under the banner of Roy's. Roy and his brothers and sons have taken over the town. Here is Roy's Toys, Roy's Hardware, Roy's Porno … (Not the last one. I made that up.)

I crossed the road and dived into Roy's Food Hall, "the largest village shop in the world". Inside it was indistinguishable from Tesco, the largest bypass shop in the world.

We were out of season. A flock of retirees had occupied the fruit and veg console, but I was happy enough avoiding fruit anyway. I was provisioning for a very particular tourist experience. I had hired a small boat, part of the Norfolk Heritage Fleet, from Hunter's Yard on Womack Water. It was one of a collection of wooden sailing boats originally built by Percy Hunter in the 1930s. Even today, with no electricity or engine, the mahogany vessel enabled the purist (and few purer than me) to experience the real spirit of the Broads – or possibly a semi-defunct form of early package holiday.

I had an urgent demand for loads of cans. My father's favourite one-pot, cruising-boat grub, based no doubt on experience in Burma with the Royal West African Regiment, required beans, frankfurters, mincemeat and Spam. I threw plenty of tins of beans in my trolley – but, better than that! Here they were: tins of breakfast beans with sausages and bacon already aboard. It was Heinz Breakfast in a Tin. And here was Heinz Spaghetti Bolognaise, with the soggy melt-on-the-tongue spaghetti and that unforgettable grainy brown tomato sauce. (My mouth is watering as I write this.)

The boat did not disappoint. Clutching my carrier bags and pulled sideways by the dog, I walked through a massive shed smelling of creosote, varnish and damp. The fleet was drawn up in the little private creek beyond and Ian Grapes was standing by to show me the ropes.

Wood Rose had a big mainsail with a massive gaffe and a fractional jib on a little boom. The mahogany bright-work was a lustrous chocolate colour. Lying on her deck was a long "quant pole" for manoeuvring her into anchorages and moorings. She was designed like a piece of exquisite office furniture, a 1930s chairman's desk on the water. Every level opened to a cleverly thought-out, partitioned cubby-hole. The cockpit seat to port hinged upwards to reveal a gas cooker. The bottle was stowed in the rear lazarette, to avoid filling the boat with explosive fumes. The doors came off. In the bow was a fine pump-action lavatory with a porcelain bowl. The cabin ceiling was a mere three feet wide by ten feet high but, most ingenious of all, it hinged upwards. I gave out involuntary murmurs of approval as Colin showed me how to lift the entire roof on my back, swing its English oak supports into place and, with the help of fixed canvas gussets, provide myself with an extra two foot of headroom.

She was handy under sail too. The following day in a strong breeze I shot across Barton Broad with Tom Williamson on board, happy, as an expert on landscape, to hang on to his berth in the corner of the cockpit and admire the landscape as I helmed. We were sluicing across one of the forty-odd lakes that make up the Broads. Tom pointed out how the banks were now largely clothed in trees.

"This is a relatively recent development," he said. "The ideal management of the Broads has changed."

Some Broads were now being closed to traffic, to allow a respite from diesel spillages and silt disturbance so that fish and wildlife could return. There was a new emphasis on nature conservancy and a new plan to maintain traditional "harmonious" development. There had always been dispute over the "proper ownership" of the Broads. Tom was fascinated by how modern management might freeze the landscape in a particular state, when there had been a long tradition of continuous change and development. The greatest illustration of this was that the Broads themselves, it had only recently been discovered, were a wholly artificial creation.

I had to interrupt him in mid-flow because we had literally run out of water. The breeze was so strong. We had rushed across the available space and I had to put the boat completely about. Lovely boat, though. She had hardly any keel and a lot of sail up but she sat steadily in the water. I pushed the tiller over and we swung around close to a tree-crowned bank.

"It was the banks that gave the game away," Tom said. "People had long assumed that they were some sort of natural phenomenon, but in the 1960s they started proper investigations."

Lambert, Jennings, Green, Hutchinson and Smith (not an advertising agency but a consortium of landscape historians) made the extraordinary discovery that these lakes were all dug by hand. They are old peat mines.

"The sides are steep and if you look closely you can see where they were cut out at different levels," Tom explained.

In the early Middle Ages this whole lake was essentially a huge open-cast mine. The rivers carried the fuel to where it was needed. Norwich was the second-largest town in England and the population used the peat to heat their houses during the winter. We were sailing through a disused industrial landscape.

In the intervening centuries these pits have become so beautiful everybody wants them. Anglers, boatmen, water authorities, nature buffs, conservationists, farmers, tourists and sailors expect to use these rivers and waterlogged holes. As we talked, dank rain-filled clouds scudded low across the sky and blew us across the slate-grey waters at alarming speeds, in absolute safety.

IN WHICH I HUMILIATE MYSELF TRYING TO GET UNDER A BRIDGE

Having dropped off Tom, I had to get the boat beyond a bridge at Potter Heigham where the arch was so low that, in order to get through, I would have to lower my mast and use my quant pole.

I came at it, bowling down the river. Cadbury sat in the well and rested his jaw on my leg. I was almost sorry I didn't smoke a pipe because we made a crusty pair. I could successfully tack the thing, though clearly I had rigged the funny little self-tacking jib incorrectly. It had a clew

FOR PEAT'S SAKE

You can really smell the peat in Scotch whisky – particularly if you happen to be sitting on a mound of the stuff at the time.

Peat is formed by the remains of plants, which rot into a brownish-black mass. Instead of continuing to rot, however, the peat then stays in this state for hundreds if not thousands of years, as long as it remains in standing water. Eventually over millions of years it can turn into coal.

Peat has been used as fuel for millennia, particularly when wood was in short supply. Today Finland and Ireland are among the world's largest users of peat for energy generation. Peat currently provides Ireland with around 5 per cent and Finland with 6 per cent of its energy requirements. But it has many other functions apart from stoking fires.

▶ It is used for drying malted barley for use in the distillation of Scotch whisky. It is the peat fire that gives Scotch its distinctive smoky, "peatie" quality.

▶ Peat is antiseptic and has therefore been used in surgical dressings.

▶ Hundreds of well-preserved human bodies have been found in peat bogs in Europe. Most of these are believed to have lived between 800 BC to AD 400.

▶ Peat is a highly absorbent material and has been put to use in recent years to help soak up oil spills.

▶ Also, because of its high absorbency, peat has been used by traditional peoples to make babies' nappies and even menstrual pads. Bet you didn't know that!

and a single-eye bolt and I had attached the shackle to the wrong bit or threaded it through the wrong section – but I could sort that later.

We were under way in a fresh breeze. There was nothing to tie the main sheet to. The boat was small, but I needed both my hands (and an extra one too) to control the thing. Despite having no keel to speak of and an incorrectly set jib, if I plunged the tiller hard to starboard she would come around.

Not that I really needed to come around. I was battling downriver with the wind on the beam. Only the fact that I had to stop every now and again and turn around to let the camera crew catch up slowed me down.

The Broads vacation adventure had been invented in Victorian times when Factory Acts and schools first provided the respectable classes with specified free time. The railway train pointed to English destinations, where tweedy, healthy fresh air could provide proper activities for dads and boys.

What could be better than these Norfolk waterways, only three hours from London by train and already popular with the upper classes? It wasn't coincidence that both John Betjeman and Arthur Ransome came here. Ransome wrote *Coot Club* and *The Big Six* about sailing holidays on the Broads. And in Betjeman's poems we encounter the recalcitrant John, dragging his stick along the railings, as his outward-bound deaf father drags him away for a manly experience, with "the lap lapping of the weedy Bure" outside a vessel similar to the little box I was piloting.

As a boy Betjeman, the would-be aesthete, disdained the Broads, but as a man he loved Norfolk. No doubt he would have an ambivalent attitude to the sheds that I was passing now. Some were sweet, some were slapdash. Some were beautifully made and some were cheap and nasty. The Broads put taste to the test.

But we were in the pool. There was the bridge. I had to swing the boat around into the wind and bring her alongside the bank. Where? There wasn't any space. It was like a Sainsbury's car park, but I spotted a gap. How infinitely superior I felt to all these stinkpots as I swung my little vessel around on a sharp curve, so that the wind dropped out of her sails, dropped my tiller and leapt for the bank.

Perhaps I swung her a little too freely. The boat went on swinging and crunched into the back of a big cruiser up ahead. A man in a short-sleeved shirt came out on deck and looked pointedly at his stern. I pretended to be busy tying up my boat. I hadn't damaged anything. He should have parked himself further up and left more space. He called his wife on deck. While I busied myself with my rigging, he got her to help him move his barge up a bit.

I opened a hatch on the foredeck. The mast pivoted. With a bit of jerking around I took out a metal fid and it was ready to swing. A large block of lead on the lower end acted as a counterweight. It folded down more quickly than I had anticipated, but after a couple of heaves I got all the bits of wood and most of the sail down onto the deck where I wanted it.

The rest was simple. I had to push the boat off into the pool, get a hold of my quant and use it like a punting pole. Mind you, the quant was fat. It was too fat to get a fist around easily and it was deliberately swollen in the middle, presumably to aid its tensile strength.

I had very little time to consider all these elements as I grappled it up and off the deck. Cadbury and I were drifting out into the main body of the river, directly above the bridge. The wind was no longer blowing me downstream but carrying me across towards the other bank or, rather, towards an important-looking tour and luncheon boat which was moored against it. It was difficult to get a purchase. In desperation I stuck a foot on the tiller and tried to steer us round.

I had a lack of steerage. I was experienced enough to know that I lacked it, but not quite experienced enough to know how to procure it.

The prow missed the highly polished side of the tour boat with the thickness of a quant pole to spare. A man in a navy jacket and a white cap stood on his deck and watched me impassively. I raised a lazy forearm in a casual salute (to indicate that this near miss had been part of my intentions all along) and slung the end of the quant pole between us with a gigantic splash. Just getting it up onto my shoulder had seriously unbalanced me. Now it nearly rocked me over the side. But I could lean on it. I pushed sideways and, as I heaved, the boat beneath my feet gradually moved away from the tour boat and sideways into Potter Heigham lagoon. The man in the cap wore the expression of a camel, but others on the opposite side had started shouting things like "Look at that!" "What's he doing?" and "Come and watch this!"

I got the middle of the pole up and started to hand it forward so that I could deploy it again. I simply needed to stick it back in the bottom, but now it was covered in water so it slipped through my hands and dropped straight in the river.

It takes a moment to accept an enormity. The brain is incapable of grasping a complete change of circumstances in an instant. Perhaps this is especially true if it ought to take the blame. I had changed from wobbling ineptitude to pathetic helplessness in a split second. There was an audible gasp from the watchers on the bank. Nonetheless, I still got down on my knees, leant forward and motioned ineffectually at the length of wood floating six feet behind me. I turned and looked at the bridge. It was twenty yards ahead. Now I had to get under it with neither an engine nor a pole.

The wind was still blowing. There was probably a current flowing. I had momentum from my last pole. I put out a foot and pushed the tiller. The boat moved. The nose obligingly swung around. We carried on towards the arch. I scrambled back down into the cockpit and grasped the tiller more confidently. When all was said and done I was still heading in the right direction. I dipped my head. There was less than three feet of headroom, but we were going to clear it. The boat slid through the arch and out into the lower river, utterly by herself.

Several people clapped. Thank you. For my part, I remembered the most important Rule of Boating in Crowded Inland Waters. I relaxed, scratched my bottom and gazed steadily about me, as if it had been my intention all along to sling my useless quant pole away and steer the boat with the aid of God.

The whole affair was a fine example of the gentle drama of the inland waterway holiday. Frankly, I cut a sad and pathetic figure on my own. I needed someone to shout at. I needed a couple of children cowering in the cockpit and I needed a wife in a fleece, bearing it all stoically.

BANJOLELE BLUES

If I had tried to shoot the bridge in 1951 I might have been given assistance by a solitary figure in dark glasses attempting to disguise a familiar Brylcreem slap, cap and Lancashire accent. George Formby spent part of every summer from 1947 cruising the Broads with his wife, and in 1951 occupied himself guiding boats under the bridge.

George, apparently, felt himself to be a victim of waterway snobbery. He always felt unaccepted: a low entertainer in a beautiful place.

It seems the Broads have long had a reputation as a social battleground. As I sailed about in my lovely yacht, showing off my close tacking, I disdained the stinkpot cruisers full of beer-swilling yobbos out for a noisy weekend, because I was a sailor and they were mere motorists. Cruising on the river, the motorboaters looked down on the day-trippers. The established estate owners resented the twee housing developments. The old thatched families sneered at the new brick closes. The house owners covered their banks with signs declaring their ownership ("No mooring", "Keep off", "Private"). The Broads would be great if it wasn't for the others.

I took a lift down to look at the Formby house with the local policemen in their RIB. Most of the time, they chugged about the rivers, gently calming minor territorial disputes. We cruised past a sandy area where the local boys liked to swim out from the bank to board passing pleasure-cruisers, and steal flags or hitch lifts. Tempers had risen.

Noise was an issue. Privacy was an issue. Speed was an issue. But Nathan Tuck and Jon Hopes were classic old-fashioned coppers. They were policemen from a sun-washed Sunday evening series called *Broads Beat*. The *Daily Mail* should send a reporter and give them an award. They were a clip-round-the-ear police presence: a stern warning here, a gentle remonstrance there. They clearly had no arrest targets. Sometimes they went to visit parents to have a little chat. Sometimes they wagged a finger.

Despite P.D. James and Barbara Pym littering East Anglia with fictional murderers, they had yet to discover many bodies.

OOOH, MOTHER!

Heronby, beside the River Bure in Wroxham, was once the holiday home of cheeky, banjolele-strumming, Lancashire-born comedian George Formby (1904–61). Presumably in Formby's time the house would have been named Beryldene because that was the name of every other house he ever owned, while the boat he sailed in the rivers round Wroxham was the *Lady Beryl*.

Beryl was George's wife. When they first met in 1923 she was a professional clog dancer, while the 19-year-old George Hoy Booth had recently adopted his late father's stage name of George Formby and was touring with his dad's rather antiquated music-hall act. Under Beryl's guidance, the act was updated and George Formby went on to enjoy an exceptionally lucrative career. He made 21 films and over 230 records and during the 1930s he was reportedly earning £100,000 a year. By 1941, despite never having made a picture in Hollywood, he was the world's fifth-biggest film star.

As well as his riverside villa in Norfolk, George indulged himself with buying no fewer than 130 cars during the course of his life and smoking 40 Woodbine or Capston Full Strength cigarettes every day from the age of twelve.

Beryl's absolute dedication to her husband's career led her to have a hysterectomy to ensure the couple

George Formby, the Hugh Grant of his day, fishing in the Norfolk Broads in 1952.

did not have any children. She was also a notoriously jealous woman. According to legend she always ensured that any kissing between George and the leading ladies in his films did not go on for a moment after the director called "Cut!"

Nevertheless, a few weeks after Beryl's death in December 1960, George unexpectedly announced he intended to re-marry. His new fiancée was 36-year old Pat Howson, the daughter of the man from whom George had bought several of his cars.

Sadly, George suffered a heart attack and died on 6 March 1961 less than three months after Beryl and two days before his wedding to Pat. His funeral was attended by 150,000 people.

George Formby's house, Beryldene, named after his wife like all his houses, was set back from the river beyond a long, shaved lawn. He is accepted today. Norfolk County Council wanted to knock down his former Broadlands home in 1991 but there was an outcry. Members of the George Formby Society reached for their ukuleles and there was a mass strum-in on the bank.

I played a tribute myself. It was raining. We sat in a wooden-walled boathouse, one that would very probably have outraged locals when it went up, but now, like Formby himself, represented little threat to civilised standards. Dark and slightly damp inside with discarded holiday kites and model boats and mis-matched deckchairs, I sat at a rickety table with Nigel, Forbes, Sarah and Fin who had been recruited to help me sing a Formby classic.

Everybody knows that the ukulele is an idiot's instrument. But even idiots have to keep in tune. Most of the ukes I've ever handled have irritating pegs stuck in holes up one end ineffectually holding on to a bit of nylon fishing line. You wind and twang and try to get the notes you want. Then you squash the peg into place, pluck a note and the thing immediately goes out of tune.

I really couldn't play the uke. It was difficult to explain this deficiency to proper musicians. They pondered alternative ways of teaching me the chords. When I faltered, they even offered to transpose it, or alter the whole song. This was madness. "After I have managed to just about learn one of the chords, you want to change it?" The camera crew were sitting in a rubber dinghy with the rain plopping around them, drifting in the Broad, waiting for me to gain a sudden miraculous proficiency at the instrument that any fool might play.

Devastatingly, I learned that George never played the ukulele anyway. He played a banjolele, the bastard child of banjo and uke. And one of

Horsey Windpump, a frankly inefficient but rather lovely method of drainage.

Wroxham Broad, where I picked up my boat.

Tourism in the 1930s. Though probably not John Betjeman in the foreground.

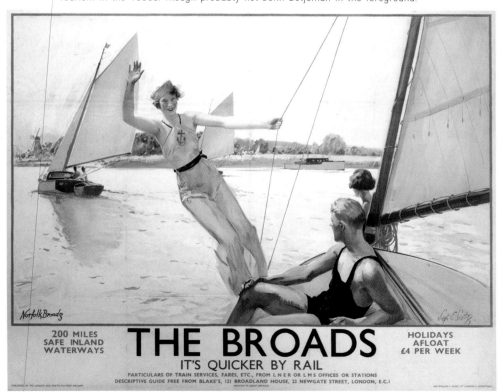

Adjusting the rig on *Wood Rose*.

A redundant industrial landscape – the Broads were created by men mining for peat.

Ignoring the authorities near Bures.

Jonah and the pike, the Antiphoner illustration in Ranworth Church.

Flatford Mill, Scene on a Navigable River by Constable.

Getting to grips with the single scull.

On the Stour: heading home with a frankly relieved Labrador dog.

the band had brought one with him. It was not a toy. It clearly cost more than five quid. It had proper frets, a smart wooden body, a white skin top and the tuning pegs turned on proper mechanical cogs. I admired it and stole it. This was easier.

In the end, I never quite mastered the art of singing the song and plucking the banjo at the same time. But this is televisual presentation. With four trained musicians twiddling, improvising, filling in and showing off around me, I didn't need to. I mimed.

No doubt having revealed this, there will be a furious campaign in the newspapers, questions will be asked in the Royal College of Music and a senior member of the BBC will be forced to resign – but we have to get on. It's a film we're making here.

THE ONE THAT DIDN'T GET AWAY

I have never been able to fish. It is not the lack of kit. It is not the lack of skill. It is the complete lack of patience.

What allows a human being (mostly male) to gawp at a luridly painted bit of cork floating in a pond for the better part of a whole day? What is it about? At peace with the world? In harmony with nature? Escaping from reality? Bored out of your skull?

I can do all the swishing stuff. I have applied myself to the art of casting and winding. I have been taught by the best. I am fully prepared.

It surprises people. When I went out with patient enthusiastic Charlie Bettell on a secret Broad and he steered his flat-bottomed boat into a secluded reach, when the camera crew readied themselves in their boat and ducked down, when the director rubbed his hands in preparation for an embarrassing tangle, I disappointed everybody.

I pulled back my rod, swished the tip and threw my tackle right out into the required place.

"No. I mean, yes. Er... That was pretty good," said Charlie.

I knew it was. I can do it. It was actually a pretty poor cast for me. It's not a very difficult thing for anybody with reasonable coordination to whip a long bendy pole back over his head and flick a weight on the end of string into the middle of a lake. I pretended to look a little disappointed for the camera.

"You need to let the rod do the work," said Charlie. I nodded. He showed me how to do it without making a little grunt. I let him teach me. Though, quite honestly, most of the knack came back anyway.

I had spent hours on the Spey with a man called a ghillie throwing a bloody line in and out of the water, casting for non-existent salmon for *Bookworm*, and another two or three long hours trying to be a fly fisherman on the Thames for *Three Men in a Boat*. I had stood in the surf on Nantucket and thrown a much bigger set of barbed nonsense out to sea for a couple of endless days, and I had done that entirely for myself.

But I had never caught anything. I expected that it would be the same with Charlie. He was a champion pike fisherman. I didn't get that idea entirely. I assumed that if you went fishing and you put your hook in the right place, the rest of it was rather up to the fish, but Charlie knew where they lived. He was terribly, terribly anxious that we caught one. He was an award winner. His reputation was on the line.

Poor Charlie. I felt sorry for him. It was one thing to sneak after your prey on a big empty pond, but quite another to go after them with another boat, three grown men, sound, camera, a novice and a dog, arguing and splashing about, trying to get a good camera angle, to learn the ropes and to do it all in exactly three hours, particularly when the rest of them insisted on tooling around exactly where you might expect the fish to be.

Charlie was undaunted. To Charlie, pike were more than a catch – they were intimate and vicious adversaries. "If conditions are right they will go after anything. They'll have frogs and even birds. In fact, don't dangle your hand in the water because I have seen them come and bite that."

I grasped my rod more firmly and warmed to the pike. It is a crocodile of the pond. I had been to Ranworth Church that morning, climbed the tower, burbled about peat barges, admired its astonishing medieval screen and stopped to look at the Ranworth Antiphoner.

This book of hymns and prayers, made by the monks of Langley over 500 years ago, was illustrated with a picture of Jonah and the Whale. But it clearly wasn't a whale swallowing the flaxen-haired old man. There was nothing out of order here. The Bible refers to a big fish. Looking closely, I could see reeds and a mud bank. This was Norfolk, not the Red Sea, and the big fish had the unmistakeable profile of a pike, which was probably the biggest fish the monks had ever encountered. There was the gaping, spoon mouth, and the row of pointy teeth in a curious smile of delight.

I assumed we were unlikely to come across a pike big enough to swallow me, though Charlie was entertaining me with stories of massive thirty-pounders upsetting boats while he threw harpoons at their blow-holes. (No, I'm making the last bit up.) I was convinced that any self-respecting pike would be lurking underneath a log sneering at us.

"Now throw them both together." The camera boat was issuing instructions. We cast in unison.

"We're coming round to the side. Just hold on."

We cast again. We dropped the tackle in front of the camera, to the left of the camera. We tied up to the camera boat and cast. We turned the boat round and cast in the other direction so that the camera boat wouldn't miss any of our chatter. And Charlie remained relentlessly upbeat.

"It's a bit colder than they like," he said. "It's critical really because if it's just right then they eat anything."

I wondered if we could get them to eat the camera boat.

"We're coming round again to your right now!"

"Let's try something else," Charlie said.

We had been working with a lure. I had become quite adept at hitting the water about twenty yards away and faking a little fish swimming across the Broad. But Charlie had endless variations. He leaned down and opened a toy box. There were hundreds of potential lures – silvery, feathery, painted, carved, moulded, plastic or tin. He'd made a number of them himself. These were the fruits of an obsession.

"Look at this one," he said. He pulled out a jointed metal contraption. "When I pull it in, it wiggles. You just have to wind in the reel at the right speed and as it floats on the top it looks like a frightened snake heading for the shore and the pike can't resist it."

"In the right conditions."

"In the right conditions, of course. It's a little cold today."

The camera boat was coming alongside, and we caught a pike.

It just happened. There was something silvery darting about twenty yards away and the rod was bending alarmingly.

"Oh, ho. Here we go." Charlie was rather matter of fact about it, given his previous form.

"We've got a fish!" I shouted and nearly fell out of the boat.

"You have it. Your rod. And you're supposed to be catching it on film."
Charlie passed me the rod, now bending almost in half.

"What do I do?"

"Reel her in gently. Get her alongside. Not too fast. Wear her out
a bit. I'll get the net. We'll just get that under her …"

And that was that. We had a pike in the folds of the keep net.

"About four pounds."

She was small by Charlie's championship standards, but female,
apparently. Her back was a muddy sage green, spotted with deep orange
markings. Her mouth was a wide, frog-like maw. There were the slender
sharp teeth from the Antiphoner.

Charlie lifted up the net and brought it on board. He got the hook
out and cooed over her. "There we are, now we have to get her up for
the photo – carefully, because we don't want to harm her. We have to get
her back as soon as possible."

This was a vital part of the ritual. The pike would go back in the
Broad. It was the short sequence I had just experienced that counted,
the minor fight and landing and, of course, the photographs.

"Put your thumb right there, Griff. That's it, on her cheek, fingers up
into the gills. Get a good grip. Now lift her up to your shoulder. Closer
to the face. She's not a dog, she won't bite you now."

But she gave an almighty sudden flip and the slippery, glistening
slimy predator fell out of my hands.

Charlie was devastated. He rescued her from the bottom of the boat
and checked her over with infinite care. She was alright.

We got our photograph and then we put her back into the keep net
as quickly as possible and held her over the side. This was my favourite
moment of the chase: the release. It wasn't because I felt squeamish on
behalf of the fish, but because there was a short period when the pike

took stock and recovered her poise and breath. There was no expression. Fish don't make faces. She lay still. I worried for her.

"She's just recovering," Charlie said.

In her element again, floating near the surface in my hands, she was an elegant, superbly marked and built creature. She didn't shoot away but finally, gently, with a languid flexing of her body, swam on. Her back almost instantly blended with the murk and she disappeared from sight.

We caught two more in quick succession. The second fish I got alone and unaided, a bigger ten pounder. And the giant of the trip at fourteen pounds was hooked by Charlie, who was well pleased.

"Magnificent," he said. He smiled at me and looked directly into my eyes, searching for something. "You must have got it now, Griff. You must see what it's all about. I bet you can't wait to get back and go after some of the big ones, can you? That was real excitement, wasn't it? You can't help but be hooked, can you?"

I smiled. I nodded. I enthused. I said that maybe it would only take a few more days casting that tackle on the Broad and hauling the big ones to build a real burning need into my system.

But somehow I doubted it.

AS EASY AS FALLING OFF A LOG: SCULLING FOR BEGINNERS

When I first got a canoe it was simply to explore the upper reaches of the Stour, which flows out of East Anglia from near Cambridge, through the great wool towns of the Essex/Suffolk border to Manningtree, where it becomes an estuary, and runs out to sea, past my house.

As a child my father's great adventure had been taking us to sail in the low-lying, slow-flowing rivers of the east coast, exploring the smelly creeks up as far as Snape and the estuaries of the Deben, the Alde and the Orwell. We had to go adventuring with him. He had paternal rights. But the Stour was the first stop. We turned left past Harwich and ventured up into the wide shallow inlet like Vikings on a raid.

Great woods came down to the water on the southern banks. We were no more than ninety miles from London but this was clearly a magical place. The heart of Anne Boleyn was supposed to buried in the church at Erwarton. Mistley at the tidal head had tried to become a mud spa. It boasted a church by Robert Adam and a huge flock of swans. Harwich itself had a distinguished history in a whole series of naval wars.

I have sailed the estuary, explored it, walked it, fished it, gazed on it and swum in it for most of my life, but until ten years ago I had never ventured up the river, inland. Now I was going to finish my television journey on the Stour, which I considered to be the quintessential English river.

I took the canoes off down a side road lined with timber-framed houses and turned left past a bowling green and a sports field. We were on an unmetalled track before we got to the warehouses and the premises of the Sudbury Rowing Club, on a little creek off the river, way upstream.

About forty years ago, the local water authorities had decided that they owned the River Stour. They certainly used it. Water is pumped across from the Ouse to join the river near Kirtling Green and the river becomes essentially an open-water conduit. The deluge from the Fens makes its way overland to refresh the heavily populated urban hinterlands of Essex. I was going to float down to my house on drinking water.

In the early 1970s the Anglian Water Authority decided to extinguish any navigation rights, and a mighty battle ensued. A petition was taken to the House of Lords, where it was decided that there was an inalienable right of navigation on the Stour, and because of that I could now go for a row with the Sudbury Rowing Club. What I wanted to do was master the single scull.

I had tried this once before. The principle is simple. You sit in a tiny seat and rest two very long oars out to either side until you are evenly balanced. Then off you go. The last time I tried this, someone held the stern of the boat and pushed me off a little and I promptly toppled sideways into the Thames. It seemed so absurd, and so little to do with me, that I assumed I was missing some trick. It had to be a matter of gyroscopic momentum. If you got moving, then suddenly balance would be restored, surely.

There have been rowing races for as long as there have been boats. Neolithic man probably raced dug-outs for bronze beakers. The sport was formalised amongst water-men or working ferryboat operators. One of the oldest races is Doggett's Badge, on the Thames. It was established by an actor. (Actors always seem to have time on their hands.) But the twin inventions that changed rowing were the result of heavy competition between universities. The first was the sliding seat, which enables a follow-through. The second was the extended cantilevered arm. With these two developments the boat could get narrower and longer. It is difficult to tip up an "eight". Perhaps the ones I have been in were controlled by extremely well-balanced men. But they seem to have broader bottoms. They sit lower in the water. A single scull, however, is very narrow and very round. You do not sit in a single scull. You sit on top of it. When you first get in, it feels as if you are balancing on a plastic floating log.

The coach at Sudbury was sympathetic. He had a training boat for me to start on. This was a chopped-down version of the real thing. It was flatter, shorter and just as unstable. While he put his weight on the cantilevered rowlock bracket, now resting on the shore, I clambered past him to get in. My toes had to be stuffed into worn (moderately disgusting) over-large shoes nailed to the floor. These would hold my feet in place while the seat beneath me slid back and forth. But to get on that sliding platform (not a seat – don't dignify the scooped tea plate with that reassuring name) … to get on that buttock saucer, I had to sit on the shell of the boat first and drop myself down while, at the same time, holding on to my outer oar, which was counter-balancing me in the water.

I began to realise why the scullers I had seen on the river were all beautiful young women. A certain willowy flexibility was a big help. I couldn't twist any part of my anatomy sufficiently to see the actual boat beneath me, so I had to rest my lower half on the requisite half-inch of bottom platter by feel alone.

"That's it, Griff. There we are. Drop down. You're on it."

I took Mike Arnott's word for it. I sensed what he meant. By flexing my knees I could bring my body up to join my thighs.

"Keep both blades flat on the water, Griff."

I drifted out into the narrow black creek. I had the handles of the oars in each hand. They were extremely long and ungainly. And for some reason they were so long they crossed over each other.

"I think I've got the wrong oars."

"No, they're supposed to do that. It gives you extra reach. You have to keep the right hand above the left at all times."

Great. The slightest twitch in any direction was sufficient to tip the boat over. Everything else was counter-intuitive. It was no use leaning too far to counter the tip. This made the tip worse. Somehow I had to twist my torso so that the centre of gravity was adjusted and the log stopped rolling, but I didn't have a centre of gravity. I had read in a magazine that after the age of fifty one's sense of balance went, and mine had gone.

"Now, leaving the blades floating in the water and holding the handles of the oars, just practise rolling from side to side, swing your body and rock the whole boat from side to side underneath you."

I did this carefully (obviously) testing my limits. They were one inch to the left and half an inch to the right.

"No, no, a bit more. Let yourself go a little."

The man was clearly crazy, but I was on television so I did what I was told and gradually increased my arc. After a while I could convincingly rock my own boat. Children paddled past in mini kayaks, electric launches came and went, ducks and moorhens skittered off into corners of overhanging willow to settle in for the night.

"Now it's time to row a few strokes. Don't go too far. I have to get into the training boat to follow you."

Mike went off behind the shed. Alone and vulnerable, I drew back my oars and with extreme difficulty, like a tightrope walker with two balancing poles instead of one, I got the oars back, dipped them in and drew the blades through the water.

With three wobbly strokes and three near capsizes I slid out into the main river.

The Stour is surprisingly broad at this point of its course. As I crept out I heard the familiar huffing and thudding noise of a rowing boat powered by eight hefty men crossing the water towards me. The club's male eight passed within inches, like an express train.

"Downstream on the right!" someone bellowed and I eased myself in that direction.

And my confidence was growing. I was beginning to master the scull beneath me. I pulled more confidently. I even began to slide a little on my seat. Mike was now following me in a dinky narrow motorboat. He egged me on.

"Pull. That's it. Nice even strokes. Follow through. Make sure you finish well."

All the familiar phrases, none of which meant very much to me, but I was picking up speed.

Forward, in, pull, slide, up, feather, slide, forward, in… Rowing is brutally simple. It's the body that does it. Once you're up and going you can perfect all the little twiddles, but the aim is to turn yourself into a tireless human machine. The more you become a robot, the faster you go.

Now I was no longer fretting about my lack of ability or my balance. I had the measure. No, I was fretting about Peter, Jamie and James, my camera crew. They were still back at the brick wharf trying to launch their blasted rubber dinghy. What was the point of me mastering a skill that most fourteen-year-olds can manage standing on their heads unless they were there to film it?

We turned and headed back down the river. I was soaring along now.

"Do you want to have a go at the proper boat?" Mike shouted.

Oh, yes. The proper boat. I had forgotten that. I was actually sitting in the training boat. This was the dumpy ugly ducking.

"Yes, Mike, never mind filming this now. Let's get me out into the real thing." It was time for me to become a swan. "Don't wait for the camera. They're probably fiddling around trying to get it onto its waterproof housing. We can film the real thing."

I swung back into the little creek with aplomb. I swooshed under the bridge. The real scull was waiting. I was helped out of the practice boat and with minimal bashing about I levered myself into the genuine commodity. As before, Mike pushed me out into the water.

"Oh, this is difficult."

"Yes, the other boat is far more stable."

I was back at the beginning. This was absurd.

"Rock the boat a little, as before," Mike instructed.

The others were floating up in the rubber dinghy. The camera was rolling.

"But this seems much heavier and it won't settle at all."

One oar started to sink into the water.

"Now use the other oar to balance yourself! You're going to have to lift that oar out."

But it wasn't really an option; with a graceful swing the boat simply continued to dip. The oar plunged into the mud and started to lift out of its bracket and I rolled over and into water.

"You're all right. You're OK."

"Yes." I was in the water, not in the boat, and they were watching me from another boat. So this confirmation of my position seemed untoward, but it was meant to reassure me that I was quite capable of getting myself back into the boat. I had to grasp both oars in one hand to balance myself and then heave myself up onto the scull.

Exhausted and fighting the propensity of the fibreglass log to roll straight over, I grasped the sharp metal edges of the cockpit while Mike spoke encouragement from twelve feet away. "That's it. Don't lose the oars. Lie across a bit. Now twist yourself round."

I slithered on to the hull.

"Now, get the feet in. Leave your bottom there."

I was sliding around unhappily, but finally managed to get first one foot then the other into place. I heaved myself forward and delicately balanced my buttocks on the two dessertspoons of a seat, grasped the oars and pulled myself upright.

"That's it. Get your breath. Now take the oars."

I reached forward. The port hand oar slipped under the water, the boat lurched and I toppled straight in again.

It was all captured faithfully on camera. Then the director called it a day.

None of it appeared in the final film.

CANOEING DOWN THE STOUR

Down beyond Sudbury the River Stour closes in. It slinks through a perfect English landscape: Essex to the south, the much more mythically rural Suffolk to the north. "Suffolk" sounds eggy, bucolic, lost and lazy. Essex is equally good, just not so equally named. I glimpsed wool merchants' ochre or pink half-timbered hall houses. I slid into great mill ponds. There were plenty of startling grand churches, some paid for out of the profits of the local weaving industry, some, like Stoke-by-Nayland, by rich medieval aristocrats. But mostly, despite the hard-won navigation rights, I was alone, hemmed in by tall banks of reeds, picking my way through over-hanging willows, negotiating passage rights with arrogant swans.

Frequently a stretch would open out ahead with bullrushes standing up on either side, below whispering aspens. The way was clogged with waterlilies in full bloom: buttercup-coloured buds the size of small fists, and open petals like dishes, lying on flat floating leaves. The water itself was clear and waving with green cabbage-like undergrowth that ceaselessly, yearningly, writhed in the current. I could see right down to a river bottom reflecting sunlight off mother-of-pearl freshwater mussel shells.

The path once ran along one bank at a time. It meant that a tow-horse had to jump into a barge and then out on the other side to carry on pulling the barge, a feat captured by Constable in the *The Leaping Horse*. Even that path had gone. The banks were fringed only by inaccessible fields. This was untouchable England.

I slipped downstream past the back of Bures, just visible in a slew of bright red brick and ranch-house eaves on the other side of a wide recreation ground. Two boys were jumping from the bridge. They had just finished exams. What they were doing was strictly illegal, of course. But boys had jumped from this bridge for a hundred years and the water authorities were trying to protect themselves against claims which the boys had no intention of making. So they jumped.

Before Nayland I had to negotiate a sluice, paddling up to the lip and letting the water drag me over down the flume. The farmer on the bank asked me if I had seen the otter further back. I hadn't. I must have seen the kingfisher. I had. He had recently caught some great trout further up. The tree just round the bend was perfect for pike. He owned five miles of the banks, "But that's the trouble, the river can easily become a bit of an obsession. I'm always drawn down to it. It takes up so much time."

I liked gliding into the black waters of the mill approaches. There was a sense of impending rush in their gloom. The mills were now stockbrokers' houses, with swing seats and weeping willows overlooking the mill pond, but, however private they wanted to be, they were supposed to provide a route for us canoeists to get past their old, disused weirs.

Nobody legislated that it had to be easy. Sometimes, the path lay through a seemingly specially cultivated bed of nettles. At one high white lapped mill I came alongside under huge oaks and alders at a wooden landing stage. Cadbury bustled ashore. I reached behind, hauled the canoe out of the water and dragged it along the path.

Ahead was a locked picket gate protecting some kind of approach drive, fenced on either side. For a moment I suspected that they wanted me to shoulder my canoe and clamber over two fences and a hedge to get back to the water, but I noticed that this drive crossed a ditch to the right. There was a very low bridge. It was a pipe, in fact. I thought I could see daylight on the other side. It was part of the overflow system for the mill pond and was currently dry. I lugged my canoe down, slung it under and then crawled through myself.

Twenty yards further on there was another little wooden jetty standing on the mill race. I had cracked the puzzle. I was back on the Stour, and I could paddle on.

CONSTABLE COUNTRY

Now I swept through flat watermeadows, stumps of willow leaning from the bank and the distant square tower of Dedham away on my right.

I was leaving the unknown, rarely travelled world of the inland Stour and arriving at perhaps the best-known river scenery in the world.

It is said that when John Constable was riding home in a stagecoach towards the end of his life, he pulled aside the blind and looked out of the window. A fellow passenger nudged him: "See, sir," he said, "we are entering Constable Country." Constable himself was probably flattered, given that he had struggled to achieve recognition for most of his life. His best-known paintings are all of a stretch of river no more than nine miles long, from Higham down to Manningtree. He painted what was within walking distance of his father's house.

The river was his subject. Since then, Flatford Mill, Willy Lot's House and the Hay Wain have decorated tea towels and teapots and tea trays. They have become jigsaws and magazine covers. Why? Perhaps because they seem to epitomise an idealised vision of rural England. And yet Constable himself wanted to paint the river as it was. He wanted to capture reality, not fantasy. He went out and made preparatory sketches in the open air, so that he could be true to the momentary changes in the weather. His effect on the Impressionists, his place in art books, his value as a great master are all based on scrupulous truth to life. He wanted to depict the damp corners, the trickling lock gates and the green weed.

I moored near Flatford Mill. The river had become the very opposite of what I had been exploring up to then. The place was crowded with tourists. The car parks were well hidden up the hill, the café was discreetly folded into a half-timbered cottage, the great red-brick millhouse owned by his father had been very carefully transformed into a lecture centre, but when I stood with Edward Jackson and compared postcards of the famous paintings with the scenes in front of me, it wasn't the lack of mould on the side of Willy Lott's house, or the trees that had colonised the side of the towpath or the thick undergrowth on the far bank of the mill pool that I noticed most but the people – the coach parties and the tourists.

Constable depicted a working river. His father was part of the Navigation Board, and had ships which exported grain from Mistley and, on return, imported coal that was stored at Cattawade. The famous picture of Flatford Mill is titled *Scene on a Navigable River,* emphasising that the picture is no romantic version of the countryside. Constable has been accused of ignoring the agricultural struggle that was going on during the first half of the nineteenth century and these are not scenes of hardship, but they are scenes of work. Far in the back of *The Hay Wain* you can just make out another wagon and harvesters in the fields. In other pictures the barges are being poled into place. The working lock, the mill, the run-offs, the horse, the canal-like sides of the improved river, the cargo and the mill race are all included. He painted a boat being repaired in a dry dock. All the details of how the lock worked and how the boat was repaired are captured. That dock has been discovered, filled in, just where he had recorded it.

And yet, these are exquisite pictures. The skies are filled with rain. The wind can be felt in the trees. There is huge vibrant life on display. Constable evokes a spiritual union with the river through art. The moment is always poised. The absence of urgency is the core of his painting. They are about routine. They are about rhythm. Somewhere in Old Master Constable is the spirit of Ol' Man River. And that is surely what we find so satisfying.

On my own journey to this place I had met a huge number of people wanting things from today's rivers. Each had an urgent priority. The water authority, the farmer, the nature conserver, the angler and the rower – everyone needed something. Many felt that the others were a threat to them. Many wanted new freedoms or new restrictions. But Constable seemed to know that the variety of the river would add to its vitality and that our spiritual connection to it was not easily quantified. This is the riverness of rivers, possibly completely undefinable except through art. Our most celebrated artist painted rivers because they were beautiful, spiritually nurturing things. That seems to me to be the value we ought always to bear in mind as we seek to drink, extract, cross, exploit, control, fish or canoe them.

While I was talking on the bridge I'd left Cadbury in the canoe. He sat nervously watching a particularly bad-tempered swan fluffing himself up, curling his neck and cruising about in front of his hen and her cygnets. The swan hissed at Cadbury. Cadbury looked guilty and rolled his eyes. The swan crossed the river and Cadbury decided to leave. He stood up to get out of the canoe, and just before he managed to scramble up onto the landing platform, the swan swam back over and pecked him sharply on the bum.

It was time to paddle on. We were only a few miles from home.

A word of thanks in several hundred words

You may be forgiven for thinking, like Margaret Thatcher, as you watch the credits roll at the end of television series "What on earth do all these people do?" I am in the privileged position of knowing exactly what everybody does, but there isn't room to tell you here. I do want to sincerely thank them for doing it though. I could not even have started on this book without the imagination of the directors Jamie Muir, Jim Funnell, Ross Harper, Konrad Begg and Suzanne Phillips. They thought out the voyages and searched out the stories and made great films under trying conditions of which this is only an imperfect record. I'm going to mention the camera and sound crew because I love them and we have fun. And the researchers and APs, the boat boy, Siobhan and Yvonne, Nicola and more Jameses than you can throw an oar at, all of you, because you are the young people without whom the thing would feel old. Clare Paterson and Ludo Graham were the executive producers. Simon Mansfield was one too, but he also kept things going and along with Valmai put the Modern stamp on this project. I salute you. Mike Haskins wrote the boxes. Rupert gave his tact and support, Gill her skill in cutting down my flatulence. Cat made it all happen. My wife Jo worked harder on this book than I did, copy-editing and pointing out my errors, but despite all her dedication the mistakes are mine. I make them in the excitement. It was an exciting project to do. This is dedicated to Paul and the dog, both of whom keep up with me beyond the limits of canine loyalty.

Picture Acknowledgements

Text illustrations (numbers refer to page numbers)

Alamy: 19, 171. Amphibious Ancients Bathing Association: 61. Bournemouth News Picture Service: 113. Bridgeman Art Library: 149 (Staatliche Gemäldegalerie, Berlin), 161 (Roy Miles Fine Paintings), 185 (Private Collection), 245 (Yale Center for British Art, Paul Mellon Collection). Britain on View/L. Beel: 123. © British Library Board: 14-15, 68-69, 126-127, 230-231. Corbis: 83, 257. Getty Images: 131. Hatfield House, reproduced by courtesy of the Marquess of Salisbury: 178-179. Mary Evans Picture Library: 89, 199, 215. Science & Society Picture Library/RPS: 237. SCRAN.ac.uk/J. Gardiner: 49

Colour plates (plates section/plate number)

Alamy: 3/1, 3/2, 4/2, 5/1, 5/6. Bridgeman Art Library: 1/8 (Bourne Fine Art, Edinburgh), 2/9 (Southampton City Art Gallery), 4/1 (British Library Board), 5/4 (Agnew's, London). Britain on View: 7/6 (R. Edwards), 8/1 (D. Sellman), 8/6 (L. Beel). Corbis: 2/8. Hatfield House, reproduced by courtesy of the Marquess of Salisbury: 6/2. Modern Television: 5/11, 5/12. Photolibrary/Jon Arnold: 2/1. Science & Society Picture Library/NRM Pictorial Collection/Septimus Scott: 8/3. Science Photo Library/R. Brook: 7/5. Skyscan: 1/7 (E. Nägele), 1/9 (R. West), 2/7 (J. Webb), 3/1 (I. Bracegirdle), 3/6, 3/8 (Blom Aerofilms Ltd), 4/5 (T. Calvert), 6/1, 7/2, 8/2. Tate, London © 2009: 8/9. Visit Wales © Crown Copyright 2009: 5/5

Map of Britain's rivers on p.8: © Neil Gower

All other photographs were taken during filming by Paul Cornwell © Modern Television

Index

Figures in *italics* indicate captions.

Abbey Mills Pumping Station, East London 214, 216, 228
Adam, Robert 271
Adamson, Daniel 83
Aire & Calder Navigation 117
Albert, Prince 212
Albert Dock, Liverpool 78, 79
Alde River 209, 270
Amlwch Harbour, Anglesey 70-71
Amwell, Hertfordshire 197-8, *199*
Amwell Magna Fishing Club 200, 201
Andrian, Barrie 38, 39
Andy (cameraman) 73, 93, 118
Anglesey 70-71
Anglian Water Authority 271
Apperley, Gloucestershire 175
Archer, Thomas 104
Arkwright, Richard 97
Arnott, Mike 272-6
Atholl, Earl of 24
Atholl, "Planting Dukes" of 54
Atlantic Conveyor 72-5, 77
AVRO aeroplane company 210

Banks, Gary 111-12
Bannister, Jonny 112, 114-16
"Barge River" 204
barges 92-6, 116-19, 169, 185, 192, 218, 225-6
    Thames sailing barges 207-10
Barrowman, John 61
Barton Broad 254
Barton-upon-Humber, Lincolnshire 122
basins 93, 94
Bazalgette, Sir Joseph 214, 215-16, *215*

Bedford, 4th Duke of 246
Begg, Konrad 137, 142, 151, 152, 159, 167
Betjeman, John 258
Bettell, Charlie 265-70
Black Rock area 166, 168
Blair Atholl, Pitlochry 47
Blair, Tony 229
Blake, William 98
Bliss, Greg 251, 252
bog-snorkelling 153-4
Boleyn, Anne 271
bores 169-74, *171*
Bow Back Rivers 226
Bow Bridge 221
Bow Cemetery 212-13
Bow Creek 227, 229
Bow Lock 221
Bow Marshes 228
brewing industry 192-6
Brian (sound man) 224
Bridge of Gaur 26, 29, 31
Bridgnorth, Shropshire 150
British Canoe Union 158, 161
British Waterways Board 224, 226
Broads 252-70
Brown, Lancelot "Capability" 99-100
Bruar, waters of 43-6
Bure River 258
Burleigh, Lord 183-6, 189, 192, 206
Burns, Robert 43, 44, 45-6
Buxton, Derbyshire 100

cabin cruisers 124, 192
Cambridge 232-3
Cameron clan 24
canoes 25-35, 39, 135, 136, 218, 243
    on the Lea 186, 188, 193

Shrewsbury 142-4
    on the Stour 277-9
    on the Trent 109-11
Car Dyke 242
carp 112-16, *113*
Carter, Peter 234-6, 238-40
Chalmers, Frank 62-7
Chantrey, Sir Francis 200
Charles, HRH The Prince of Wales 252
Chatsworth 98-105
Ching Brook 210
chub 200
Clifford, Mike 16, 17
Cluny House Gardens, Aberfeldy, Perthshire 54-5, 58
Clywedog tributary 142
Coalbrookedale 147
coasters 226
Codding, Alan 117, 118, 119
Conacher, Mary 31-4
Constable, John 278, 279-82
Cook, Beryl 85
Coppermills Water Treatment Works, Walthamstow 211
coracles 137-41
Cornwell, Paul 11, 12, 13, 134-5, 136, 152-3, 186, 188, 252-3
Cotman, John Sell *245*
crannogs 36-9, *37*
crayfish 187, 223
Cromford Mills, Derbyshire 97-8
Crossness Pumping Station, south-east London 216-17

Dagenham Brook 210
Darby, Abraham 147, 148
Darby, Abraham, III 148
Davies, Tamsin 210-11

Dear, Bob 201, 202
Deben River 270
Dedham, Essex 279
Defoe, Daniel 96
Derwent River 96-8, 99, 105-9
Devis, Arthur *161*
Devonshire, Amanda, Duchess of 98
Devonshire, Andrew Cavendish,
   11th Duke of 100
Devonshire, Deborah, Duchess of 101
Devonshire, Georgiana, Duchess of
   100-101
Devonshire, Peregrine Cavendish,
   12th Duke of 98, 99, 100
Devonshire, William Cavendish,
   4th Duke of 104
Dickens, Charles 212
Dobson, Ian 121
Doggett's Badge race 272
Doxey, Sean 102-5
Druids 150-54, 169
duck punts 234-5, 239-41
Dunalastair, Perthshire 31

Eas a' Chual Aluinn, Sutherland 19
eels 155, 223, 234-9, 237
Egerton, Dr John 159
Eliot, George 109
Elizabeth I, Queen 197, 213
Ely, Cambridgeshire 242-3
Emerson, Peter Henry *237*
Engine Farm, Cambridgeshire 251
English Bridge 14
English Heritage 206
Environment Agency 168
Erwarton, Suffolk 271
Evans, Mike 166-8
Evans, Simon Bennett 128, 129, 130

Farr, William 212, 215
Feast, Alan 84, 85

Fen Tigers 246, 252
Ferriby, east Yorkshire 124
Fife, William, III 125
Fisher, Lee 47, 48, 50, 51, 52
fishing 200-203, 265-70
Five Springs, Luton 181
Flatford Mill, East Bergholt, Suffolk
   280-81
Forget Me Not (working barge) 92-6
Forman, Lance 222-4
Formby, Beryl 262, 263
Formby, George 261-4, *263*
Forty Foot Drain 248
Franklin, Benjamin 195
French and Jupp's, maltsters 193-4, 196
Funnell, Jim 233, 275

Garry River 46, 48
Gifford, John 117, 119, 121
Gilpin, William 43, 159, 160
Glen Lyon 40
Glen River 235
Goyt River 87, 95
Graham (of British Canoe Union)
   158-9, 160, 162, 163-4
Grapes, Ian 254
gravadlax 223
gravel barge 116-19
Great Drainage Scheme 252
Great Fen Project 251-2
Great Ouse 235, 243
Great Stink (1858) 213-14, 215
Greenwich Dome 229
Grey Mare's Tail 16-22, *19*

H. Forman & Son 222-4
Hafren Forest 130, 132-4
Hafren River 139
Halliday, Stephen 212-13
Harcourt Williams, Robin 183
Harper, Ross 17

Hatfield House, Hertfordshire 182-5,
   186
Hay, Duncan 44-6
Helen (coracle expert) 138, 140
Hertford 186-8
Herts Canoe Club 188
Hodges, Simon 217
Hogarth, William *195*
Holme Fen, Cambridgeshire 251-2
Hopes, PC Jon 262
hovercraft 121
Huddersfield Narrow Canal 93
Hull 125
Humber Bridge 122, 123, *123*
Humber Estuary 120-22
Humber River 12, 117, 119, 125
Hundred Foot Drain 246
Hunter, Percy 253
Hunter's Yard, Womack Water 253
Hutton, Roy 56-7, 58, 60
Hutton, Val 57-60
hydroelectricity 40-43
Hyslop, Steve 169, 170

Ierne 124-5
Irk River 87
iron-making 145-50, *149*
Irving, Joe 124, 125
Irwell River 86, 87

Jackson, Edward 280
Jackson, Eric 164, 165, 166
James, P.D. 262
James I, King 197, 198, 199, 211
Johansson, Stefan 73
Johnson, Boris 227
Jones, Huw 125

kayaks 106-9, 158-60, 162-4, 274
Keegan, John 26
Kenmore, Perthshire 39

Kevin (cameraman) 153
King, Steve 169-70, 172, 173, 174
Kinlochleven, Argyll, Scotland 19
Koch, Robert 214

Lady of the Lea 207-10
Ladybower Reservoir 96
Latham, Dave 26-31
launches, electric 274
lave fishing 166-8
Lea Bridge 211
Lea River 180-229, 221
    Amwell and the New River 196-9
    angling 200-203
    end of the 228-9
    and Hatfield House 183, 184-5
    and London's 1866 cholera outbreak
    211, 214
    origin of 180-82
Lea Rowing Club 218-20
Leah, Chris 93, 94, 95
Lee Navigation 185, 192, 225, 227
Leven River 19
Liddard, John 196-7
lighters 226
Liverpool 74-7, 83, 84, 85
Loch Leven 16
Loch Rannoch 23, 24, 25, 31
Loch Tay 36-9, *37*
locks 93, 94-5, 189, 224-7
    flash 184, 189, 191
    pound 189, 191, *191*, 205
    working 191
Lowry, L.S. 85, 86
Luton, Bedfordshire 180-82

McDonough, Beth 64, 65, 66
McIntosh, Joyce 61
Manchester 85-6, 96
Manchester Ship Canal 82-5, *83*
marker buoys 121-2

Marple Junction 95
Martin, Chris 106
Matilda, Queen 221
Matlock canoe club 106
Mattingley, John 53, 54, 55, 58
Mattingley, Wendy 54, 55, 56
meanders 143, 144, 147, 158, 189
Medlock River 87
Mersey River 12, 71, 72, 74-82, 87
Middle Level Drain 235
Middlesex Filter Beds, East London
    210-11
Milne, Duncan 175, 177
Morley, Andy 188-90
Morton Brook 87, 88, 91
motorboats 192, 228
Muir, Jamie 233, 275
Myddelton, Sir Thomas 197, 198

narrow boats 188, 208, 244
National Trust 241
Natural Heritage 206
Nene River 235
New Bedford River 246
New Gauge House, near Ware,
    Hertfordshire 196-7
New River 197, 198, 199, *199*, 211
Newark 110
Norfolk Heritage Fleet 253
North, Mark 193-4, 196
North Sea 67
Northern Outfall Sewer 228

Old Bedford River 246
Old Ford Lock 227
Olympic site, east London 226, 227,
    228
O'Neill, Jimmy 219, 220
Orwell River 271
Ouse River 120, 237, 242, 271
Outwell, Cambridgeshire 234, 237, 238

paddles, paddling 27, 29-31, 147, 188,
    190
Pain, Brian 208, 209
Paine, James 99
Park, Chris 151
Patrick (researcher) 224
Paxman, Jeremy 201
Paxton, Joseph 102, 104
peat 156-7, 255-6, *257*, 257
Perthshire 53
Peter (cameraman) 233, 275
Phibbies (Ye Amphibious Ancients
    Bathing Association) 61, *61*, 62
Phillips, Suzanne 224
pike 266-70
Pippa (coracle expert) 138, 140-41
Pitchforth, Joanne 155
pleasure cruisers 243, 259
Plynlimon massif 128, 129, *131*, 131,
    175
Portland basin 94
Potter Heigham, Norfolk 256, 260
Powell, John 164-6
Prescott Lock 224, 225-6
Pudding Mill River 228
punting 232-4
    duck punts 234-5
putchers 164-6
Pym, Barbara 262

Rafferty, Geoff 71-5
Ransome, Arthur 258
Ranworth Church, Norfolk 267
rapids 26, 140-41, 162-3
Regent Canal 244
RIB (Rigid Inflatable Boat) 119, 227,
    262
Richard (cameraman) 20
Riddell, Alastair 40-43
Robin Hood Theatre, Averham 110
Robinson, Ben 246, 247, 248

Roch River 87
Roe, A.V. 210
Ross-on-Wye 158, 159
rowing boats 218-20
Royal Gunpowder Mills, Waltham
    Abbey, Essex 203-6
Royal Seaforth Docks 75, 77
Rutter, Richard 225-7

sailing boats 253-6
salmon 46-53, *49*, 55, 133, 165, 166-8,
    200
    curing 222-4
    lave fishing 166-8
Sandman, Dave 78-81
Scottish Crannog Centre, Aberfeldy
    37, 38
sculling 270-77
Severn Bore 169-74, *171*, 175
Severn River 12, 23, 129, 130, 133,
    134, 139, 144, 146, 157, 164,
    168, 176, 177
    and coracles 137, 140
    the first metal boat 148, 149
    "a natural river" 141-2
sewers, sewage 87-92, 89, 213,
    214-18, 228
Shardlow, Derbyshire 109
Sharkey, Feargal 201
Shrewsbury 142-5
Slaughter, Graham 113, *113*
Smeaton Bridge (Perth Bridge) 57, 65
Snow, Dr John 215
Spey River 266
Stanstead Abbotts, Hertfordshire
    193-4, 200
Starkie, Ben 16, 17, 21
stilt-walking 241-2
Stour River 270, 271, 272, 274, 277-9
Stratford Bridge 222
sturgeon 116, 223

Sudbury Rowing Club 271, 272
Summers, Dr David 47
surfing 170, *171*, 172-4
Swarkestone Causeway 110-11, 122
Symonds Yat 159, 160, 162

Tame River 87
Tay River 23, 50, 56-8, 60-67, 133
Telford, Thomas 148
Thames River 23, 181, 195, 200, 207,
    213, 216, 221, 227, 229, 266, 272
Thames sailing barges 207-10
Thames Water Authority 198
Thatcher, Margaret, Baroness 226
Theobalds palace 183-4
Thornhill, Sir James 99
Three Mills Cut 228
Trent Falls 120
Trent River 96, 109-11, 116-19, 120
Tritton, Willie 48
trout 201, 202, 203
Tuck, PC Nathan 262
Tudor (cameraman) 190, 204, 224
Tummel River 25, 31-5, 40
tuna 223
turning bays 93
Tweed River 133
Tween, Trevor 181-2

Upwell, Cambridgeshire 234

Valiant (gravel barge) 117
Vermuyden, Cornelius 250
Vyrnwy tributary 142

Waltham Abbey, Essex: Royal
    Gunpowder Mills 203-6
Walthamstow, Greater London 207,
    208
Walthamstow Water Company 211-12
Walton, Izaac 113, 200-201, 202

Waterworks River 228
Watt, James 149
Weil's disease 90, 91, *91*
weirs 182, 184, 188, 191, 196
Welland River 235
Welney Wetland Centre 239
Welsh Bridge 143, 144
West Highland Line 25
Whytock, Ronnie 51
Wicken Fen, Cambridgeshire 241-2
Wilkinson, John "Iron Mad" 148, 149,
    149, 150
Williamson, Tom 254-6
Witham River 235
Wolfit, Donald 110
Wood Rose 254
Woods, Ray 156, 157
Woodwalton Fen 252
Wordsworth, William 159
Wroxham, Norfolk 252-3
Wye River 129, 142, 146, 154, 157-60,
    164, 168, 175, 176